The Innocence of Kaiser Wilhelm

(In the First World War)

Christina Croft

© Christina Croft 2015

A Hilliard & Croft Book

Contents

Who's Who 5

Prologue 9

Chapter 1 – 'Determined to Keep Peace with Everyone' 11

Chapter 3 – 'The English Woman' 28

Chapter 4 – 'The Whole World Misjudged Me' 37

Chapter 5 – 'The Will To Do Right And Good' 51

Chapter 6 – 'The Only Guarantee Against Invasion' 61

Chapter 7 – 'The Queen is Constantly Praising the Emperor' 70

Chapter 8 – 'A Place in the Sun' 84

Chapter 9 – 'To Secure Us Peace On The Seas' 95

Chapter 10 – 'The Old Peacock' 105

Chapter 11 – 'He Has Invariably Worked for Peace with England' 117

Chapter 12 – 'I Am Convinced That He Sincerely Loves Peace' ...130

Chapter 13 – 'In Favour of an Understanding With Serbia' 139

Chapter 14 – 'It's Nothing…It's Nothing' 146

Chapter 15 – 'An Invention of Malevolent Persons' 154

Chapter 16 – 'The Most Sorrowful Man in the World' 166

Chapter 17 – 'A Sentimental Subterfuge' 180

Chapter 18 – The Defamation of Kaiser Wilhelm 194

Chapter 19 – 'America is More Indebted to Germany than to Any Other Nation' 211

Chapter 20 – 'Proof Against the Theory of Barbarity and Cruelty' 220

Chapter 21 – 'The American People Do Not Desire It' 231

Chapter 22 – 'They Are Afraid of the Kaiser's Kind Heart' 245

Chapter 23 – 'That I Should Most Faithfully Serve Germany' 255

Chapter 24 – 'Conceived in Lust and Born in Lies' 268

Chapter 25 – 'Innocent Before God & Men' 275

By the same author:..288

References...289

Who's Who

Royalties

ALBERT I (1875-1934) King of the Belgians
ALEXANDER (1888-1943) Prince Regent and later King of Serbia
ALIX (1872-1918) Empress Alexandra of Russia; wife of Tsar Nicholas II; first cousin of Kaiser Wilhelm II
AUGUST-WILHELM 'Auwi' (1887-1949) 4th son of Kaiser Wilhelm II
CAROL I (1839-1914) King of Romania
DONA See 'Victoria Augusta'
EDWARD VII 'Uncle Bertie' (1841-1910) King of Great Britain; uncle of Kaiser Wilhelm II
EITEL-FRIEDRICH (1883-1942) 2nd son of Kaiser Wilhelm
ELLA (1864-1918) Grand Duchess Elizabeth of Russia; sister of Tsarina Alexandra; cousin of Kaiser Wilhelm II
FERDINAND (1841-1928) King ('Tsar') of Bulgaria – Austrian born Prince of Saxe-Coburg-Kohary
FRANZ FERDINAND (1863 -1914) Archduke of Austria-Este; heir to the throne of Austria-Hungary
FRANZ JOSEF (1830 -1916) Emperor of Austria-Hungary
FRIEDRICH WILHELM/FRITZ (1831-1888) – Crown Prince of Prussia, Emperor Friedrich III. Wilhelm's father
FRIEDRICH WILHELM (1893-1916) Prince of Hesse-Kassel; nephew of Kaiser Wilhelm II
GEORGE (1865-1936) King George V of Great Britain; first cousin of Kaiser Wilhelm II
HENRY (1862-1929) – Wilhelm's younger brother
KARL (1887-1922) Archduke and later Emperor of Austria-Hungary
MARIE (1875-1938) Queen of Romania. Kaiser Wilhelm II's first cousin
MAXIMILIAN (1902-1962) Elder son of Archduke Franz Ferdinand
MAXIMILIAN 'Max' (1867-1929) Margrave of Baden
MAXIMILIAN 'Max' (1894-1914) Prince of Hesse-Kassel; nephew of Kaiser Wilhelm II
NICHOLAS 'Nicky' (1867-1918) Tsar Nicholas II of Russia
NIKOLAI NIKOLAEVICH (1856-1929) Grand Duke and Commander-in-Chief of the Russian army.

SOPHIE CHOTEK (1868-1914), Duchess of Hohenberg; morganatic wife of Archduke Franz Ferdinand

SOPHIE (1870-1932) – Queen of the Hellenes, Wilhelm's sister

VICTORIA (1819-1901) – Queen of Great Britain. Kaiser Wilhelm II's maternal grandmother

VICTORIA/VICKY (1841-1901) –Empress Frederick. Eldest child of Queen Victoria. Wilhelm's mother

VICTORIA AUGUSTA/DONA (1858-1921) German Empress; wife of Kaiser Wilhelm II

VIKTORIA LUISE (1892-1980) Princess of Prussia; only daughter of Kaiser Wilhelm II

WILHELM I (1797-1888) Regent, then King of Prussia; German Emperor; Kaiser Wilhelm II's paternal grandfather

WILHELM II/WILLIAM (1857-1941) German Emperor, Kaiser, King of Prussia

WILHELM (1882-1951) Crown Prince of Prussia; eldest son of Wilhelm II

ZITA (1892-1989) Archduchess and later Empress of Austria-Hungary; wife of Archduke Karl

Politicians, Court Officials and Military Leaders

ASQUITH, Herbert Henry (1852-1928) British Prime Minister

BALFOUR, Arthur (1848-1930) British Foreign Minister

BERCHTOLD, Leopold von (1863-1942) Austria Foreign Minister

BISMARCK, Otto von (1815-1898) Chancellor of Germany

BETHMANN-HOLLWEG, Theobald von (1856-1921) Chancellor of Germany

BUCHANAN, George (1854-1924) British Ambassador to Russia

CHURCHILL, Winston (1874-1965) British politician

CZERNIN, Count Ottokar von (1872-1932) Hungarian Minister to Bucharest, later Foreign Minister

FALKENHAYN, Erich (1861-1922) German Chief of General Staff

GIESL, Wladimir (1860-1936) Austrian Foreign Ministry official

GROENER, Wilhelm (1867-1939) German Chief of Staff

HARRACH. Franz von (1870-1934) Bodyguard to Franz Ferdinand in Sarajevo

HINDENBURG, Paul von (1847-1934) German Chief of General Staff

HÖTZENDORF, Franz Conrad von (1852-1925) Austrian General and Chief of Staff

HOYOS, Alexander von (1876-1937) Austrian Foreign Ministry Official; adjutant to Berchtold

JAGOW, Gottlieb von (1863-1935) German Foreign Minister

LANSING, Robert (1864-1928) United States Secretary of State

LLOYD GEORGE, David (1863-1945) British Minister for Munitions; later Prime Minister

LUDENDORFF, Erich (1865-1937) German Joint Chief of General Staff

MOLTKE, Helmuth von (1848-1916) German Chief of Staff

PACELLI, Eugenio (1876-1958) Papal Nuncio to Bavaria

POINCARÉ, Raymond (1860-1934) French President

POTIOREK, Oskar (1853-1933) – Austrian Military Governor of Bosnia-Herzegovina

POURTALÈS, Friedrich (1853-1928) German Ambassador to St. Petersburg

SAZONOV, Sergei (1860-1927) Russian Foreign Minister

TIRPITZ, Alfred von (1849-1930) Admiral and Secretary of State for the German Navy

TISZA, Istvan (1861-1918) Hungarian Prime Minister

TSCHIRSCHKY, Heinrich von (1868-1916) German Ambassador to Vienna

WOODROW WILSON, Thomas (1856-1924) President of the United States

ZIMMERMANN, Arthur (1864-1940) German Foreign Minister

8

Prologue

Shortly after seven a.m. on Sunday 10th November 1918, an agitated man emerged from a motor car at the Dutch border and surrendered his sword to an approaching officer, Major van Dyl. The once All-Highest Kaiser and Supreme War Lord had arrived as a broken and disillusioned refugee, seeking asylum from the Queen of the Netherlands.

The journey from his military Headquarters at Spa could hardly have been more humiliating. Not only had he had to contend with the threatening jeers of the crowds who gathered at the stations en route, but also, as news arrived of the devastating terms imposed upon Germany in order that an armistice might be agreed, he could only reflect on whether his decision to leave the country had been as beneficial for his people as he had hoped.

For four years, he had been vilified in Allied propaganda, which had been so readily absorbed by his enemies that he was widely viewed as one of the most hated men in Europe; and now, it was only the hospitality of Queen Wilhelmina and her refusal to extradite him to the Allies, which would save him from an ignominious trial, the result of which could easily have been a death sentence. In the years that followed, his sole consolation was his firm belief that he was innocent of all the charges levelled against him and, as he told his hosts in Holland,

"My conscience is clear before God, and what other people think cannot be helped."[1]

Almost a century later, however, Kaiser Wilhelm II is still viewed as either a warmonger or a madman as the hundred-year-old propaganda posters remain fixed in the general consciousness. Was he, though, truly responsible for the catastrophe of the First World War, or was he in fact a convenient scapegoat, blamed for a conflict which he desperately tried to avoid?

Chapter 1 – 'Determined to Keep Peace with Everyone'

There could not have been a more propitious time for an eager and ambitious young man to ascend the dual throne than June 1888, when Kaiser Wilhelm II succeeded his father as King of Prussia and German Emperor. After a decade of conflicts, culminating in a resounding victory in the Franco-Prussian War, the German states had been unified into one Empire, which, by the time of Wilhelm's accession, had known peace for seventeen years. Industry was thriving; coal was plentiful; new methods of iron and steel manufacture had been developed; advances were being made in the chemical industry; and a highly-efficient railway system benefitted trade and communication. The population of forty-eight million was rapidly increasing, and already measures were in place to provide old age pensions, compensation schemes, employers' liability acts, and hygienic housing for workers. Even the lowliest labourers in Germany were beginning to amass savings in one of the most flexible banking systems in the world; while a highly-disciplined and effective army was prepared to protect German interests.

Wilhelm was not, however, prepared to rest on the laurels of his predecessors. Much remained to be done to nurture the infant Germany and turn her into one of the most dynamic countries in Europe.

"If I rest, I rust," was his motto, and, even before his accession, he had developed so clear an image of the nation's progress that he could hardly wait to ascend the throne. Several years earlier, he had scrawled across his own photograph, *I bide my time*; and, now that his hour had come, he was prepared to fulfil his plans for the betterment of his people. With the brash naiveté of youth, he intended to lead Germany into a new Golden Age of prosperity and advancement by improving education, promoting the arts,

11

encouraging sports, supporting freedom of religion, developing a strong foreign policy, and making his opinions count in domestic politics.

"I do not think," wrote the Austrian diplomat, Ottokar von Czernin, "there is another ruler who had better intentions than he had. He lived only for his calling – as he viewed it. All his thoughts and longings were centred round Germany. His relations, pleasures and amusements were all subservient to the one idea of making and keeping the German people great and happy, and if good will were sufficient to achieve great things William II would have achieved them."[2]

Inspiring all his endeavours was the conviction that he and his dynasty, the Hohenzollerns, had been called by God to protect and lead the German people and to promote their material and intellectual interests. This was not, as his detractors often suggested, an arrogant tyrant's assertion of the Divine Right of Kings, but rather an awareness of the responsibilities of his position and a belief that in his role as Kaiser, he embodied the spirit of the country. Based on this conviction, during the early years of his reign, he was prone to making melodramatic statements, calling for absolute obedience from his armed forces, even to the point where he stated that he would expect them to kill their own families if he demanded it, but this was not personal vanity – nor had he ever had any intention of making such a horrendous request! – it was rather a dramatic means of expressing his belief in the importance of loyalty to the country which, as Emperor, he embodied. Like his grandmother, Queen Victoria – 'Queen by the Grace of God' – he felt it to be a sacred obligation to perform his duties with diligence and commitment, knowing that one day he would be answerable to the Almighty.

"I regard my whole position and my task," he said, "as laid on me by Heaven, and that I am appointed by a Higher Power to whom I must later render an account.'[3]

He was equally well aware, however, of the limitations of his position, recognising the differences between his roles as King of Prussia and German Emperor. As the former, he was an autocrat, supported by a two-tier government, comprised almost exclusively of wealthy and titled landowners (Junkers) and industrialists, renowned for their conservatism and allegiance to the Crown. On the other hand, as German Emperor – rather than Emperor of Germany – his role was similar to that of a constitutional monarch – 'the first among equals' of all the German sovereigns.

Following unification in 1871, the kingdoms, grand duchies and principalities, which comprised the new German Empire, retained much of their autonomy and their individual rulers. The Emperor's primary duties consisted in representing the country abroad; appointing ambassadors; and, in the event of Germany being attacked, issuing a declaration of war. To curb his authority a parliament was established, comprising two houses – the Bundesrat (or federal government), consisting of representatives of the different states; and the more democratic Reichstag of three-hundred-and-ninety-seven members, chosen by a wider electorate than anywhere else in Europe. With the exception of criminals and paupers, all males over the age of twenty-five were eligible to vote in a secret ballot; and, since the Reichstag controlled the purse-strings, it became the most powerful body in the Empire, prompting one observer to remark that 'Germany is in many ways more democratic than England.'[4]

Nonetheless, Wilhelm was eager to adhere to the vision of his role as leader of a dynamic and prosperous Germany and, in order to maintain economic progress, an increase in overseas trade was essential. To achieve that end, he recognised four vital factors: a contented and productive workforce; advances in science and technology; a strong navy to secure foreign markets; and, perhaps, most importantly of all, a continuation of the peace which Germany had enjoyed since 1871.

From the start of his reign, he set out to create a co-operative workforce by improving benefits and raising wages, and his first proclamation to the people included a promise that he would support legislation to protect workers and the weak. At the same time, he understood the importance of guarding employers' profits, to give them an incentive to invest in industry, create more goods and increase employment.

"I am resolved," he said, "to lend my hand toward bettering the condition of the German workingmen as far as my solicitude for their welfare is reconcilable with the necessity of enabling German industry to retain its power of competition in the world markets...The loss of such foreign markets would deprive not only the masters but the men of their bread."[5]

True to his word, for the next twenty-five years, he continued to argue in favour of the workers, despite his deep mistrust of socialists whom he viewed as anarchical and detrimental to Germany's progress. During his reign the humblest labourers became the most secure and highest paid in Europe. In Hamburg, for example, dock labourers, who were viewed as the most dispensable workers, were employed by the week; in Belgium, by the day; and in Britain only by the hour.

The new Kaiser's vision was not confined to the industrialised cities, for he was acutely aware that, over the past century, the people of rural communities had endured increasing poverty and, unable to support themselves, several million Germans had emigrated, mainly to the United States. Since forty-three per cent of Germany's food was imported, Wilhelm believed that, with adequate investment, he could eventually make the country self-sufficient and at the same time revive the dwindling agricultural communities. He arranged, therefore, the importation of the most advanced threshing and mowing machines, and encouraged the study of crop and soil sciences, fertilizers and various innovative forms of farming. His efforts proved so successful that emigration from Germany rapidly declined and, although he did not achieve his target of self-sufficiency, by 1914, he had reduced the need for food imports to twenty-five per cent.

While domestic issues occupied much of his time, he was equally keen to involve himself in Germany's foreign policy. If overseas markets were to be maintained and increased, international co-operation was essential and, therefore, from the start of his reign, he sought to impress on the world his overriding desire to maintain peace. Ten days after his accession, he summoned the Reichstag to an extraordinary meeting in which he laid out his plans, stressing that he intended to follow in the footsteps of his grandfather, Wilhelm I, who 'ruled with a love of peace,' and who 'won for himself the trust of his allies, the love of the German people, and the kindly recognition of foreign countries.' Three months later, at the official opening of the Reichstag, he spoke of having secured an agreement with England to combat the hunting and transportation of African slaves; and, again, emphasised the need for good relations with his European neighbours.

> "It is incompatible with my Christian faith," he said, "and with the duties which as Emperor I have assumed towards the people needlessly to bring upon Germany the sorrows of a war, even a victorious one."[6]

Despite these pacific professions, however, the foreign press was quick to note that the first address of his reign had been made to the army.

"We belong to each other, I and the army. Thus we are born for one another and thus we will stand together in an indissoluble bond in peace or storm as God may will it."[7]

To Wilhelm, military might was not incompatible with his desire for peace, for he believed that strong defences were the best deterrent against war[a], but the speech sent a ripple of anxiety through the Empire and beyond, provoking a good deal of speculation about what kind of ruler he intended to be.

To the majority of his subjects, he was largely unknown, having ascended the throne far sooner than anyone had anticipated. In March 1888, his aged grandfather, Wilhelm I, had died after a short illness, and his successor, Wilhelm's father, reigned for only ninety-nine days before succumbing to cancer of the throat. The 'year of the three Emperors' had seen a ninety-year-old sovereign succeeded by a middle-aged man who was already dying, followed by a dashing twenty-nine-year-old Hussar whose manner and appearance contrasted sharply with those of his predecessors. To many Germans, Kaiser Wilhelm II reflected the spirit of a young and dynamic nation, but others – especially those who had been close to his parents – were disconcerted by his youth and inexperience, viewing him as nothing more than 'Bismarck's tool', a puppet of the elderly 'Iron Chancellor', whose ultra-conservatism had won many enemies including Catholics, socialists, democrats and, most significantly, perhaps, Wilhelm's own mother.

To the outside world, too, Wilhelm was largely unknown. As Queen Victoria's eldest grandson, he had gained a measure of popularity in England, where, throughout his childhood and youth, occasional favourable stories had appeared about him in the press; but in recent

---

[a] See Chapter 6

months, his alleged mistreatment of his English mother and his apparent disregard for his well-loved father's liberal opinions, had tarnished his reputation.

The French, still reeling from their defeat in the Franco-Prussian War, initially hoped that so inexperienced a monarch might be prevailed upon to return to them the provinces of Alsace- Lorraine, which had been annexed by Prussia after the conflict. Some believed him so gullible that they went so far as to tell him that this had been his late father's intention, and they were shocked when Wilhelm adamantly refuted the claim and vowed that Germany would not 'cede a single stone' that had been won 'by the sword'. This statement, combined with his opening address to the army, quickly gave rise to the fear that this mercurial young man saw himself as a latter-day Napoleon who intended to expand his Empire still further across the French border.

On hearing that, so soon after his accession, he was being described as a warlord, Wilhelm was deeply distressed and anxious to allay such fears. He reiterated his commitment to the army but emphasised that its sole purpose was the defence of the realm.

"In foreign policy," he said firmly, "I am determined to keep peace with everyone so far as in me lies. My love for the German army and my position in it will never lead me into the temptation of robbing the country of the benefits of peace, unless some attack on the Empire or her Allies forces war upon us."[8]

To press the point still further, he had no sooner completed a tour of the various German states than he prepared to embark on a series of visits to foreign courts to assure his European neighbours of his peaceful intentions. In May 1889, while entertaining the King and Queen of Italy, he raised a toast to 'our unchanging friendship'; in St. Petersburg, he assured Tsar Alexander III that he hoped to continue the hundred-year-old friendship between their countries, and stressed that:

"I never think of increasing German territory. I intend to devote my time to Home Reforms which are so necessary in Germany."[9]

In Stockholm, he spoke of the 'traditions binding the Swedish and the German people together' and invited King Oscar II to be the godfather of his fifth son. In Denmark he was so passionate in expressing his desire for peace that he succeeded in winning over several members of the Royal Family, despite a long-standing dispute concerning the Prussian seizure of Schleswig-Holstein from the Danes a quarter of a century earlier. He flattered the aged Emperor Franz Josef of Austria-Hungary by describing him a great soldier, notwithstanding the fact that he had lost virtually every war in which he had been engaged; he cultivated a friendship with the King of Romania; in the Netherlands, he told Queen Wilhelmina of his appreciation of the close ties between their countries; and, when he visited England, he spoke of Queen Victoria as 'a very superior lady in her wisdom and counsel', before reminding his hearers that:

"The friendship with the English, which had been sealed in my blood, my honoured grandfather maintained to the end of his life."[10]

So emphatic and impressive were his messages of goodwill that they were reported around the world; and in the United States, where a large a large population of German emigrants had settled, journalists could not praise him highly enough. One article, which appeared in the American *New Review* in 1889, would have pleased him above all others, for it compared him favourably with his hero and ancestor, Frederick the Great:

"In force of character and intellectual power, the present Emperor surpasses any of his predecessors, certainly up to the time of the Great Frederick."[11]

Even in France, despite the deep-rooted hostility towards Prussia, some journalists were impressed not only by his pacific speeches but also by his genuine interest in the welfare of the poor[b].

Convinced that his tours had been successful and his messages well-received, Wilhelm returned home triumphant, confident that his words and his personal charisma were sufficient to eradicate decades of international hostility. In 1891, in an attempt to continue to ameliorate relations with France, he encouraged his mother to travel to Paris to invite French artists to exhibit at the forthcoming Berlin exhibition. It came as a rude awakening when he heard that she had met with such violent protests from the League of French Patriots that she had all but been forced to flee the country.

Even worse was to follow when the Imperial Chancellor, Otto von Bismarck, shocked by Wilhelm's naïve belief that he could resolve years of conflict simply by speaking of peace, advised him that it was impossible to please everyone, and rather cruelly told him that his visit to Russia had not been as successful as he had imagined. While Wilhelm had proudly been relishing his role as a diplomatic genius, he had been unaware that the Tsar believed him to have outstayed his welcome in St Petersburg, and had belittled him by describing him as a 'badly brought-up boy'.

At home, too, he was not without his critics. For all his expressed interest in the welfare of workers, and his support for the Workingmen's Insurance Act – twenty years before similar legislation was introduced in Britain – the socialists were dissatisfied by the limitations of the act, while Bismarck, felt that, rather than appeasing the socialists, the Kaiser – whom he patronisingly referred to as 'the young man' – should heed his advice and take strong

---

[b] See Chapter 5

action to bring them to heel. Throughout his reign the Junkers continued to criticise his concern for ordinary workers, and as late as 1914, the renowned playwright, George Bernard Shaw, wrote that:

> "The Kaiser has been openly reviled as a coward by his Junkers because he falls short of Mr Asquith[c] in calm indifference to Liberal principles and blank ignorance of working class sympathies, opinions and interests."[12]

The greatest criticism of all came from his own mother, who, unimpressed by his speeches and flamboyant declarations, believed him incapable of understanding the intricacies of foreign or domestic politics. He was, she claimed, Bismarck's creature, reading only the papers that were set before him, and following instructions from militaristic intriguers. Her opinion, however, was undoubtedly tarnished by her grief at the untimely death of her husband, and long-standing tensions in her relationship with her son, which would come to mirror with remarkable accuracy his relationship with her native England.

---

[c] Herbert Henry Asquith - a British Liberal politician and later Prime Minister.

Chapter 2 – 'A Thousand Pities That He Should Be So Afflicted'

The whirlwind tour of foreign courts not only provided Wilhelm with an opportunity to demonstrate his newly-acquired authority and carry his messages of peace, but would also, he hoped, win him the admiration of his fellow sovereigns and the affection of their people. In spite of his bravura and the powerful image he attempted to portray, his exaggerated belief in his own abilities was tempered by a deep-rooted sense of inadequacy. This lack of self-confidence had blighted his formative years and given rise to a lifelong pattern of feeling rejected and misunderstood by those whose affection and attention he most craved.

Born into a loving family, the first child of Queen Victoria's eldest daughter, Vicky, and her husband, Prince Friedrich Wilhelm ('Fritz') of Prussia, Wilhelm was welcomed into the world with great rejoicing on 27th January 1859. His paternal grandfather – then acting as Regent for his brother, the incapacitated Prussian King Friedrich Wilhelm IV – was so excited by the news of his birth that he hurried from a meeting at the Foreign Office and hailed an ordinary cab to take him at once to see him. According to a witness, the festivities in Berlin had the atmosphere of a 'great family festival', and when the proud father, 'radiant with happiness' presented his son to the crowds, the general rejoicing, through all classes of society, was boundless[13].

In Britain, too, the baby's birth prompted such celebrations that an extra verse was added to the National Anthem, which was performed by the London Opera Company to great applause:

"Hail the auspicious morn,
To Prussia's throne is born
A Royal Heir.

May he defend its laws,
Joined with old England's cause,
And win all men's applause!
God save the Queen!"

His maternal grandparents were delighted and, as Queen Victoria wrote countless letters asking for every detail of his health and appearance, her consort, Prince Albert, was moved to utter a prayer of thanksgiving.

> "God be praised and thanked that He has ordered all things so graciously, and may He continue to shield the mother and the child!"[14]

What neither his grandparents nor the crowds of well-wishers initially realised, however, was the extent of the near-fatal agonies that Wilhelm's eighteen-year-old mother had suffered bringing him into the world, nor the long-term effects of the trauma that the baby had endured. In the midst of a harrowing and protracted labour, the attending English and German doctors discovered that Wilhelm was in the breech position but none was prepared to perform the customary caesarean section, which almost invariably resulted in the death of the mother. Unwilling to risk killing a daughter of Queen Victoria, the German doctor, Martin, chose instead to use forceps and, by the time that the baby was dragged from the womb, he appeared more dead than alive. In a desperate effort to revive him, Martin rubbed him so vigorously that the nerves and muscles of his left shoulder – already weakened by the forceps – were irreparably damaged.

The resulting disability was not immediately apparent, and those who saw the infant prince in his first few months were struck by his attractive appearance.

> "They say all babies are alike," wrote one German observer. "I do not think so: this one has a beautiful complexion, pink and white, and the most lovely little hand ever seen! The nose rather large; the eyes were shut, which was as well, as the light was so

strong. His happy father was holding him in his arms."[15]

Soon, though, his mother observed that the child was incapable of crawling, and seemed quite unaware that he had a left arm at all. Concerned that the nerves had been damaged, a German physician, Dr Wenger, stuck pins in his hand to see if he could feel pain, before binding his right arm to his side in the hope that it would compel him to use the left. The experiment failed, and, as Wilhelm grew, the disability became more pronounced and more inconvenient. His gait was awkward; he could not keep pace when running with younger boys; his head sometimes jerked involuntarily to one side; and his weak left arm was noticeably shorter than the right, resulting in an inability to use a knife and fork or to dress himself easily. His lack of balance, exacerbated by chronic and painful ear infections, hindered his ability to learn to swim or ride; and, as word of his difficulties spread through the court, cruel mutterings were heard in some quarters that, 'a one-armed man can never be king.'

Frantic with worry, his mother became obsessed with his problems, fretting about him 'night and day' and desperately seeking a cure.

> "It is a thousand pities he should be so afflicted," she wrote gloomily to Queen Victoria when Wilhelm was five years old, "...it disfigures him so much, gives him something awkward in all his movements, which is sad for a prince...and it is hard that it should be our eldest that has this misfortune."[16]

Over the next five years, she continued to fret as doctors subjected him to all kinds of treatments, ranging from the barbaric to the utterly bizarre. He was strapped into a machine with a metal rod pressed to his spine, while attempts were made to straighten his neck by means of a screw; weights were hung from his arm in an effort to make it grow; surgery was performed to cut a nerve in his neck; and, most bizarrely of all, his arm was tied to the corpse of a recently-slaughtered hare, which, according to an ancient superstition, had the power to restore withered limbs.

The long and painful treatments often left him too exhausted to attend his lessons and, to his highly-intelligent mother's chagrin, he consequently appeared 'backward', failing to learn to read or write as quickly as she would have hoped.

Eventually, realising that little could be done for the injured limb, his parents sought to help him to adapt to his difficulties and to conceal the disability as far as possible. Raised pockets were sewn into his clothes to disguise the shortness of his arm; and, later, following his accession, he often wore a cape during his public appearances. When sitting for a portrait or a photograph, his small hand was either gloved or hidden in his pocket, and he learned to adopt a striking pose, which not only concealed the deformity but also gave the impression of powerful grandeur.

Refusing to pamper him, his parents aimed to treat him as they would any other child, drawing little attention to his difficulties and encouraging him to endure his challenges without complaint. When, at the age of five, his pony reared, throwing him to the ground, a witness observed that:

> "Both parents remained quite calm, and apparently took no notice; the Prince mounted again and went on riding."[17]

Under the guidance of a military gymnastics tutor, Captain von Dresky, he learned to swim and row a boat; and, with the help of an assistant to load his rifle, and a tripod on which to rest the barrel, he soon became a skilled marksman. Despite frequent and painful falls from his pony, his academic tutor, Hintzpeter, forced him to remount again and again until at last he became such an accomplished horseman that he could outride many cavalry officers, and easily took jumps which even the most skilled equestrians hesitated to attempt. Notwithstanding his atrophied arm, his fingers were supple enough to play the piano; and, compensating for the weakness of the left limb, he developed such a powerful right arm and hand that those whom he greeted with a handshake were shocked by the strength of his grip.

Still, his mother continued to bemoan his fate to Queen Victoria. It was dreadfully sad, she said, that he would always be dependent on servants for so many daily activities, and, to some extent her prediction proved accurate. Throughout much of his life, a footman stood behind him at the table to cut his food, until a spoon with a serrated edge was designed especially for him, and, to avoid drawing attention to his problems, the same piece of cutlery was provided for all his guests during banquets. Dressing was always difficult, particularly for man who liked to change his clothes several times a day:

> "We would not care if [he] changed his uniform ten, instead of three or four times per day," said one of his attendants, "it's the fear of injuring his lame hand that makes us nervous and gradually wears away our usefulness. And, besides, we must always be prepared to forestall the collapse of the all-highest master when he balances himself on his left leg, as is his wont sometimes, when he is in a hurry to put on a different pair of trousers."[18]

For the most part, though, he succeeded in overcoming his physical handicaps, but the psychological scars of his painful treatments and the humiliation of being 'imperfect' never truly left him. His tutor, Hintzpeter, repeatedly reminded him that a King must be in every way superior to his people, which instilled in the little boy a desperate need to appear strong and to conceal not only his disability but also his naturally sensitive nature. For a while

25

he became so shy and insecure that his aloofness was mistaken for arrogance, and as he learned to hide his inner turmoil behind a mask of bravado, he was viewed as precocious with too inflated a sense of his own importance. Laughing too loudly, talking too quickly, dominating conversations and plying his hearers with questions as he 'practically stood on one's feet, glaring into one's eyes'[19], the hyperactivity of his mind seemed to compensate for the weakness of his arm; and his thoughts leaped so quickly from one idea to another that his childhood playmates and cousins nicknamed him 'William the Sudden.' It was a pattern that would continue into adulthood when, to his wife's despair, he would unexpectedly decide that they were to move from one palace to another without a moment's notice[d].

Even at the height of his power, he could not forget the shame of his disability. During the First World War, when he discovered that surgeons were making prosthetic limbs for wounded soldiers, he expressed a particular interest in artificial arms, wondering whether such an appliance could be made for him.

The greatest tragedy of all, however, was the effect that his disability had on his relationship with his mother. Mistaking her corrections of his behaviour for personal criticism, and her anxious expressions for revulsion, he came to the erroneous conclusion that she found his arm so repulsive that she could not love him. That thought, which developed throughout his childhood, was devastating for a little boy who longed for her affection and relished every moment that he spent in her company. While he was picnicking with his friends in the gardens one day, an

---

[d] A joke was often heard in Berlin: What is the Emperor's favourite saying? *Suffer without complaint.* What is his second favourite saying? *Duty, duty, duty.* What is his third favourite saying? *Hurry, Augusta* [his wife] – *start packing!*

26

observer noticed how proudly he told his companions that his mother had baked the cake they were enjoying, and:

> "When the Crown Princess and her husband made their appearance, no face lighted up with more pleasure than that of Prince William."[20]

Sadly, her numerous duties and frequent confinements[e] prevented her from spending as much time with him as she would have wished; and, to make matters worse, his paternal grandparents, influenced by the formidable Otto von Bismarck, were not only determined to keep him untainted by 'the English woman's' liberal opinions, but seemed to actively turn him against her as they insisted on retaining overall charge of his upbringing.

---

[e] By the time that Wilhelm was fourteen years old, his mother had given birth to seven more children: four girls and three boys, two of whom – Sigismund and Waldemar – died in childhood.

Chapter 3 – 'The English Woman'

It was Vicky's misfortune that her arrival in Prussia coincided with Bismarck's rise to power, for, at the time of her marriage, she had naively believed that she and her equally liberal-minded husband, Fritz, could be instrumental in fulfilling her father's dream of a unified Germany headed by tolerant and constitutional Prussia. While Bismarck shared their hopes for a Prussian-led Empire, his plans for the future of Germany and the methods he would adopt to achieve his ends were totally at odds with Vicky and Fritz' vision. Ambitious for himself and for his country, his meteoric rise to power was due largely to his staunch loyalty to the crown, which earned him the unfailing support of Fritz's father, who succeeded his brother as King Wilhelm I in 1861. The following year, he appointed Bismarck as Minister-President, before raising him to the position of Imperial Chancellor when Germany was unified in 1871. So dependent was the King on his manipulative Chancellor that he was even prepared to side with him against his own son, whose constitutional views were dismissed as either irrelevant or subversive, culminating in his being virtually banished from the court.

> "The object of Bismarck has been, and is, to isolate the Crown Prince from all persons not immediately under his (Bismarck's) influence," a British diplomat wrote to Queen Victoria. "He knows that the Prince is a man of unsanguine character, and that this isolation acts upon him in a depressing manner, and he believes that he can depress him into submission."[21]

It was typical of Bismarck to use such underhand methods to attempt to control the Crown Prince, for he was equally ruthless in destroying all of his critics. Having taken control of the press, he had derogatory articles printed about his opponents, ruining their reputations with real or invented scandals. Vicky soon fell victim to his ruse when, irked by her tactless comparisons between Britain and Germany, and her willingness to express political opinions not in keeping with his own, he let it be known that 'the English woman' was emasculating her taciturn husband and infecting him with her 'un-Prussian' ideas. Worse was to follow when, during the Franco-Prussian War – which Bismarck had deliberately engineered in order to unite the German states against a common enemy – he went so far as to accuse her of divulging military secrets to the French, resulting in her being so reviled in Berlin that she was not even permitted to assist in the organization of hospitals for the wounded.

Distressed as she was by Bismarck's slanders, nothing was more wounding for Vicky than the way in which he treated her husband, undermining his credibility, claiming his triumphs and distancing him from the court. Almost equally distressing were the Chancellor's efforts to alienate Vicky's eldest children from her by implying that 'the *English* woman' was too attached to her homeland to show any loyalty to Germany. Playing upon Wilhelm's insecurities, Bismarck flattered his frail ego by reminding him of his position as a future Emperor and telling him tales of military victories and Prussian heroes. As these blandishments began to instil in the boy a sense of his own importance, his mother's efforts to correct his arrogance sounded harsh and unfeeling, while his father's liberal opinions appeared weak compared to Bismarck's tales of masculine glory.

Wilhelm's apparent disdain for his parents, however, was symptomatic of his desperate longing for their attention, for, in spite of Bismarck's efforts, he loved them deeply and revelled in their company. In his later years, he would fondly recall reading to his mother as she painted, and how happily they laughed together; and when the family were able to escape from the intrigues of court to the simplicity of their country estate, Wilhelm appeared happy and healthier than ever. More memorable still were the days that he spent visiting his grandmother at her seaside home, Osborne House, on the Isle of Wight. There, he and his brother, Henry, watched the merchant and naval fleets sailing out along the Solent, inspiring in them a dream to create an equally magnificent German navy. Despite once announcing in a fit of pique that every last drop of English blood had gone from his veins during a nosebleed, Wilhelm loved England, and more particularly Queen Victoria, who, from the moment of his birth, had never failed to shower him with affection. Holidays with 'dearest grandmamma' were always a delight as the Queen took a great interest in his progress and, as well as arranging treats and entertainments, made a point of defending him against his sometimes hypercritical mother.

> "Oddly enough," said Lady Warwick, "when there were family quarrels in Berlin, the Queen always sided with her grandson against the Princess Royal."[22]

Wilhelm was thrilled when the Queen affectionately addressed him as 'my dear boy', but she was not above correcting his behaviour and one occasion wrote that he deserved 'a good skelping.' For his part, there times when he would criticise her interference, even referring to her as 'the old hag', but their mutual devotion was unwavering and he never forget the kindness she showed him as a child nor the support that she would give him at the start of his reign[f].

While Vicky's mother did her utmost to smooth relations between her and her son, Fritz's parents exacerbated the tension by pandering to Wilhelm's whims to the point where Vicky could only excuse his 'laziness and conceit' by explaining that his faults had been 'more

---

[f] See Chapter 7

30

encouraged than checked'. Their over-indulgence was so at odds with Vicky's frequent reprimands that, as Wilhelm came to hero-worship his grandfather, he viewed his mother as increasingly 'stern, cold and distant'.

Unfortunately, he was unaware of the way in which she had been prevented from playing as great a part in his upbringing as she would have wished. He did not know that she had been forbidden from breast-feeding him, nor that she regularly wrote to Queen Victoria, bemoaning the fact that she and Fritz were not permitted to raise him according to their own ideas. He probably never read the numerous compliments she paid him in her epistles to her mother, describing him as 'a dear, sweet child', with a 'charming countenance and pleasing expression', and proudly explaining that:

> "He is growing so handsome and his large eyes have now and then a dreamy expression and then again they sparkle with fun and delight."[23]

During his adolescence, torn between his natural feelings for his parents, and the attention of their archenemy, Bismarck, Wilhelm's turmoil resulted in desperate attempts to win his mother's attention by writing her love letters, which were so unnerving that she felt the best course was to ignore them. Since his outpourings of love had been so easily dismissed, he became more aloof in his dealings with her, fearful of showing emotion lest it should be followed by feelings of rejection. When, for example, on the eve of his wedding, she expressed sadness that he would never again sleep in the family home, he dismissed her concerns, and, as she told Queen Victoria:

> "He thinks me absurdly sentimental to observe this and says it is all the same to him in what place or house or room he lives."[24]

His emotional turmoil and deep-rooted sense of inadequacy was heightened when, while studying at the University of Bonn, he fell madly in love with his fourteen-year-old cousin, the beautiful Ella of Hesse. Ella was horrified by his proposal of marriage, leaving him so utterly devastated that his opinion of his own attractions reached its nadir. Some years later he told a mistress that he was amazed that she could love him since he had always believed himself to be unappealing to women; and it was, perhaps, significant that in 1881, he married 'beneath him' – his bride, Princess Augusta Victoria ('Dona'), being the daughter of the somewhat impoverished and insignificant Duke of Schleswig-Holstein. A pious and charitable woman with few political opinions, Dona, like Bismarck, flattered his ego by agreeing with everything he said. Her brother observed that Wilhelm and Dona never fought because 'he sees to it that his slightest whims are obeyed, nay, more, anticipated.'[25]

Fortunately, Wilhelm's relationship with his father was far less complex than that with his mother. Fritz, a hero of the Franco-Prussian War, had all the qualities that Wilhelm most admired. Tall and striking in appearance, respected not only by his subordinates but also by his enemies, his courage had not hardened him or blinded him to the horrors of war. Wilhelm watched enraptured when he returned to Berlin at the head of a triumphant army but, as the thrill of victory imprinted itself on the little boy's mind, Fritz was quick to dispel any illusions about the glories of battle. Years later, Wilhelm would announce:

> "Never have I had warlike ambitions. In my youth my father had given me terrible descriptions of the battlefields of 1870 & 1871. I felt no inclination to bring such misery, on a colossally larger scale, on the German people and the whole of civilized mankind."[26]

On a personal level, Fritz probably understood Wilhelm better than anyone, and he knew exactly how to correct him without injuring his pride. When, for example, his anxious nursemaids reported that their young charge

32

refused to be bathed, Fritz instructed the palace sentries to abandon their usual custom of presenting arms when Wilhelm passed by. Shocked at their apparent negligence, Wilhelm complained to his father, who told him that the soldiers had orders never to salute an unwashed prince.

The bond of affection between father and son was strengthened by the hours that they spent in each other's company, for, not only did Fritz calmly accompany him to his medical examinations but also made the time to share his interests and studies. Wilhelm loved to sit beside him as he pointed out pictures in colourful history books; and, when Fritz' duties permitted, they passed many happy afternoons walking, swimming and enjoying boating outings together. Sadly, though, as Fritz was increasingly ostracised from the court, he had more time to spend with Wilhelm, who, while savouring his attention, was simultaneously drawn to those responsible for his exclusion.

The greater part of the Kaiser's youth was spent in the company of his brother, Henry, and their tutor, the austere Calvinist, George Hintzpeter, who had been chosen by his parents on the recommendation of an English diplomat. Thirty-eight-year-old Hintzpeter firmly believed that a Spartan regime would benefit his princely pupils, whom he treated with strictness bordering on brutality. Despite his uncouth table manners and his being, in Vicky's opinion, 'not very bright', Wilhelm's parents were happy with Hintzpeter's methods, but the princes found his lessons joyless and uninspiring. Studying from dawn until evening, their days were interspersed with recreational rides or walks but even then Hintzpeter insisted on continuing their education by compelling them to recite from the classics. The rigidity of the regime was stifling to the impetuous and free-spirited Wilhelm, leaving him with a lifelong 'feeling of restlessness under every kind of restraint'[27]. Nor was Hintzpeter's influence quite as beneficial as Vicky and Fritz believed, for he constantly reminded Wilhelm that, as a future Emperor, he must be superior to his people, simultaneously exacerbating his sense of his own importance, and compounding his feelings of inadequacy by setting him unattainable targets and never offering a word of praise. To counteract Bismarck's influence on the boy, Hintzpeter encouraged him to think for himself rather than accepting advice from others, but his efforts backfired when Wilhelm took him to mean that he should disregard his parents' opinions and admonishments. Moreover, it appeared to some observers that, while objecting to the Chancellor's influence, Hintzpeter himself 'nursed serious hopes of one day ruling over Germany in the name of his pupil'[28] and he added to the tensions between Wilhelm and Vicky by stating that she was too wrapped up in her husband to show any genuine affection to her children.

For all his faults, however, Hintzpeter adhered to Vicky and Fritz's instructions to provide their sons with a well-rounded education which was far more comprehensive than the purely militaristic schooling that was common among Prussian princes. Each week the boys were taken to a factory to see the working conditions and to learn the basics of manufacture and marketing. There, they were expected to behave as apprentices rather than princes, and at the end of the day they would doff their caps and thank the workers for their time. The experience served Wilhelm well, for, following his accession, he not only retained an interest manufacturing processes but also displayed an ability to speak easily with people of all classes. An English member of his household noted that:

> "...the Emperor and his family possess in an unusual degree what Kipling calls the 'common touch.' They know how to talk to poor men, working men, without any shadow of that

patronizing affability often mistakenly employed by one class when trying to be nice to another which is not on the same social plane."[29]

Hintzpeter also believed that Wilhelm and Henry would benefit from the competition of their peers, and, despite their parents' reservations and initial objections from the court, the princes were eventually enrolled in a gymnasium in Kassel. There, sitting on 'uncommonly hard benches', they were treated like any other pupils and, although Hintzpeter remained with them, he was not permitted to interfere in their lessons to help them in any way which would give them an advantage over their classmates. As it happened, Wilhelm had little need of the tutor's assistance, for, notwithstanding the fact that his mother had once described him as 'backward', he was an able student who excelled in subjects that interested him.

Years later, his detractors would revile the Kaiser as an unintelligent buffoon, but in truth he had clearly inherited at least some of his mother's intellectual genius. His excellent memory enabled him to become a proficient historian, and his passion for archaeology made him something of an expert in that field. Following his accession, a Harvard theologian was amazed by his deep understanding of various theologies; while the professor of a reputable American technical college was equally impressed by the extent of his knowledge of engineering. A pioneer of applied psychology was happily surprised by his understanding of how the new science could benefit medicine, education and the law:

> "The questions which he asked and the criticisms which he expressed, showed a more thorough grasp of the essentials, and a more helpful insight into the new science than any which I have heard from scholarly or unscholarly men."[30]

Moreover, his skill as a linguist not only enabled him to speak fluent French and English with no trace of an accent, but also impressed many academics who were amazed by his ability to discuss complex subjects in several languages.

His intelligence was commented upon by many who met him during his childhood and youth, but they were equally struck by his unassuming manner, describing him as 'an amiable playfellow', and 'a plucky, hearty, unaffected lad' who was able to sparkle in conversation and entertain his hearers.

From Kassel, as Henry embarked on a naval career, Wilhelm moved on to the University of Bonn to study jurisprudence and political science before commencing what was to be one of the happiest periods of his life – a course of training at the most prestigious military academy in Potsdam[g].

---

[g] See Chapter 6

Chapter 4 – 'The Whole World Misjudged Me'

During the reign of Wilhelm's uncle, King Edward VII, the image of the once 'amiable playfellow' was gradually distorted as his alleged cruel treatment of his mother and disregard for his father was used by propagandists to suggest that a man who could behave so heartlessly to his parents was capable of any horrific atrocity. To this day, the myth, based solely on Vicky's account of events, continues to be believed but, in reality, in the weeks leading up to his father's death, Wilhelm was earnestly trying to do his best for his country.

Vicky and Fritz were married at a time when the British Royal Family was at an apex of popularity, and as the Queen's eldest daughter, Vicky, the young and pretty Princess Royal, was held in great affection by her mother's subjects. Fritz, too, quickly endeared himself to the British people, who, enraptured by his prepossessing appearance and kindly manner, widely and justifiably believed that he was Queen Victoria's favourite son-in-law.

> "He was so kind to me always," the Queen wrote sadly, following his demise. "...I see him always before me with those beautiful loving blue eyes."[31]

Never did Fritz make such an impression on the English as when, in June 1887, dressed in the brilliant white uniform of the Cuirassier Guard, he led a mounted procession to Westminster Abbey for Queen Victoria's Golden Jubilee thanksgiving service. An article in Lloyd's newspaper captured public opinion by describing him as sitting 'with the firm easy seat of a cavalry soldier; an ideal prince among princes.'[32]

His appearance in the procession was all the more striking because, by then, rumours had begun to circulate that the fifty-five-year-old Crown Prince was seriously ill. Few who saw him at the Jubilee, however, would have believed that he was already in the grip of terminal cancer, and that he had barely a year left to live.

Throughout the mid-1880s, he had frequently been troubled by colds and hoarseness, and, in the early spring of 1887, doctors had attempted to cauterize a small growth on his larynx. In May, seeing little improvement, Vicky invited a British throat specialist, Sir Morell Mackenzie, to Berlin to carry out an examination. On discovering further tumours, Mackenzie performed a biopsy, promising to see Fritz again when he arrived in London for the Jubilee.

Realising that his father was unwell, although not yet aware of the severity of his illness, Wilhelm eagerly thrust himself forwards, offering to replace the Crown Prince as the Emperor's representative at the celebrations. Vicky, incensed by his pushiness, complained bitterly to her mother, whose initial response was to deny Wilhelm an invitation to the jubilee, until Vicky relented and persuaded her to change her mind. Although Wilhelm's behaviour was brash and somewhat unfeelingly opportunistic, it is possible that he genuinely believed that his father was not fit for the exertion of the journey and subsequent celebrations. Vicky herself was so concerned for his health that she feared the London air would exacerbate his condition and it would be better if they were housed in the outskirts of the city. Nonetheless, whatever Wilhelm's motives might have been, his keenness to replace the Crown Prince implanted in Vicky's mind the belief that he was using Fritz's illness to usurp his position and further his own ambition. It was a belief which would become an *idée fixe* for her in subsequent months, and one which has, ever since, done great damage to her son's reputation.

Mackenzie, meanwhile, carried out a further examination of Fritz's throat, and following the Jubilee celebrations, advised a period of recuperation far from the dust of Berlin or the smog of London. Vicky and Fritz, therefore, spent some time on the Isle of Wight, before joining the Queen at Balmoral where, it was hoped, the freshness of the mountains would help to alleviate his symptoms. Although, by early autumn, he appeared to have improved, he was not yet fit to resume his duties and so he and Vicky took their younger daughters to the Austrian Tyrol, until, as winter set in, they migrated to the warmer climes of San Remo in western Italy.

Doctors regularly examined his throat, offering a variety of conflicting diagnoses and disagreeing about the best course of treatment to the point where Vicky lost faith in the ability of the German medics, and placed all her trust in the English Morell Mackenzie.

By then, the Crown Prince had been absent from Germany for almost six months and, as his aged father's normally robust health began to decline, journalists and ministers demanded to know why the heir was neglecting his duties. Since no official diagnosis had been given, speculation was rampant – some pressmen suggesting that he was suffering from venereal disease; or, still more salaciously, that Vicky was having an affair with her chamberlain and had enlisted the help of her English doctor to do away with her husband. For Fritz's father, the Emperor, the most disturbing report claimed that the Crown Prince was suffering from an inoperable cancer. Understandably anxious, the Emperor wanted to discover the truth for himself and, therefore, according to Mackenzie:

> "His Royal Highness, Prince William, was commanded to repair at once to San Remo with the confidential physician, Dr Schmidt of Frankfort, who had been selected by the physicians of the Emperor."[33]

For Vicky, under immeasurable stress and refusing to accept the seriousness of her husband's condition, Wilhelm's arrival served only to aggravate an already painful situation. Exhausted with worry, she accepted the warning of her associates who falsely claimed that Wilhelm, as Bismarck's puppet, had come to San Remo solely to usurp his father's authority. When, on the Emperor's orders, Wilhelm summoned a meeting of all the attending physicians to obtain an authentic report on the Crown Prince's condition, Vicky wrote plaintively to her mother, complaining of his arrogant high-handedness. It was this description of Wilhelm's behaviour that was later used to discredit the Kaiser, suggesting that he was motivated solely by a lust for power. Ironically, though, when the future Tsar Nicholas II was attending *his* dying father, he was accused of weakness for allowing the doctors to report to his mother rather than directly to him.

According to his memoirs, Wilhelm was filled with 'grief and sorrow' on hearing the doctors' devastating diagnosis, for, by then, although several were reluctant to admit it, most concurred that he was suffering from terminal cancer. Having little faith in Mackenzie, and keen to stem the gossip in Berlin, Wilhelm suggested that only German doctors should attend him. His advice did little to placate his mother, who, incensed by his perceived interference, responded by denying him access to his father.

In fact, Wilhelm was not the only one to doubt Mackenzie's abilities. Queen Victoria, realising that Vicky's anxieties were probably clouding her judgement, told her that, 'Some people also think that Sir M. Mackenzie's judgement is not quite equal to his skill in the internal operation'[34]; and her close friend, Lady Mary Ponsonby, tactfully suggested that it might be better to prevent Mackenzie from attending the Crown Prince alone. Vicky chose to ignore their advice but continued to blame Wilhelm for causing much distress to her husband.

Already saddened at not being allowed to talk alone with his father, it was even more painful for Wilhelm to see that foreign journalists were allowed to come and go freely into his room   while 'every obstacle was placed in my path, to keep me from [his] side and even to prevent me from keeping in constant touch with him by my writing'[35]. His letters to Fritz were intercepted and, to make matters worse, articles appeared in French newspapers stating that he was behaving as though the Crown Prince were already dead.

The German press was equally guilty of mischief-making, printing false reports that Wilhelm had left San Remo with a signed Act of Abdication from his father, and, although Wilhelm had had nothing to do with the invention or the printing of the stories, Vicky erroneously believed that he had sanctioned their publication.

Meanwhile, in Berlin, a coterie of ministers who had long been opposed to Vicky's political views, feared that if Fritz ascended the throne in such a poor physical condition, all authority would effectively be passed to his wife. It would be better for Fritz and for the country, they claimed, if the Crown Prince abdicated as heir and allowed the crown to pass directly to Wilhelm. Although many were motivated by self-interest, their suggestion, viewed objectively, was not without merit. Already there was talk of the potential necessity of performing a tracheotomy to enable Fritz to breathe, which could easily result in his losing his voice altogether. On his return to Berlin, Wilhelm had questioned whether a man who could not speak would be able to perform his duties as Emperor; and, callous as his words might have sounded, it was not an unreasonable question. The immense burden of responsibility would surely exacerbate Fritz's condition, and in Prussia, as in Russia, the Emperor was expected to epitomise the strength of the country and to rise above the physical frailties of ordinary mortals.

During the cold winter of 1888, the ninety-year-old Emperor contracted a chill, and, aware that his health was beginning to fail, recognised the need to prepare for a regency. In view of the physicians' reports about the seriousness of Fritz' condition, the Emperor, like the majority of his ministers, had come to believe that he would outlive his heir and, as Wilhelm was next-in-line to the throne, he would be the obvious choice of regent. Already, twice a week, he had been trained in 'kingcraft' by his grandfather and by Bismarck, and, despite his youth, he was proving himself capable of carrying out a monarch's duties under the Chancellor's guidance. With Fritz still far away in San Remo, therefore, the Emperor appointed Wilhelm as *Stellvertreter des Kaisers* (Vice-Emperor) and gave him authority to sign declarations 'By Order of the King.'

As his mother continued to deny him access to his father, Wilhelm duly dispatched his brother, Henry, to Italy to explain the Emperor's decision. Appalled by the news, Vicky again complained to her mother that Wilhelm and Henry had behaved so badly that Fritz was 'much upset, very angry, and much excited..."[36] In her anguish, as she bemoaned the fact that Wilhelm was now issuing orders without consulting his father, she failed to take into account that it was impossible for him to refer to Fritz since she had ensured that his letters were intercepted, and he was not permitted to see him.

Bismarck, eager to see his protégé in a position of power, pressed the Emperor to go further by involving Wilhelm in all affairs of state, but aware of how distressed Fritz had been at Wilhelm's promotion to *Stellvertreter des Kaisers,* he refused to be rushed into making a decision. He would, he told Bismarck, have liked to have his grandson participate in all his duties but was reluctant to cause the Crown Prince greater pain.

Throughout this time, despite Vicky's complaints, Wilhelm did nothing to promote himself but made it clear that he would willingly accept whatever role the Emperor chose to give him. His grandfather wisely decided that the best course of action was to continue his kingly education by gradually introducing him to the different government departments by allowing him to spend a brief period with each in turn.

> "That…would not, I feel," he told Bismarck, "irritate my son quite so much as the [plan] that you suggest."[37]

Clearly, both Wilhelm and the Emperor were doing their utmost to take Fritz's feelings into account while seeking to ensure that the business of running the country continued unimpeded. Vicky, however, was surrounded by friends who constantly told her that the Emperor and his court were ignoring Fritz, and that Wilhelm 'sought to anticipate his birthright, and was lending himself to an intrigue, the object of which was to wrench the sceptre from his father's dying hand.'[38]

In February 1888, as the growths in his throat continued to proliferate, Fritz was forced to undergo a tracheotomy. He endured the operation with fortitude but barely had time to recover when, in early March, a telegram arrived in San Remo, telling him to return at once to Berlin as his father was dying. Mackenzie warned that the journey would prove too much for a man in his condition, but Fritz felt duty-bound to return and began to make the necessary arrangements.

Wilhelm, meanwhile, was in constant attendance on the Emperor, who urged him to do his utmost to ensure that, whatever happened, Germany should remain on good terms with Russia. It was for this reason, as Wilhelm explained later, that he made a point of visiting St Petersburg so soon after his accession.

On the morning of March 9th, as Fritz was about to depart for Germany, a further telegram arrived, informing him that his father had died and he was now the Emperor. As soon as he heard that his parents were approaching Berlin, Wilhelm went to the station to meet their train, and as the new Emperor Friedrich III emerged from his carriage, he rushed forward to embrace him. Barely able to speak, Fritz responded graciously but when Wilhelm moved to greet his mother, she pointedly turned away, making a show of attending instead to her husband.

Some days later, when Fritz, exhausted by the exertion of the journey and subsequent meetings with ministers, had been forced to retire to bed, Wilhelm sought out his mother at the Charlottenburg Palace, and begged her to explain what he had done wrong to provoke such anger in her. Vicky accused him directly of attempting to dethrone his father, and when Wilhelm protested that this was far from the truth, his mother merely shrugged and replied that, 'one more lie more or less was, after all, a simple matter to one who had carried ingratitude to such an extent.'[39]

In truth, Wilhelm would have had little to gain from attempting to 'dethrone' his father. Everyone knew that Fritz was dying and, as one contemporary stated:

"Prince William never thought of putting himself in his father's place...Whatever may have been his faults and mistakes at that period of his life, he was certainly no fool, and it would have been folly to jeopardise his future reputation for the sake of reigning a few months earlier."[40]

On 1st April, during Bismarck's seventy-third birthday celebrations, Wilhelm tactlessly raised a toast to the leader to whom the country looked for guidance since the old chief had died and the present one 'lay wounded and incapable of presiding over destinies.' Even the Chancellor was embarrassed by such insensitivity, but in Wilhelm's mind, it was far more complimentary to portray his father as a wounded hero rather than a frail man who was dying of a painful cancer. To Vicky, the statement was further evidence of Wilhelm's intentional cruelty and she berated him so vehemently that their relationship appeared to be irreparably shattered.

In spite of his wife's reluctance to face the truth, Fritz knew he had not long to live and understood the necessity of preparing Wilhelm to succeed him. He began to entrust him with more and more duties, and, in view of his youth and inexperience, asked Bismarck – to the Chancellor's great surprise – to remain in office to guide him.

Towards the end of April, Queen Victoria, longing to see her son-in-law for one last time, defied the advice of her ministers to pay a private visit to Berlin. In conversation with Vicky, she gently tried to explain that the dispute between her and Wilhelm was not solely his fault, since she, too, must bear some responsibility for the breakdown of their relationship. The Queen pointed out that, if Wilhelm had been swayed by the intriguers in Berlin, Vicky, too, had been misled about her son by a coterie of advisors. Vicky, outwardly at least, remained unmoved by her words but, within a few days of the Queen's departure, Fritz granted his eldest son even greater authority.

In May, the dying Emperor had the pleasure of attending the wedding of his second son, Henry, but soon afterwards, as Mackenzie noted, he began a rapid decline and asked to be moved to his favourite home, the New Palace, which he renamed Friedrichskron. There, the wrangling between the German doctors and Mackenzie intensified, as they disagreed about which kind of cannula would be most effective in helping Fritz to breathe. Eventually, a German doctor named Bergmann, forced in the new tube with such roughness that it caused profuse bleeding, leaving Fritz coughing painfully for several hours. As a result of the criticism that he received, Bergmann resigned, prompting the press to condemn both Mackenzie and Vicky for conspiring to be rid of such a skilled professional.

By mid-June, as Fritz was approaching death, Bismarck warned Wilhelm that Vicky had entrusted many of her diaries and other personal papers to Mackenzie to take back with him to England as soon as the Emperor died. Since these papers contained sensitive information and details of Germany's military capabilities they posed a serious threat to national security, and must, therefore, be retrieved the moment that Fritz breathed his last. In fact, unbeknown to either the Chancellor or to Wilhelm, Vicky had already had the documents sealed into locked boxes which her mother had taken back to England following her visit the previous April.

On 15th June 1888, as Fritz was fading rapidly, Wilhelm organised a regiment to surround the palace to await his instructions. According to his own somewhat unlikely account, he had assembled the Infantry to march past his father's window in order to bring him pleasure:

"I gave the dying Emperor his last joy on earth when I had the Second Infantry Brigade march past him led by me in person. These were the first and last troops seen by Frederick III as Emperor."[41]

In response, Wilhelm wrote, his grateful father sent him a little card, thanking him for his consideration, but he failed to mention that, as soon as he heard that Fritz had died, he ordered the troops to prevent anyone from leaving the palace until the incriminating documents had been found.

Naturally, a broken-hearted Vicky was horrified when she saw what Wilhelm had done, and her recounting of these events did much to damage his reputation within his extended family and in Britain at large. Stories of his 'imprisonment' of his grieving mother abounded, but, in fact, within an hour the cordon was lifted and Vicky was left to mourn in peace. Queen Victoria, though askance at Wilhelm's heartlessness at such a time, understood why he had been driven to adopt such extreme measures, and, shortly after his accession, she returned the boxes to him with their contents undisturbed and their seals intact.

Shortly before Fritz' death, Mackenzie, desperate to protect his reputation from further attacks in the German press, had asked Vicky if it would be possible for a post-mortem to be performed to clarify the exact nature and extent of the Emperor's illness. Reluctantly, she had agreed, but now, in her grief, she changed her mind and begged Mackenzie that 'her beloved husband's body should not be touched.'[42] The doctor duly forwarded her request to Wilhelm, who responded that there was no need to distress her with such a procedure. The following day, however, the German physicians who had also attended the late Emperor obtained an audience with the new Kaiser and stressed that they were legally bound to perform an autopsy to specify the exact cause of death. The arguments were so persuasive that Wilhelm consented to their request – a decision which his mother described as another act of deliberate cruelty, although, as Mackenzie recorded, 'The Emperor William II...yielded out of scrupulous regard for the law.'[43]

Grieving, bitter and angry with her son, Vicky was still more distressed when he asked her to vacate her beloved home, the Friedrichskron, on the grounds that the most impressive palace in Berlin should rightfully become the residence of the Emperor. Vicky repaired to England, telling her mother that she was now 'homeless', notwithstanding the fact that Wilhelm had offered her a choice of five other palaces in the city. While the episode demonstrates Wilhelm's lack of understanding of his mother, it is interesting to note that his cousin, Britain's George V, was later criticised severely for permitting his widowed mother to retain Sandringham House, while he, the King, remained with a far larger suite in the cramped rooms of York Cottage.

47

Relations between Wilhelm and Vicky remained fraught throughout the first decade of his reign. As far as possible they avoided one another and, if their carriages happened to pass on the road, he failed to acknowledge her. Since the majority of the accounts of their relationship in that period are based on Vicky's letters and First World War propaganda, even today Wilhelm is almost invariably portrayed as the guilty party. In reality, as Queen Victoria had observed, he was not solely to blame for the unfortunate situation; and, as he later commented, he and his mother were too alike and shared the same stubborn nature.

For thirty years since her arrival in Prussia, Vicky had endured Bismarck's slanders and the criticism of the court, sustained only by her devotion to Fritz and their plans for a happier future when he eventually became Emperor. By a cruel twist of fate, her hopes had been dashed at the last minute, and as all the dreams that they had shared failed to come to fruition, it is unsurprising that she resented seeing Wilhelm in a position which she believed rightfully belonged to his father. Having already – unjustly – accused him of being a liar and usurper, she closed her mind to the possibility of his becoming a successful Emperor, and, rather than offering him support, she made it clear that she had little faith in his ability to reign. He was, she said harshly:

> "...utterly ignorant of social, agricultural, commercial and financial questions etc., only occupied with military things, with a little smattering of foreign affairs, continually travelling and being feted, dinners, receptions etc...Oh what a tragedy it all is!"[44]

Distressed by 'the flatterers' who surrounded him, Vicky withdrew from public life and, while dedicating herself to philanthropy and artistic endeavours, she continued to pour out her disappointment to Queen

Victoria, complaining of the direction in which the Kaiser was leading the country.

Despite his bravado and show of indifference, Wilhelm was obviously wounded by her low opinion of him.

> "With grave anxiety, I placed the crown on my head," he said ten years after his accession. "Everywhere I met doubt and the whole world misjudged me."[45]

Fortunately, after years of estrangement, a measure of harmony was restored as Vicky was nearing the end of her life. When he discovered that she was dying of cancer, he visited her regularly and behaved with perfect tact and kindness. It has often been stated that, during her final hours, he cruelly exacerbated her pain by ordering her doctors to reduce the dosage of morphine. Her own letters, though, disprove this allegation, as she not only wrote of the regular injections that she was receiving, but also of all the other treatments that were administered in an attempt to ease her agony. 'I have had to have morphia every two hours in the night,' she told her daughter, Sophie; and some weeks later explained that:

> "The injections of morphia dull the pains a little for about a quarter of an hour, sometimes not at all, then they rage again with renewed intensity, and make me wish I were safe in my grave, where these sufferings were not. So my nights are spent! The electricity does no good, nor poultices (hot), nor ice-bags, nor embrocations, nothing, nothing. It is fearful to endure."[46]

At the beginning of August 1901, Wilhelm did all he could to make her final hours as peaceful as possible. At her request he asked the English cleric, Canon Teignmouth-Shore, to attend her; and, for thirty-six hours he remained by her side until she passed away at six o'clock in the evening of 6th August. After her death he carried out all her

49

wishes for a simple funeral at her home in the Taunus Mountains, during which, as she had requested, her coffin was draped in the Prussian ensign, and the music of her favourite composer, Felix Mendelssohn, was played. A touching moment occurred during the service when four of Wilhelm's sons suddenly rose from their seats and donned their helmets to stand, swords-drawn, at the four corners of the bier as a Guard of Honour.

Two years later, Wilhelm unveiled a bronze statue of his mother in her coronation robes, opposite a similar monument to his father at the Brandenburg Gate. In his memoirs he wrote fondly that, although, during her years in Prussia there had been 'a want of give and take on both sides', she was:

> "...a woman of great gifts, full of ideas and initiative. If, however, she was never quite appreciated as she deserved...I am convinced that history will give her the full recognition that, like so much else, was dirtied in her lifetime."[47]

Chapter 5 – 'The Will To Do Right And Good'

In carefully cultivating his public image as the face of a powerful new Germany, Kaiser Wilhelm II unwittingly set himself up as a target for caricaturists, and, later, for propagandists who would use his distorted image to support their accusations of all kinds of barbarity, including responsibility for the outbreak and atrocities of the First World War. His striking moustache – created for him by his barber, Herr Hapy in 1894 – lent itself to the Victorian stereotype of a theatrical scoundrel; and, just as the enemies of England's King Richard III exaggerated the curvature of his spine to portray him as 'crook'd-back villain', so, too, did Wilhelm's detractors use his disability to imply that he was not only deformed but also repulsive. One French journalist cruelly suggested that he tried to emulate prominent men of action in an effort 'to forget the infirmity of his one useless arm'[48]; and in October 1914, the *New York Times* advised readers to:

> "Rid yourself of the idea that the Emperor is a heroic figure. He is a man not exactly of small stature but distinctly below the average and rather fat....The deformity [of his arm] strikes the eye unpleasantly."[49]

His love of uniforms[h] gave rise to the belief that he was a bellicose war lord, and lines from his histrionic orations were taken out of context to portray him as either insane or supremely egotistical.

Unfortunately, while the negative aspects of his character have often been emphasised, his more positive traits have been dismissed as merely a charade of magnanimity. If, however, the Kaiser were truly as cruel as the propagandists would have his enemies believe, he would surely have behaved with equal monstrosity towards

---

[h] See Chapter 6

the people with whom he came into contact on a daily basis. This, though, was not the case, for he was respected and even loved by his servants, and frequently showed great kindness, particularly to 'the lower orders'.

Following his grandmother's death, he spotted a seamstress shivering as she stitched the pall, and immediately arranged for a fire to be lit in her room. The staff at Osborne and Windsor were amazed by his munificence when he left them more than ten thousand marks[i] in tips; and he organised a fund to provide holidays at seaside resorts for the domestic staff in all of the palaces that he visited. His dentist, too, was impressed by his generosity when he not only refused to accept the offer of free treatment, but paid double the amount on the bill.

At Christmastime, he wandered through the streets and palace grounds, handing out gold coins to children, gardeners and anyone whom he met, until it occurred to him that, when they attempted to spend the money, they might be suspected of theft. He arranged, therefore, to have the equivalent amounts made up in lower denominations, much to the relief of the recipients. Many of his closest companions also witnessed his spontaneous and unpublicised acts of kindness, such as when he spotted a poor man shivering in the street and immediately handed him his own coat.

On a wider scale, he consistently worked for the improvement of living and working conditions for the poor. Having become a patron of the Imperial Automobile Club, he established a fund to provide for the families of deceased drivers; and he was delighted to found the Kaiser Wilhelm Children's Home to provide annual month-long holidays for the children of the poorest families in Berlin:

"Weakened, pale, needy children," he wrote, "were transformed there into fresh, blooming, happy little

---

[i] Approximately £3848, which would be worth over £400, 000 today.

beings of whose welfare I often joyfully convinced myself by personal visits."[50]

When, within a year of his accession, a miners' strike erupted, he arranged to meet with representatives of both the employees and the employers, and, while declaring that the strike was illegal since the strikers had not given the statutory fourteen days' notice but had, 'through force and by means of threats' prevented those who wished to continue working from so doing, he promised to examine all their demands and report back to them forthwith.

Keen to find an alternative to socialism, he arranged for an international conference about working conditions to be held in Berlin. Delegates gathered from all over Europe, and, after a fortnight of discussions, recommended legislation governing working hours, maternity leave, and raising to fourteen the minimum age at which children could be employed in mines. Throughout the proceedings, Wilhelm made a particular point of showing courtesy to a French delegate, Jules Simon – to whom he later sent a gift of the compositions of Frederick the Great – in the hope of ameliorating relations between Germany and France[j]. Although he was not entirely successful, the French were impressed by his sincere concern for the welfare of workers, reporting that:

> "Kaiser Wilhelm II has the will to do right and good. He works hard, and he understands exceedingly well conditions with which sovereigns as a rule do not trouble themselves."[51]

Even his detractors had to agree that he committed himself wholeheartedly to his work, taking his duties seriously and accepting the responsibilities that came with privilege. Contrary to public opinion, he was not so arrogant as to dismiss advice or to ignore the opinions of his ministers, whom he often met informally, walking

---

[j] See Chapter 6

around the gardens of his palaces. Usually, in matters of importance, he expressed his own views first, but was not, according to his one-time Ambassador to St. Petersburg, 'inaccessible to objections or adverse opinions; he was, on the contrary, always ready to give due weight to his responsible advisors' suggestions and generally approved them.'[52]

In public, he recognised the importance of playing to the full the role of Emperor, and he revelled in the minutest details of pageantry and displays of the wealth of his nation. Within his own home, though, he lived very simply, sleeping on a 'commonplace' bed purchased from a local bazaar, in a rather Spartan room, filled with ill-matched 'furniture from museums and modern furniture from Berlin shopkeepers.' Even his mother was astonished at the simplicity of his tastes, complaining that his room was like 'the back of a suburban shop dealing in antiquities.'[53] Many who stayed with him as private guests, noticed that he ate sparingly, rarely touched meat and had an abhorrence of an excess of alcohol[k]; and they saw, too, his dislike of ostentation, as he urged his wife to wear no jewels but her wedding ring when they were alone.

Impulsive and passionate, his mind frequently leaped from one thought to another, which made him a scintillating and sometimes formidable conversationalist.

---

[k] According to his dentist, the Kaiser had become virtually teetotal because once, while young, he was intoxicated while aboard a ship and had given the captain orders to steer a particular course. When the captain explained that such a course was too dangerous, Wilhelm insisted that his orders should be obeyed, leaving the unfortunate captain torn between risking the lives of all on board, and disobeying a command from the heir to the throne. He opted for the former course, and, having thereby brought the ship safely to harbour, he climbed to a clifftop and threw himself to his death, rather than facing the shame of a trial for insubordination. Horrified, Wilhelm vowed never to overindulge again, and he became such an ardent promoter of temperance that lavish banquets appeared to him vulgar and distasteful.

Habitually biting his lower lip, he had a habit of firing questions at those with whom he spoke, which was taken by his detractors as a deliberate attempt at intimidation. Others realised that this was simply a result of his genuine interest in people, for, despite his sometimes unnerving manner, working men and others with whom he conversed were often happily surprised by his uncondescending tone and his eagerness to learn of their experiences. His American dentist, Arthur Davis, for example, was extremely anxious at the thought of treating such a prestigious patient, but, within minutes of their first meeting, the Kaiser behaved so graciously that the dentist soon relaxed and, from then on, looked forward to his appointments 'because of the extremely interesting views he expressed.'[54]

Equally impressed by his manner was the young Romanian poet, Hélène Vacaresco, who had been so overawed at the prospect of meeting him that she had not slept the previous night. When Wilhelm was told of her nervousness, he immediately paid her a compliment before engaging her in a subject with which he knew she was familiar and would be able to speak freely.

"This very young and imposing lady," he said, "has already known so many great, so many remarkable men, far greater and more remarkable than myself. She has seen many Emperors, too, I hear, so one more or less cannot be of much account."[55]

This self-effacing comment, which seems so at odds with the customary portrayal of the Kaiser's self-importance, was, in fact, typical of him, for, as one man who knew him well observed, 'there is not the least haughtiness in the Kaiser. He is genial and cordial and thoroughly human.'[56]

The insecurities which had plagued him throughout his childhood were often concealed behind a façade of bluster and joviality, which created the image of a larger-than-life character, dominating and steering conversations to distract from his own ignorance. Frederick Ponsonby, equerry to King Edward VII, was unimpressed by 'his brilliance', assuming that:

> "...he anticipated what subjects of conversation would crop up and then got his staff to look up statistics, which he afterwards brought out in conversation, with the result that people were astounded at his knowledge."[57]

In fact, as was already shown, he was able to discuss a wide variety of subjects impromptu, and, whether he was talking with university professors, sailors or workmen, his hearers were often amazed by his spontaneous conversations which demonstrated the extent of his interest in and knowledge of their specialities. Naval officers were astounded when, while formally visiting their ships, he busied himself in the engine rooms discussing the intricate details of their engineering, and was not averse to climbing into the dustiest or oiliest spaces to study more closely the workings of specific instruments. Moreover, even if Ponsonby were correct in assuming that the Kaiser prepared his conversations in advance, it could be argued that, since his position necessitated meeting numerous people from many different backgrounds, it was a sensible precaution to take to avoid any awkwardness and to set his guests at ease. Even today, monarchs and politicians use the same method to facilitate easy exchanges.

The majority of those who dined with the Kaiser were fascinated by his conversations and equally struck by his quick and sometimes shocking sense of humour. With a love of amusing anecdotes, he was particularly fond of the writings of Mark Twain, and he frequently made witty remarks and puns in a variety of languages. When, for example, his son's tutor complained to the Kaiser that the prince had used the offensive word, 'Schcisskerl', Wilhelm replied:

"The devil! He must be broken of that; but where did the little Schcisskerl hear that expression?"[58]

His daughter's governess was equally shocked when her pupil began to make 'unladylike gurgles' and, on being corrected, explained that she had learned the trick from her father.

There were times, though, when his exuberance and love of practical jokes went too far. On one occasion, when he slapped the pompous Ferdinand of Bulgaria on the bottom, the self-styled 'Tsar' took such offence that he promptly departed for Sophia. Still more disconcerting was the moment when an overweight general, whom he had asked to dance dressed in a tutu, collapsed and died of a heart attack.

Although his humour sometimes appeared cruel to those closest to him, he was never, the Austrian diplomat, Czernin, noted, offensive or cruel to strangers or to his servants and social inferiors; and, as one observer recorded, 'He possesses in a supreme degree the art of pleasing, and yet at the same time hurting people's feelings.'[59] Witnesses noted, too, that, while his unpredictability and erratic nature often distressed his wife, Augusta Victoria ('Dona'), he never ceased to make public and private demonstrations of support and affection for her. Whenever she spoke, his eyes never left her as he gave her his full attention, and all were impressed by the 'chivalrous way he always makes his wife the leading personage present.'[60]

As his duties and travels occupied much of his time, his sons viewed him as a somewhat distant, aloof and even frightening figure, but this did not reflect the reality of his feelings for them, for he loved them deeply and missed them when he was away from home. 'I shall have soreness in the heart until I see my wife and youngsters again,'[61] he told a companion during one of his foreign tours; and he delighted in recounting tales of their exploits to visitors and guests at his banquets. At Christmas, he gave them money to purchase gifts for one another, and asked them to compile lists of what they most wanted, from which he personally chose the most appropriate presents.

As they grew older, there were many clashes of personality, particularly with his eldest son and namesake, Crown Prince Wilhelm, who, in later years as he understood his father better, came to respect and admire him. Ironically, many of their disagreements sprang from the Kaiser's determination to maintain peace with Germany's neighbours, for, while his hot-headed son frequently warned him that the French were readying themselves for battle, the Kaiser insisted that nothing must be done to provoke an international conflict. When war eventually erupted, the general consensus of opinion in Germany was that Wilhelm was 'the peace Kaiser' who had sought to avoid the conflict, while the Crown Prince was a man of war, who was eager to spring into action.

If at times his relationship with his sons was fraught, he was totally at ease with his daughter, with whom he took regular carriage rides simply for the pleasure that it gave her. From her 'snug place in his heart,'[62] she was able to tease him in a manner which would, from anyone else, have earned a reprimand, and, following her marriage in 1913, he missed her so deeply that, according to her governess, the entire house felt empty and lonely in her absence.

'In his home life,' wrote his Ambassador to St. Petersburg, '[he was] a good man whose simplicity and refreshing candour were very attractive.'[63] It was an opinion shared by the psychologist, Hugo Munsterberg, who noticed that 'the beauty of his family life...irradiates through all his personal feeling.'[64]

On a wider scale, as was typical at the time, he viewed his role as Emperor as similar to that of a father of his people, for whom he felt responsible and whose welfare was of vital importance to him. Modelling himself on his hero and ancestor, Frederick the Great[1], he was keen to promote education and culture for the masses. He opened free libraries and art galleries; upbraided the Prince Regent of Bavaria for his failure to acquire and display paintings; and supported rising artists by visiting their studios and funding exhibitions. Although he was criticised for his interference in education, his advice to students was both practical and ahead of his time. When, in 1911, he returned to his old gymnasium in Kassel, he warned against the dangers of an excess of alcohol and such games as seeing who could 'gulp down the greatest number of intoxicating drinks', drawing attention to parties in the American universities where 'no wine is seen on the table and they get along very well without it.'[65] Understanding, too, the necessity of balancing study with physical activity, he urged the students to take up sports, and, should they become overwhelmed by their schoolwork:

"I advise you to withdraw from them for a time – travel or go on a walking tour. Then when you return you will have a clearer vision."[66]

This advice was drawn from his own experience, for, amid the stresses of his office, he found solace in the simplicity of nature, walking or riding daily in the countryside or the gardens of his palaces, where he relaxed by studying botany and the cultivation of crops and flowers.

Despite his typical restlessness and constant need to be active, Wilhelm also took time to reflect, and thought deeply about the best means of serving his people.

"Since my accession I have thought a great deal," he told a Frenchman in 1894, "and I have come to

[1] The Kaiser treasured every relic of Frederick the Great and was delighted to have found his study, but, as he told a visitor, he had not yet succeeded in recovering his flute.

the conclusion that for a man situated in my position, it is worth a great deal more to do good to mankind than to inspire them with fear."[67]

The Crown Prince confirmed that his father quite simply 'desired to do his best, and he regarded as the best, the peace of the realm;'[68] and an independent American witness reported to Washington that the Kaiser was 'the greatest servant of all' whose character typified the spirit of the country as the 'one great and promising phenomenon of civilization, the shining hope and assurance of the progress of mankind.'[69]

Chapter 6 – 'The Only Guarantee Against Invasion'

Kaiser Wilhelm's love affair with the army began when, at the age of ten, in the tradition of Prussian princes, he donned a miniature uniform of the First Regiment of Infantry Guards to receive his commission and the prestigious Order of the Black Eagle from his grandfather, Emperor Wilhelm I. His heart pounded with excitement as the Emperor described the significance of the occasion, and in his childish imagination he saw himself as a hero of old receiving a knighthood from his liege. Such was his joy in that moment and the pride he felt in his military garb that over the next half century he would amass over four hundred uniforms, which he changed several times a day to strut about like an actor playing the protagonist in a grand heroic drama.

His obsession with military attire and pageantry had little to do with creating a militaristic state, for he was as happy to be seen in one of his many foreign uniforms as he was to appear in the helmet of the Death's Head Hussars. He could not have been more delighted than when Queen Victoria created him Admiral of the British Fleet; or when his uncle, King Edward VII, presented him with the uniform of a British Field Marshal. His regular letters to the Tsar of Russia were interspersed with trivial details of the colours and styles of various regimental tunics and jackets, and suggestions as to how Russian soldiers might adopt similar accoutrements to their uniforms. Moreover, considering the self-consciousness he felt about his disabled arm, he naturally chose to dress in a manner that most accentuated his more attractive features, and, as an English member of his household observed, he never suited civilian clothes, which were 'distinctly unflattering'[70] to him.

There were, however, those who feared his enjoyment of these military trappings. The controversial journalist and pacifist, W.T. Stead, prophetically stated in 1899 that:

> "...He does not altogether realise where this tin-soldier parading and blowing-of-trumpets-and-horns may lead. That one day he will wake up very much astonished that his pet playthings are not tin and have become too strong for him to manage. It may well be that William II, like Frankenstein, is unconsciously creating a monster that will one day turn and devour him."[71]

His love for the army ran deeper than his passion for uniforms and display. It combined his longing to recapture a mythical Age of Chivalry with a genuine appreciation of his fellow officers and gratitude for the happy days he had spent at the Military Academy at Potsdam. There, for the first time in his life he enjoyed true camaraderie and felt entirely at home. His former insecurities were forgotten, and, as he wrote later:

> "I really found my family, my friends, my interests – everything of which I had up to that time had to do without."[72]

While his mother found his obsession with Potsdam distasteful, Queen Victoria believed it to be a passing phase but Wilhelm never forgot the comradeship of the officers, and, from the start of his reign, he was determined to repay the army by offering his unstinting support and introducing reforms for the benefit of the ordinary rank and file. On his orders, the period of conscription for the Infantry was reduced from three to two years; and, having taken the time and trouble to listen to the concerns of junior soldiers, he took measures to prevent a continuation of the brutality with which many of them had been treated.

> "In my army," he said, "every soldier should be justly, lawfully and worthily treated, so as to arouse

62

and promote in him delight in, and devotion to, his calling, love and confidence in his superiors"[73]

For the first time, foot soldiers were provided with water bottles and fireproof, waterproof tents; and their kit was enlarged to include five uniforms to ensure that they would have sufficient garments to accommodate different weathers. He was keen to enable young men from poorer families to gain promotions by reducing the considerable expenses required by officers; and all soldiers who received an honourable discharge were guaranteed well-paid positions as state officials.

Such was his just treatment of his troops that he was even held up as a model to British officers. When, for example, in 1891, a German officer was shot dead by one of the men whom he had just been drilling, a British Member of Parliament, Captain Norton, recounted to the House of Commons the Kaiser's response to the incident as an example of good sense and fairness:

> "The German army is the first army in the world, more especially where discipline is concerned. The German Emperor, who is the head of the army...and who, besides being a man of great ability is of undaunted courage, having a free hand, did what? He did not punish the regiment collectively, but he sent special detectives from Berlin to inquire into the character of the particular squadron, and into the sayings and doings of the men. Four months afterwards three men were brought to trial, and acquitted. Why? Because there was a reasonable doubt."[74]

While his critics would later suggest that the Kaiser had no genuine grasp of modern military practices, he introduced some of the most innovative schemes of the era, including the use of war dogs, smokeless gunpowder, mobile steel forts, and the erection of wire fences to prevent enemy charges. Moreover, his commitment during

63

manoeuvres exceeded that of all other officers, for, despite frequent interruptions from ministers of state, he was always first on the field at dawn and last to leave at the end of the day. An American, who witnessed him in action in the autumn of 1888, observed that:

> "He commanded not by occupying a conspicuous eminence and nodding assent to the suggestions of vulnerable subordinates...on the contrary he was obvious master of the situation, carrying out a plan previously matured by himself, and ordering such modifications during the day as his quick perception and logical will suggested. Every day...from sunrise till late afternoon, one conspicuous figure was always hard at work, and that was the Emperor, earning his soldier's pay as hardly as any of the poorest Brandenburgers."[75]

His passion for all things military was born of the place and era in which he was raised. He had been devoted to his grandfather, Emperor Wilhelm I, whose service as a soldier had earned him the epithet, 'Grapeshot Billy', and whose courage on the battlefield had been rewarded with the Iron Cross. Often his grandfather regaled Wilhelm with stories of his experiences in the Napoleonic Wars, during which he had been an active participant in the Battles of Ligny and Waterloo. From these accounts and from his own historical studies, Wilhelm understood that due to its physical location, Prussia had, for centuries, had come under attack from both the east and the west. Over time, 'the Eastern hordes' and the vast Napoleonic armies had swarmed across the borders and the memory of the ravages wrought by the French Emperor's troops were still fresh in Prussian minds many decades later as Wilhelm described to his daughter's governess the way in which they had stripped stately homes and burned all the artistic treasures, Unlike Britain, Prussia had no oceans to protect her from potential enemies, and consequently the need for strong defences had engendered a certain militarism that was an accepted part of Prussian culture long before Wilhelm ascended the throne. One foreign observer noted that:

"The people of the fatherland all serve in the ranks, not merely because their Kaiser wishes it, but because they themselves are convinced that this sacrifice is the only one that can guarantee them against invasion."[76]

Following the success of the Franco-Prussian War, Wilhelm I had been keen to strengthen his army in the hope that by so-doing he would prevent reprisals from the French; and his grandson, Wilhelm II, was equally convinced that military might was necessary to deter would-be attackers and to sustain the peace which his ancestors had won by the sword. As he offered support to the ancient regiments, he was deeply aware that he was continuing a tradition handed down through many generations.

"Imagine a monarch," he declared in 1898, "holding personal command of his army, disbanding his regiments, sacred with a hundred years of history."

To Wilhelm, therefore, there was no incongruity between his reiterated desire for peace and the expansion of his army, which doubled in size between 1870 and 1914. The fact that during those years, Germany enjoyed four decades of peace – while Britain fought in more than forty conflicts – appeared to justify his belief that strength was the most effective deterrent against war.

Two years after his accession, while insisting that the country had no need for further military glory or conquests since 'she has already obtained once and for all, on the field of battle, the right to exist as a united and independent nation'[77], he emphasised his determination to protect what his predecessors had won. Stressing that he desired to live on good terms with his neighbours, he let it

65

be known that he was also prepared to fight to maintain the peace that he valued so highly, announcing that Germany's blows would 'fall like hail' on anyone who dared to disturb it. The same year, he stated dramatically that:

> "I will not permit that any one should touch my eastern provinces and he who tries to do so, will find that my power and my might are as rocks of bronze."[78]

It was a theme to which he returned in Bremen, fifteen years later:

> "When I came to the throne, I swore that, after the heroic times of my beloved grandfather, bayonets and cannon would, so far as was in my power, be laid aside, but these bayonets would be held so sharp and these cannons ready, so that when cultivating our garden and extending our beautiful house, we should not be disturbed by envy and jealousy from outside."[79]

The idea that Germany could easily come under attack was not merely the paranoid imagining of a would-be warlord. Even one of Germany's greatest critics, Britain's David Lloyd George, acknowledged in 1908 that the Kaiser's army was to Germany what the Royal Navy was to Britain – 'her sole defence against invasion. Here is Germany in the middle of Europe with France and Russia on either side with a combination of armies greater than hers.'[80]

The threat from France was a constant concern as, since 1871, there was a feeling that the French would seek to avenge themselves for their defeat in the Franco-Prussian War, and, more specifically, retake the provinces of Alsace-Lorraine, annexed by the Prussians at the height of their victory. The annexation was not simply a matter of conquest or humiliating the enemy, for, as the Prussians argued, a large percentage of the population spoke German and were of Germanic origin. More importantly, with

Napoleon's ravages still fresh in their minds, the Prussian generals saw the provinces as a buffer between the French and the newly established German Empire. This was why, as Bismarck – who initially opposed the annexation – told the Reichstag in 1873, that it was necessary to control the territories in order to erect 'a rampart against the incursions which a passionate and warlike people have been making into our country for two hundred years.'[81]

What neither the French nor the Germans had initially realised, however, was that Alsace-Lorraine contained the largest iron-ore deposit in Europe, and the second largest in the world. Under German rule, the territories prospered as not only did the output of grain and coal dramatically increase but, on the back of the discovered deposits, the chemical and textile industries thrived.

> "The soil of the lost properties," claimed Sydney Brooks in 1918, "has made Germany's fortunes. She has derived from it her metallurgical ascendancy, the motive powers for her industries, her wealth, and as a consequence, her naval, military and political power."[82]

By 1913, the majority of the Alsatians viewed themselves as more German than French, and at the National Congress of United Socialists, the former deputy, Francis de Pressence, stated, 'Time has done its work. Alsace-Lorraine no longer wants to return to French rule.'[83] Wilhelm, therefore, despite constant pressure from Paris and regular exhortations from other foreign governments, had three valid reasons for refusing to relinquish the territories: to honour what his predecessors' armies had 'won by the sword'; to keep a defensive buffer between Germany and France; and to maintain the economic advantage of the region's natural resources.

The French, however, continued to condemn the seizure of the provinces, and, in 1899, one journalist

67

expressed the widely-held belief that 'Alsace-Lorraine has made us the irreconcilable enemies of Germanism.'[84] Such statements highlighted the very real possibility that at some point the French would attempt to avenge their wounded pride and regain the lands they had lost, particular since they were rapidly increasing the number of regiments in their army.

Prussian militarism is often cited as a major contributing factor to the outbreak of the First World War, but Wilhelm began to strengthen his forces in response to similar moves from the French, and, while much emphasis has been placed on the expansion of his army, far less attention has been given to the fact that, after 1871, the French army also doubled in size. In 1895, the Kaiser was shocked to discover that the French were re-forming certain divisions along Germany's western border, and rumours were rife that, if the French attacked, they would have the support of Russia. Writing frantically to his friend, Tsar Nicholas II[m], Wilhelm warned that:

> "Such a serious danger will cause me to strongly increase my army, to be able to cope with such fearful odds...God knows I have done all in my power to preserve European Peace but, if France goes on, openly or secretly encouraged like this, to violate all rules of international courtesy and peace in peacetimes, one day my dearest Nicky, you will find yourself suddenly nolens volens embroiled in the most horrible of wars Europe ever saw!"[85]

Although he would never relinquish Alsace-Lorraine, Wilhelm was still eager to maintain peace with the French. He was quick to send condolatory messages on the deaths of presidents and other prominent ministers; and in 1897 he was among the first to send a letter of sympathy following a horrific fire at a Paris bazaar, which resulted in

---

[m] See Chapter 11

the death of a hundred-and-twenty-six people, including the Bavarian-born Duchess of Alençon. Three years later, his efforts appeared to have paid off when many Germans were well-received at the Paris Exhibition; and in 1907, he sought to allay the ghosts of the Franco-Prussian War when, referring to the French as an 'honourable enemy', he laid a wreath on a monument to their soldiers who had died in the campaign.

Such were Wilhelm's efforts at reconciliation that many of his ministers and even his own son, convinced that the French were preparing for war, accused him of 'prudence, political pusillanimity and over-careful regard for other people's feelings.'[86] Nonetheless, Wilhelm continued to work for harmony with Germany's neighbours; and, by cultivating his friendship with the Russian Tsar and remaining on a good footing with his grandmother in England, he believed that family ties would be strong enough to maintain peace throughout the continent. With Queen Victoria's death, however, cordial relations between the nations began to crumble and, when Britain allied herself to France, the Kaiser would feel himself betrayed by the country whose friendship he had most treasured.

Chapter 7 – 'The Queen is Constantly Praising the Emperor'

By the turn of the twentieth century, Queen Victoria's influence extended far beyond the borders of her Empire. Her grandchildren were highly placed in the courts of Russia, Denmark, Greece, Romania and Germany; and within a few years of her death, her granddaughters would be prominent figures in the Royal Houses of Norway, Spain and Sweden. Even in her own lifetime, numerous kings and princes stood in awe of 'the Grandmamma of Europe,' and, while she did her utmost to support the disparate members of her extended family, she expected due deference from them in return. When, therefore, soon after his accession, Wilhelm informed her of his plans to visit Russia, the Queen reproved him, pointing out that once the year of mourning for his father was over his first port of call should be Britain.

When Wilhelm showed his grandmother's letter to Bismarck, the Chancellor was so incensed that he offered to dictate a reply, informing the British Queen that she had no authority over the German Emperor. Wilhelm, however, had always been close to his grandmother, and, declining Bismarck's offer, he wrote a respectful reply, explaining that his planned visit to Russia was in accord with his late grandfather's last wish that he should maintain good relations with the Tsar. Impressed by this gracious response, the Queen accepted his reasoning and agreed that, since he must put his country before all other considerations, she would be happy to see him at a later date.

> "From that day onwards," Wilhelm wrote, "my relations with the Queen…were of the best imaginable; from that day onwards she never treated her grandson except as a sovereign of equal rank with herself!"[87]

This was not self-delusion, for, although Queen Victoria was often amused by his theatrical and sometimes grandiose behaviour, she regularly urged other members of the family to show him the respect that his lofty position deserved. In the early months of his reign, for example, she tactfully advised his younger sister, Moretta, to accept Wilhelm's refusal to allow her to marry a particular German prince – a stand which earned him much criticism from the rest of the family.

For several years, Moretta had been desperately in love with the dashing Prince Alexander ('Sandro') of Battenberg, but, as the Battenbergs were the children of a morganatic marriage[n], Emperor Wilhelm I had adamantly refused to sanction the match. When Vicky, who, like Queen Victoria, was particularly fond of Sandro, persisted in pleading his cause, the exasperated Emperor declared that, if the marriage ever took place, Moretta and her mother would be banished from the court.

For a long time, Wilhelm's father was equally opposed to the match but, when he eventually succeeded to the throne, Vicky prevailed upon him to change his mind and one of his final acts as Emperor was to write to Wilhelm, telling him that:

> "I entirely acquiesce in the betrothal of your second sister with Prince Alexander of Battenberg. I charge you as a filial duty with the accomplishment of this my desire, which your sister Victoria [Moretta] for so many years has cherished in her heart."[88]

---

[n] Prince Alexander of Hesse had married Julia Hauke a lady-in-waiting to his sister, the Russian Tsarina, but due to their unequal statues, the marriage had been deemed morganatic, which meant that neither his wife nor their children could inherit his titles. The Grand Duke of Hesse eventually bestowed upon Julia the title Countess – and later, Princess – of Battenberg, which was the name by which her children would be known.

On his accession, however, Wilhelm ignored this request – an action which Vicky viewed as a betrayal of his father's wishes, and a deliberate act of cruelty towards his sister. In fact, though, Wilhelm was acting for the benefit of his country rather than out of any desire to distress Moretta. At that time, he was doing his utmost to fulfil his grandfather's exhortation to maintain good relations with Tsar Alexander III, who had vehemently expressed his dislike of the Battenberg prince. A decade earlier, with the backing of Tsar Alexander II, Sandro had been appointed Sovereign Prince of Bulgaria, but following the Tsar's assassination in 1881, his successor, Alexander III, withdrew Russian support and Sandro was ousted from the throne. Realising that by sanctioning the marriage he could jeopardise Russo-German relations, Wilhelm had no qualms about refusing to honour his father's mandate, and although Queen Victoria had long been Sandro's champion, she understood that he was acting for the good of Germany. When a broken-hearted Moretta arrived in England, her grandmother gently told her that she could not contravene the Emperor's order, and advised her that, if she truly loved Sandro, she should now 'set him free'°.

Devoted as she was to her eldest grandson, there were times when the Queen was amused or exasperated by his behaviour. She laughed at his obsession with uniforms, and made it clear to him that she had no time for his Hohenzollern pretensions, reprimanding him for signing his personal letters to her as an Emperor, rather than simply her grandson. Nonetheless, as he stated, she never attempted to undermine his authority but ensured that his position as Emperor was respected.

° Broken and disillusioned, Sandro returned to his native Hesse where, soon afterwards, he married an actress, and died at the age of only thirty-six in 1893. Two years after Wilhelm's accession, Moretta married Prince Adolf of Schaumburg-Lippe.

For his part, Wilhelm returned her affection and, in the early years of his reign, he was grateful for her advice and 'superior counsel'. During his first visit to England after his accession, the Queen upbraided him for his treatment of his mother and father, but she let him know that she was also aware that he had been unjustly treated and slandered by his parents' friends and advisors. She warned him against being taken in by those who had deliberately sought to alienate him from his family, and those who would willingly use him to further their own agendas. It is likely that her words planted in his mind the first seeds of doubt about the wisdom of continuing to listen to Bismarck.

"It was after his visit to Queen Victoria," wrote one contemporary observer, "that he began to reflect seriously on his former conduct, to perceive how very liable to reproach it had been, and to find rising within him an intense aversion to all those who had encouraged him in his ways."[89]

At the time of his accession, many people believed that he was merely a cypher for the Chancellor, who was convinced that he would manipulate 'the young man' with even greater ease than he had formerly manipulated his grandfather. Several times Vicky described her son as 'Bismarck's creature', but she, like the Chancellor himself, underestimated Wilhelm's intelligence and strength of character. He was not so unobservant as to be unaware of the way in which Bismarck had treated his parents, nor, despite his admiration for the elderly statesman, did he believe that the Chancellor was totally infallible or trustworthy, and, after only two years on the throne, he was tiring of Bismarck's machinations and his assumption that his own authority exceeded that of the Crown. When, for example, in his eagerness to improve housing, transport and industry, the Kaiser gave individual ministers free rein to act as they saw fit within their own departments, he was shocked to discover that Bismarck constantly impeded their efforts by insisting on having to sanction every decision they made. Worse was to follow when Wilhelm discovered that every letter and report addressed to him was intercepted and censored by the Chancellor, and that his own authority was frequently undermined when Bismarck secretly issued contradictory orders. Matters came to a head when Wilhelm learned that, rather than supporting his efforts on behalf of workers, Bismarck was attempting to provoke the socialists into an uprising so that he would have an excuse to crush them by force.

> "The conflict between the Chancellor and me arose because of his belief that the social problems could be solved by the severest methods, and, if the worst came to the worst, by means of soldiers, not by following principles of general love for mankind or humanitarian nonsense, which he believed he would have to adopt in conformity to my views."[90]

Refusing to turn his troops on his own people, Wilhelm realised that it was time to distance himself from the man who believed that his position was unassailable because the young Kaiser could not possibly manage without him.

In the winter of 1889-90, as Bismarck was suffering from rheumatism, Wilhelm advised him to withdraw to his country estate, providing him with an opportunity to withdraw gracefully from public life. From there, though, he continued his intrigues until, in March 1890, the exasperated Kaiser summoned him to Berlin where a restrained but tense exchange took place, culminating in Bismarck attempting to demonstrate Wilhelm's need of him by revealing the contents of a disparaging letter about him from the Tsar. Rather than buckling under such criticism, Wilhelm calmly made it clear that Bismarck's position was now so untenable that he had no alternatively but to resign.

This was not, however as has often been supposed, merely the whim of an arrogant young Kaiser, since, by then, a recent election in the Reichstag had returned so great a number of socialists that it was clear that the country no longer supported the Iron Chancellor's domestic policies.

"...Whatever his merits were as a foreign minister," wrote one observer, "they dwindled painfully when it came to treating the more delicate questions of finance, socialism, press laws and internal improvement."[91]

Ironically, in the light of all that had happened, Bismarck desperately turned to Vicky for help, asking her to use her influence over her son on his behalf. Vicky must have gained some satisfaction in natural justice when she replied in all honesty that she no longer had any sway over Wilhelm since Bismarck himself had long ago alienated him from her.

Bismarck's resignation enabled the Kaiser to increase his efforts to maintain good relations with his grandmother, whom the ex-Chancellor had always viewed with a combination of mistrust and disdain. From the early 1890s, he made regular speeches reminding the British of his close relationship with the Queen and his lifelong love of England.

"I have always felt at home in this lovely country," he told an audience in London's Guildhall in 1891, "being the grandson of a Queen whose name will ever be remembered as the most noble character and a great lady in the wisdom of her counsels...Moreover the same blood runs through English and German veins."[92]

He was quick to praise her Royal Navy, telling the officers at Portsmouth that his plans for a fleet of his own owed much to all he had learned from them, and how deeply he admired Britain's naval heritage. This was not mere flattery. He thoroughly enjoyed his holidays in England, whether attending the regatta at Cowes, visiting his grandmother, or staying with friends at Highcliffe Castle near Bournemouth, from where he often wrote letters to the Queen, telling her how 'thoroughly at home' he felt, and describing:

> "…his delight in the pretty English children he met, his pleasure in the tea he gave to the boys and girls on the estate, his astonishment at their well-dressed appearance, their reserved, composed manners, at the way in which they sang grace, at the clergyman who controlled the proceedings and knew how to box and play cricket."[93]

For the first eight years of his reign, the British people reciprocated his warmth and affection, and agreed with his often expressed sentiments that 'the peace of the world depends upon the maintenance of good relations between Germany and England.'[94]

By the mid-1890s, however, relations between the two countries were becoming increasingly strained, due partly to Britain's resentment of Germany's burgeoning economy, and partly to the Germans' reaction to the British actions in southern Africa.

For centuries, British and Dutch (Boer) industrialists had been colonizing parts of present-day South Africa, which, by the 19th century, had been divided into four territories, two of which – Cape Colony and Natal – were governed by the British, and two of which – the Orange Free State and the Transvaal – were governed by the Boers. In 1886, the discovery of gold in the Transvaal prompted an influx of British prospectors, hoping to make their fortunes, in response to which the Boers, objecting to the inrush of outsiders 'stealing' their gold, imposed taxes and other restrictions upon the foreigners. The restrictions provoked much resentment in neighbouring Cape Colony, and, in December 1895, a group of six hundred armed mercenaries under the leadership of an Englishman, Leander Starr Jameson, assembled at the border, intending to incite an uprising of all the foreigners in the Transvaal. In a plot which would have been worthy of Bismarck, Jameson planned to use the ensuing chaos to take over the government of the Transvaal under the pretext of restoring order. His plan was foiled when the uprising failed to materialise and, in the resulting fiasco, thirty of Jameson's men were killed, while he and many of his followers were arrested and returned to England to stand trial. Despite his being found guilty of orchestrating the raid, the British press portrayed Jameson as an archetypal swashbuckling hero, who had been acting solely in the interests of his country.

The event was viewed very differently in Germany, where many people shared the Kaiser's opinion that the British had long been planning to colonise the whole of the region by driving the Boers – who shared the same Germanic origins – from the country. Even in Britain there were those who viewed the raid and the subsequent Boer Wars with scepticism, as the journalist W.T. Stead observed:

> "It pleases us to fritter away our forces in wars like the so-called Great Boer War, which has nothing great in it except the enormous money-hunger of a few wretched financiers."[95]

The failure of the raid prompted rejoicing in Berlin, and, in response to public sentiment and to the expressed wishes of the Reichstag, the Imperial Chancellor, Prince Hohenlohe, prepared a congratulatory telegram for the Transvaal's President, Paul Kruger.

Although he agreed with the sentiments of the telegram, Wilhelm refused to sign it for fear that it would create ill-feeling in Britain and damage Anglo-German relations. The Chancellor, however, insisted, explaining that as a constitutional Emperor, he was bound to carry out the wishes of the Reichstag:

> "...otherwise there was a danger that the excited attitude of the German people, deeply outraged in its sense of justice and also in its sympathy for the Dutch, might cause it to break down the barriers and turn against [the Kaiser] personally."[96]

To press the point, Hohenlohe told him that his relationship with Queen Victoria and his obvious affection for England had given rise to rumours that he placed British interests above those of his own people. Still, Wilhelm hesitated until, eventually, pressed by several members of the Reichstag, he realised he had no option but to sign.

No sooner had the telegram been sent than the British press printed its contents in full and whipped up such a wave of anti-German feeling that, for over twelve months, Wilhelm was subjected to such vitriolic attacks that even some British journalists were aghast.

> "The Kaiser will not easily forget the English vulgarities of which he has been the victim," wrote the editor of the *Daily Chronicle*. "...The Kaiser has accomplished great things. One of them was to weld Germany into the most compact and dirigible entity on the Continent. He has never suffered a defeat and Germany has steadily progressed under him."[97]

Nonetheless, the criticism intensified a year later when he expressed his support for the Turks (Ottomans) in the Turko-Greek War. British journalists portrayed him as a petulant child, whose antipathy towards the Greeks sprang from his annoyance with his sister who, on marrying the heir to the Greek throne, had contravened his wishes by converting to Orthodoxy. In reality, as Wilhelm wrote to the Tsar, he believed that the Greeks were seeking to expel all the Muslims from Crete in order to seize their property and '...give it to the Christians who were till now their own paid tenants and labourers who revolted against their masters.'[98] Since, on more than one occasion, he had assured the Muslims that they had a good friend in the Kaiser, he felt it was his duty to support them. He was also keen to maintain good relations with Turks and, when he congratulated the Sultan on his successes and was photographed viewing a collection of captured Greek guns, the British journalists were probably correct in claiming that he was currying favour with the Sultan to gain support for his plans for the Baghdad Railway[p].

For the most part, Wilhelm ignored the journalists' attacks but he was deeply wounded when, in view of the country's hostility towards him, Queen Victoria denied him an invitation to her Diamond Jubilee celebrations in 1897. Then suddenly, the following year, the derogatory articles ceased, and Wilhelm was convinced that this was due to his grandmother's intervention. Their relationship was unshaken and, while Vicky regretted the ill-feeling that had been aroused against him in Britain, she unaccountably claimed he had only himself to blame, and, in a rather peevish letter to her chamberlain, added:

> "The Queen is constantly praising the Emperor for never missing an opportunity of being courteous and sympathetic…you know my mother is very fond of her grandson."[99]

A year later, when the Boers declared war on Britain, the German press was filled with pro-Boer articles, reflecting the general feeling throughout the country.

> "At every concert, in the course of every theatrical performance and on every possible pretext," the Kaiser's cousin, Princess Alice of Albany recalled, "opportunity was taken to say hostile things about England and to mock the British generals in Africa."[100]

---

[p] See Chapter 11

Contrary to the tide of public feeling and the wishes of many of his ministers, Wilhelm was determined to maintain and publicise Germany's neutrality, refusing to receive President Kruger when he arrived in Berlin, and issuing an order that no officer in his army was to express any bias in the South African war. Nonetheless, rumours soon spread to London from Paris and St Petersburg, warning that Germany was about to enter the conflict on the side of the Boers. This idea appealed not only to many Germans but also to the French and Russians, who, in fiercely anti-British articles, voiced their overwhelming support for the Boers, but Wilhelm, desperate to prevent a colonial dispute from sparking a European conflagration, went out of his way to maintain good relations with Britain. In November 1899, he braved the wrath of his ministers and people to accept his grandmother's invitation to England as a public demonstration of his moral support. The visit made a strong impact on the British, and, when, in an address in Brighton, the business magnate, Sir John Blundell Maple, stated that the English must never forget that the Kaiser had stood beside them in their time of need, he was greeted with loud applause.

In Germany, though, the anti-British attacks escalated, thanks largely to Bismarck's son, Herbert, who 'was one of the worst agitators against England both in Parliament and in his own Party Press'[101]; and when the possibility of an Anglo-German alliance was mentioned in the Reichstag, it raised a storm of indignation and prompted even more intense criticism of Wilhelm from his own people.

In the midst of these rising tensions, Wilhelm perceived that the press in both Britain and Germany was deliberately attempting to sour relations between the countries and undermine his efforts to maintain peace. The future British Prime Minister, Henry Campbell-Bannerman, shared Wilhelm's opinion, stating that he had 'nothing but condemnation for the action of those in either nation who by stupid and vulgar abuse fomented discord between the two nations.'

At the same time, the Kaiser suspected that the French and Russians were also involved in attempts to damage his relationship with Britain, for the sole purpose of isolating Germany. In 1899, a suspected agent-provocateur, Jules Hansen, arrived in Berlin to solicit support from Chancellor von Bulow, for a triple alliance of Germany, Russia and France to attack Britain while the greater part of her army was embroiled in the Boer War. Like Wilhelm, the Chancellor mistrusted Hansen, suspecting that his true purpose was to lure him into a trap to prove to Britain that that the Germans could not be trusted. As soon as Wilhelm heard of the plan, he wisely sent the details to Queen Victoria and the Prince of Wales, who – ironically in the light of later events – stated frankly:

> "I no longer have any doubt that everything that comes from Petersburg and Paris is only a low intrigue to set England and Germany against each other."[102]

Weighed down by a series of family bereavements and the strains and losses of the Boer War, in the winter of 1900-1901, Queen Victoria's health began to deteriorate rapidly. By New Year, those closest to her were alarmed by her sudden decline, but, as other members of the family were informed of her condition, the Kaiser was deliberately excluded from all communications. Fortunately, Wilhelm had foreseen such an eventuality and had asked the Queen's doctor, Sir James Reid, to let him know if ever his grandmother were seriously ill. In mid-January, Reid sent a telegram to the Kaiser, telling him that if he wished to see the Queen, he should come to Osborne House as soon as possible.

Aware of his unpopularity among his English relations, Wilhelm tactfully telegraphed the Prince of

Wales, assuring him that he did not wish to cause trouble but wanted to see his grandmother before she died. 'Uncle Bertie' – the Prince of Wales and future Edward VII – responded with equal grace but, rather than allowing him to go directly to Osborne, he invited him to Buckingham Palace, with the excuse that the Queen was not yet well enough to receive him.

Wilhelm was in London on 20th January 1901 when Reid sent a further telegram warning that the end was imminent. The following day, he and Bertie arrived on the Isle of Wight where numerous other members of the family had already gathered. The Queen's room was so crowded that Wilhelm was forced to stand in the corridor outside, from where he heard his aunts telling their mother the names of all who were present, but purposely failing to mention that he, too, was there. Deeply upset by the snub, he maintained a dignified silence, but Sir James Reid was so shocked by the omission that he approached him privately and told him that he would seek the Prince of Wales' permission to take him to see her when the others had left the room. That afternoon, Reid led him to his grandmother's bedside and left them alone for five minutes. On his return, the Queen said fondly to her doctor:

"The Emperor is very kind."[103]

Soon after his visit, she rallied a little then lapsed into unconsciousness. The family again assembled around her bed and this time Wilhelm was given a special place at her side. Kneeling, he supported her head on his arm for over an hour until, at six-thirty that evening, the 22nd January 1901, she died.

His sincerity and graciousness during the Queen's final hours and in the days following her death restored much of the Kaiser's popularity in the eyes of the British people. His genuine distress at the loss of his grandmother was obvious to everyone, as the British peer, Lord Suffield, noted that during the funeral 'he looked as sad as her own sons'[104].

"Difficulties there may have been, and differences may yet arise between the German people and ourselves," one Member of Parliament told the House of Commons, "but we shall not lightly forget the part which His Imperial Majesty the German Emperor has taken in the nation's grief. His Majesty may have been animated by personal and not political motives, but we value his presence and his sympathy none the less. Family ties have ever been honoured in this country, and the presence of His Imperial Majesty appealed to the people of this country with a striking force that we shall not readily forget."[105]

In Germany, however, 'the antagonistic feeling against England [remained] very pronounced'[106], and Wilhelm's attendance at the funeral led to further accusations that he was more British than German. The tensions between the two countries were steadily mounting, and, with the Queen's death, and that of her daughter, Vicky, just seven months later, the rapport between the Royal Families rapidly declined. The accession of King Edward VII would see the divisions widen, and the personal antipathy between the King and the Kaiser would be reflected in the growing rivalry between their countries. Interestingly and fittingly, though, Wilhelm made his last visit to England in 1911 for the unveiling of the statue of Queen Victoria in front of Buckingham Palace – his final tribute to the grandmother whom he loved.

Chapter 8 – 'A Place in the Sun'

Throughout the mid-19th century, while the other powers were acquiring colonies, Bismarck had been too engrossed in unifying the Empire to pay attention to overseas expansion. Even when, in 1882, a group of one-thousand-five-hundred influential figures under the leadership of Queen Victoria's nephew, Prince Herman of Hohenlohe-Langenburg, formed the German Colonial Society, the Chancellor was unmoved by their arguments, believing that colonies would create international friction and prove unduly expensive.

Within a couple of years, however, as German traders sent back reports of the untapped resources of Africa, Bismarck began to take notice. During the 1860s and 1870s, explorers and commercialists had moved into 'the dark continent', discovering a vast and largely uncolonised expanse, which they predicted would be extremely lucrative, prompting the European 'scramble for Africa'.

In 1894, as international rivalry threatened to break into armed conflict between the various European nations wanting a share of the African prize, the Portuguese proposed a meeting of all interested parties and Bismarck seized the opportunity to stake Germany's claim to colonies by offering to organise a conference in Berlin. Representatives of fourteen countries attended the discussions, which resulted in Africa being divided into zones, the rights to which were shared among the participatory nations. Germany gained modern-day Namibia and Cameroon ('German South-West Africa'); and Tanzania, Rwanda and Burundi ('German East Africa) – which, in the eyes of one contemporary author, were 'territories which other countries had deemed worthless.'[107]

This was not entirely true, but the Germans failed to make the most of their gains and, while other empires soon began profiting from their colonies, the venture proved something of a disaster for Germany. Few talented officials had any interest in travelling to an unknown land, and consequently many of those who gained positions of authority did so because, as a member of the Reichstag stated, they had 'failed to make their way at home.'[108] With few restrictions and little direct contact with Berlin, some behaved so brutally towards the native peoples that they provoked incessant revolts, which, together with a lack of productivity, led Bismarck to wish that he had never become involved in the project.

One of the most disastrous events occurred in 1904 when, in what has been described as the first genocide of the twentieth century, the German colonial troops responded to an uprising by driving over a hundred thousand people of the Herero and Nama races into the desert to starve to death. Survivors were captured and forced into slave labour in concentration camps, where conditions were so appalling that many more thousands died of starvation and thirst.

The Namibian genocide has often been described as a precursor to the Nazis' 'final solution', and in recent years it has even led to the Kaiser being compared to Adolf Hitler. In reality, Wilhelm never visited the African colonies and sent no direct orders to commit such an atrocity. He could therefore be held no more responsible for the actions of officers with whom he had no contact than any other monarch whose troops behaved with equal monstrosity in Africa.

Four years before the Namibian uprising, the British had used similar tactics against the Boers in an attempt to drive them from the land or to annihilate them completely. Apart from poisoning wells, they slaughtered livestock, leaving the carcases out in the sun to spread disease, and employed the 'scorched earth' policy of burning crops in order to starve out the enemy population.

85

"It's funny to see us with fixed bayonets, chasing the pigs round the farmyard," wrote one British trooper. "We killed a thousand sheep and put them into every house. The stench in a week will be horrible…We burn every farm that we come to, and bring the women and children to the Refuge Camps. No matter where we go, we burn the crops, leaving nothing but a waste of country behind us."[109]

Whole families of Boers were taken to concentrations camps where they were given such meagre rations that over twenty-seven-thousand men, women and children died of starvation or disease. The black Africans were treated no better, for they, too, were taken to camps where it is estimated that over twenty-thousand slave labourers were worked to death. The French also behaved inhumanely in Equatorial Africa where they burnt countless villages and forced the native peoples into slave labour, often chaining them together and ensuring discipline by means of a lash.

Nothing, however, could compare to the Belgians' behaviour in the Congo where, if slave-labourers failed to meet the expected quotas of rubber or ivory, they were punished by having their hands or feet cut off. Naturally, there were frequent uprisings and, in retaliation, vast numbers of people were slaughtered and their bodies left on display as a deterrent to others. It is estimated that between 1885 and 1908 up to ten million Congolese people died at the hands of the Belgians.

Of course, the fact that other nations were also committing heinous acts in no way excuses the Namibian genocide, but it demonstrates that the Kaiser's armies were no worse than other imperial forces and Wilhelm himself had no direct involvement in their crimes.

Unlike Bismarck, Wilhelm viewed the acquisition of colonies as necessary to prosper the country's economy and to place Germany on an equal footing with the other Great Powers. He knew that overseas expansion depended on an effective navy and so, from the start of his reign, he dreamed of creating a fleet that would equal that of Great Britain[q]. One obvious obstacle to his plans was the British occupation of Heligoland – a small island in the North Sea which had been ceded to Britain by Denmark in 1814 as a base from which the Royal Navy might protect the Scandinavian and German states from Napoleon. By the time of Wilhelm's accession, the British had little use for the island, but to Germany it was a place of strategic importance, due to its position in front of the western entrance to the Kiel Canal. The canal, which had been under construction since 1887, would provide easy access for trade from the Baltic to the North Sea, and link the German naval bases at Kiel and Wilhelmshaven. Since, at the time, Wilhelm viewed Germany's African holdings as little more than bargaining tools which could be exchanged for more useful territories, he asked Bismarck's successor, Leo von Caprivi, to strike a deal with Britain about ceding Heligoland to Germany. In return for the island, Britain gained the Zanzibar region and other parts of German East Africa, while Germany came away not only with Heligoland but also with a part of present-day Namibia which became known as the Caprivi Strip. Since the area provided access to the Zambezi River, Caprivi hoped it would be possible to create a direct trading route between the German settlements in East and West Africa but, in the event, the river proved unnavigable and, once again, Germany gained little from her African adventures.

A second consideration when creating an effective navy, was the necessity of coaling stations in various parts of the world, for there would be little point in investing in an expensive fleet if the ships were forced to remain close

---

[q] See Chapter 7

to home due to a suitable refuelling sites. Throughout the 1890s, Wilhelm instructed his ambassador to approach the British in hope of buying or leasing from them appropriate harbours but he was disappointed when each request met with a rebuttal. Even when Wilhelm himself approach the then Home Secretary, Herbert Asquith, and asked directly where Germany could 'set foot in the world without standing on Britain's toes', Asquith abruptly replied, 'nowhere', before rudely turning his back on the Kaiser and walking away.

Germany might have missed out on 'the scramble for Africa', but, by the mid-1890s, the European powers were turning their attention on China, and, this time, Germany would be at the forefront of the land-grab. Formerly China had held little interest for the imperialists, but a war with Japan in 1894-1895 exposed the weakness of the government and as the Russians, British and French began to consider expansion into the region, the Kaiser's ships patrolled the coast in search of suitable coaling stations.

In 1896, a German gunboat, the *Iltis,* sank during a typhoon near Shanghai, resulting in the deaths of seventy-seven seamen, who, it was said, went down singing hymns and calling three cheers for the Kaiser. Moved by their story, Wilhelm approached the British trading conglomerate, *Jardine, Matheson & Co.,* seeking permission for a monument to the dead to be erected on their land on the Bund – the most famous street in Shanghai. His request was graciously granted and, two years later, his brother, Henry, unveiled the bronze memorial which would stand as a symbol not only of Germany's future interest in China but also of Wilhelm's hopes for further cooperation between Germany and Britain.

The following year, an event occurred which enabled the Germans to gain a greater foothold in the East, when a gang of between twenty and thirty Chinese nationalists, angered by the huge numbers of European missionaries building churches on their land, burst into the mission of the Roman Catholic Society of the Divine Word in the province of Juye, and brutally stabbed to death two German priests. Five days later, the Kaiser dispatched a naval squadron to the region, causing the Chinese government to ask for negotiations, which soon resulted in an agreement by which the Germans would be granted a ninety-nine year lease of the province of Kaio-Chau.

Since the region was not officially a colony, it was placed under the Governorship of a German naval officer, who immediately set about making improvements which would benefit the native population as well as German commerce. In the city of Tsingtao, new houses and roads were constructed, sewers were built and, for the first time, fresh drinking water was available to ordinary people.

> "Here," wrote the Kaiser later, "everything was done to promote commerce and industry, and done jointly with the Chinese...[It] was a prospering German commercial colony where many Chinese worked side-by-side with Germans...It was a contrast to the naval stations of Russia and England, which were purely military, directed solely towards domination and conquest."[110]

While Wilhelm was proud of German endeavours in Kaio-Chau, he was becoming increasingly anxious about Japan – a country which had recently undergone successful industrialisation, developed an impressive fleet and was also seeking colonies. The 'Yellow Peril', said the Kaiser, posed a serious threat to western civilization and, having allegedly had a dream about the danger from the East, he commissioned a painting portraying the Europeans being led into battle by the Archangel Michael against the followers of Buddha. He frequently urged the Tsar to 'defend Europe from the inroads of the Great Yellow

Race'; and, in 1902, as Japanese military capabilities increased, he warned that the prospect of armies of Chinese being led by 'Christian-hating' Japanese officers was a 'future not to be contemplated without anxiety; and not impossible."[111]

Eight years later, however, a French journalist reported that in a private conversation the Kaiser told him that he had only placed such emphasis on the 'Yellow Peril' to emphasise the necessity of the European countries working together to protect their commercial interests.

> "We only wish to solve problems dividing the civilized world, to render it more easy for nations to live in harmony, to group together the forces of Europe, for it may be necessary later to use these united forces in the interest of a common economic policy."[112]

To twenty-first century readers, the use of the term 'Yellow Peril' is clearly offensively racist and, while this cannot be defended, it must be remembered that Wilhelm, living in a far more intolerant age, was voicing an opinion shared by many of his contemporaries. The Tsar referred to the Japanese as 'monkeys'; and throughout the second half of the nineteenth century, the United States was plagued by a series of violent racist riots in response to the dramatic influx of Chinese immigrants. In 1871, a mob of five hundred men stormed into Los Angeles' Chinatown, looting, destroying buildings and torturing and hanging eighteen innocent immigrants. During the next twenty years, similar scenes were enacted across the country as pogroms took place in Seattle, Denver, Wyoming and Oregon; and the entire Chinese population was expelled from Tacoma.

> "There is a real 'Yellow Peril' in existence now," wrote one columnist for the *North American Review*, "it is one that is growing and is certain to continue growing in the future...The peril is the

oldest and most natural one that can arise to disturb human arrangements: the problem of population."[113]

President Theodore Roosevelt referred to the Asian peoples as 'yellow niggers', and when, in 1906, a United States' base in the Philippines was attacked by local militia, the American commander ordered his troops into a neighbouring village to kill every male over the age of ten, and to rape all the women 'to put some Aryan blood into their race.'

French journalists were equally quick to use the phrase 'yellow peril' when warning of the rapidly rising birth rate in China; and throughout the British Empire, the Chinese were frequently portrayed as inferior beings with whom it was not possible to reason or negotiate.

Such deep-rooted racism was not aimed solely against the Asian peoples, nor did the Kaiser's sentiments appear abnormal in a world where white supremacy was largely taken for granted. The pseudo-sciences such as phrenology were used to 'prove' the inferiority of African and Asian peoples, while Darwin's theories were taken as evidence that Aryans were superior to the rest of mankind.

"I contend that we are the first race in the world," stated the British Governor of Cape Colony, Cecil Rhodes, "and that the more of the world we inhabit the better it is for the human race."

It was a view shared by the then popular British political philosopher Houston Stewart Chamberlain, whose theories of the Aryan race were later adopted by the Nazis; and President Roosevelt claimed it was the destiny of the Aryans to civilise the rest of the world.

Interestingly, too, some of the earliest proponents of eugenics – the theory of 'improving the quality of the race' by enforced sterilizations and breeding programmes – were American and British, rather than German. As early as 1798, the English cleric, Thomas Malthus, had published *An Essay on the Principle of Population,* in which he warned of the dangers of an increased population, and which was later used by the British in India when they failed to bring relief to famine-struck areas. The Philadelphian gynaecologist, William Goodell, proposed sterilising the insane to prevent mental illness from infecting the race; and the English anthropologist, Francis Dalton, argued that the Chinese were superior to the Negro peoples and should therefore be sent to Africa to displace the native population. When the First International Eugenics Conference was held in London in 1912, one of the attendees and most ardent supporters of the propounded theories was the future British Prime Minister, Winston Churchill.

As the Imperial Powers vied with one another for Chinese colonies, Tsar Nicholas II of Russia proposed a peace conference to be held in The Hague, where he hoped agreements might be reached about the reduction of military budgets, leading to disarmament. The conference was attended by representatives of twenty-six countries, and, although it did not achieve all of the Tsar's aims, it led to the creation of the Permanent Court of Arbitration for International Disputes, and The Hague Convention, which dealt with the humane treatment of prisoners-of-war and bans on the use of certain weapons such as dumdum bullets and poisonous gasses. At the height of the First World War, attention was drawn to the fact that, during the conference, Germany had refused to agree to limit the size of her army, but little mention was made of the fact that the British had been equally adamant in refusing to limit the size of their navy; and the United States had refused to pledge to refrain from manufacturing or employing some of the most horrific weapons.

In China, meanwhile, angered by the interference of foreign powers, a group of highly trained natives formed the 'Militia United in Righteousness' (the 'Boxers'), with the aim of expelling all the imperialists from their land. Initially, the Empress Dowager Cixi suppressed the Boxers but, in January 1900, she officially announced her support for their cause and called for a declaration of war against the invaders. The Boxers stormed through the country, burning Protestant and Catholic churches, and killing not only foreigners but also native Christian converts. As they swept towards the capital, the anxious Imperial Powers put all their differences aside to form an international force to suppress the uprising.

The ease with which the erstwhile rivals worked together was remarkable in the light of later events, as the first landing force of nine-hundred-and-four men comprised British, German, Japanese, Russian, Italian and Austrian soldiers, led – at the suggestion of the Germans and Japanese – by the British Commander Craddock of *H.M.S. Alacrity*. Soon afterwards, Italian troops arrived, along with American squadrons from their base in the Philippines, which had been recently annexed by the United States.

On 19th June, in the wake of much brutality from both sides, the Chinese Empress gave her commanders free rein to kill all the foreigners without taking any prisoners. The following day, Baron von Ketteler, the German minister in Peking – who had contributed to a local uprising by shooting dead an innocent boy – was killed in a frenzied attack before being flayed and having his heart ripped out, which, according to some accounts, was then eaten by one of his attackers. A month later, having read the details of Ketteler's death, Wilhelm gave one of his most notorious speeches to his troops who were departing for China, which would later be used as evidence that he incited his army to act with the utmost brutality. His words, however, may have been misinterpreted[r], and, while his men *did* behave barbarically, similar atrocities were already being

---

[r] See Chapter 24

committed by all the participating armies. The Japanese were randomly beheading innocent natives, including women and children; the Russians and French were raping and bayonetting women – one French commander excusing their behaviour by saying they were merely demonstrating 'French gallantry' – and the Americans and British were happily amassing fortunes from looting.

By September, the allied forces had taken control of Peking and, despite some opposition from her own people, the Empress Dowager agreed to accept the peace terms proposed by the international force. The following month, Wilhelm was hailed as a hero for concluding an Anglo-German agreement to prevent either country from seizing land during the upheavals in China, and to keep the harbours and rivers of the region open for world trade. A year later, he announced confidently:

> "In spite of the fact that we have no such fleet as we should have, we have conquered for ourselves a place in the sun...In the events that have taken place in China, I see the indication the European peace is assured for many years to come."[114]

The Kaiser's acquisition of colonies is often cited as a contributing factor to the outbreak of the First World War, but between 1871 and 1914, Germany acquired – primarily through leasing and treaties – only two thousand square miles of territory. In the same period, Britain, primarily through conquest, gained two million square miles; France, three-quarters of a million square miles; and even Belgium one million square miles of land.

Chapter 9 – 'To Secure Us Peace On The Seas'

During his childhood visits to Osborne and Portsmouth, Wilhelm, enchanted by his grandmother's navy, had happily spent hours sketching the details of gun ports and rigging, and listening intently to the officers who took him on guided tours of the ships. A highlight of his youth was an excursion to see Nelson's *Victory* – an outing surpassed only by a trip to the new Prussian harbour at Wilhelmshaven, where, in 1869, he 'gazed speechless' at the great ironclad, *Konig Wilhelm,* a colossal battleship purchased from Britain two years earlier. So enamoured was he of the history, power and beauty of the vessels that he dreamed of creating an impressive fleet of his own; and, as he grew older, this childhood whim took on a new importance as he recognised the value of trade to the German economy and the consequent need of a powerful Imperial Navy. Contrary to reports in the British press, Wilhelm was not inspired by a desire to challenge Britannia's dominance of the seas, but rather to learn from Britain's naval history in developing his own fleet.

Such was the importance he gave to the matter that, shortly after his accession, he spent two hours lecturing the Reichstag on the necessity of improving the navy, explaining that if the Empire were to thrive, new outlets for exports were required along with an effective merchant fleet, which in turn would require the protection of a powerful naval force. Due to her geographical situation, Germany's outlets to major oceans were limited. To reach the Atlantic it was necessary either to take a long route around the Shetland Islands or to pass through the English Channel, which could, at any time, be blocked by the French or British Navies; and to the East, the Russians patrolled the Baltic. It was vital, therefore, that Germany should have a fleet that was powerful enough to protect her trading ships in the event of international disputes.

Initially, his arguments met with little enthusiasm from his countrymen. Unlike Britain, Germany had never been a maritime nation, and, since, historically, enemies had attacked overland rather than by sea, few of his people saw a need for strong naval defences. Moreover, since Germany had neither productive colonies nor coaling stations, it would require enormous expense to make sufficient improvements to the paltry fleet to turn it into a credible resource to the economy.

One man, however, shared Wilhelm's vision: Alfred von Tirpitz who, born with few financial advantages, had worked his way up from a naval cadetship to becoming a sea captain at the age of twenty-six. Two years after Wilhelm's accession, Tirpitz was making a name for himself as the Chief of Staff at the Naval Headquarters in Kiel, where, while developing torpedoes, his greatest desire was to build a fleet of powerful battleships. Tirpitz predicted that sooner or later, Britain would become so resentful of Germany's increasing success that war would be inevitable. In all probability, he warned, the British would make use of their superior sea power by creating a naval blockade to starve Germany into submission, and the only means of preventing such a scenario was for the German Imperial Navy to become powerful enough to protect her harbours and seaways.

Due to these – accurate – predictions, Tirpitz was viewed as an Anglophobe and warmonger, but in fact, as one American commentator wrote in 1913:

> "He is a profound admirer of everything British. All his children have been educated in England. English naval traditions command his reverential respect. He has never ceased to hold them up to German sailormen as a model and inspiration. When he designed the Naval Law, he had little idea of entering the lists with Britain as an active competitor."[115]

Wilhelm was impressed by Tirpitz's arguments and invited him to Berlin where he gave him authority to outline his ideas for the future of the Imperial Navy. Although he undertook the task with great diligence, Tirpitz soon came into conflict with other members of the naval staff, and his plans were repeatedly thwarted by the Reichstag's refusal to grant him sufficient funds to bring them to fruition. In 1898, he succeeded in passing the First Naval Law but this was but a minor step towards creating the fleet of which he and the Kaiser dreamed.

In an attempt to generate more enthusiasm for his plans, Wilhelm asked his brother, Henry – a lifelong sailor – to establish and lead a 'Navy League', to educate the masses as to why the navy was so vital for Germany. School trips were organised to enable to pupils to visit ships and talk with the officers – just as Wilhelm and Henry had done at Portsmouth when they were children – and leaflets were distributed widely in public places, emphasising the connections between naval development, trade and domestic prosperity.

The League had a moderate success, and, a year after its foundation, an incident occurred which propelled the Reichstag into taking Tirpitz' ideas more seriously. In the midst of the Boer War, British cruisers stopped and searched several German mail steamers off the African coast, suspecting them of carrying weapons and supplies to the enemy. When the *Bundesrat* was detained for several days, there was such an outcry in Berlin that the British government was forced to order the immediate release of the steamer and offer compensation to the shipping company with promises that there would be no further molestation of civilian vessels.

Tirpitz used the 'Bundesrat Incident' to demonstrate the necessity of a strong defensive fleet, and his arguments, combined with the wave of patriotism that swept through Germany in response to the British actions, persuaded the

Reichstag to accept some of his recommendations. The Second Naval Bill of 1900 doubled the size of the fleet, making it a force to be reckoned with.

Wilhelm repeatedly stressed that the navy's sole purpose was to protect Germany's trading interests and to 'secure us peace on the sea'[116], and initially the British paid little attention to his plans. Sir Edward Reed, a renowned naval architect and one-time First Lord of the Treasury, was certain of the innocence of the Kaiser's intentions, stating categorically that:

> "His motive in striving for sea-power is quite simply this, that the German Empire has too many great and distantly located interests to enable it to retain its leading position without a reasonable expansion of its maritime forces....For the protection of its rapidly-expanding commerce beyond the seas, the empire requires a strong navy."[117]

With the passing of the Second Naval Bill, however, the British began to view the growing fleet with mounting unease, fearing not only the potential loss of their dominance of the seas, but also the possibility of being outstripped in exports and commerce. As rumours of the rising resentment in Britain reached the Kaiser, Tirpitz' ominous predictions took on greater importance, and Wilhelm was increasingly convinced that, as with the army, the only means of maintaining peace at sea was to create so powerful a force that 'even for the adversary with the greatest sea-power, a war against it would involve such dangers as to imperil its position in the world.'[118]

These words convinced the British establishment that the Kaiser did indeed intend to set up his fleet as a rival to their own, and throughout the early years of the twentieth century, politicians in London repeatedly called for a more intense shipbuilding programme to counter that which was taking place 'across the North Sea'. Charles Dilke, renowned for his republican views and criticism of the Royal Family, drew attention to the reduction in France's naval budget, suggesting that this placed an even greater onus on Britain to increase her own.

Not all politicians shared this view, for, as Lord Courtney stated, it was wrong of Britain to continually treat the Germans with suspicion when they stated, reasonably, that they needed a strong navy to protect their merchant fleet. He asked, "Can no trust be place in the honesty of any nation?"[119]

The First Lord of the Admiralty, Viscount Goschen, shared Tirpitz' view of the ultimate inevitability of war and, although he acknowledged that neither the Kaiser nor his ministers had any designs on Britain:

> "[Germany] requires more territory for her teeming millions. She feels that she must have colonies, that she must expand, as other growing countries must expand, that she must have outlets for her commerce, and that she must have sea power like us to hold her own against every possible effort to limit her colonial expansion or paralyse her action. Her Ministers have no desire for war. But they have an Imperial German policy."[120]

This, as Tirpitz had predicted, was at the heart of Britain's objections to the Kaiser's naval programme. Wilhelm was not, as was later suggested, creating a threat to British security but rather, simply by seeking to prosper his country, establishing Germany as an economic rival. A strong navy would enable him to find more commercial outlets and eventually outstrip Britain as 'the workshop of the world'. Wilhelm was not deliberately attempting to undermine the British economy, for his focus was fixed solely on expanding Germany's trade; and, ironically in the light of the accusations that were levelled against him, this was one of the most powerful reasons why he earnestly wanted to maintain peace. 'A merchant does not make war with his customers,' he said; and, in 1895, at the opening of the Kiel Canal, when ships of every nation were invited to pass through the waterway, he stated sincerely:

"Only in peace can the world's trade be developed, in peace only can it prosper. We desire to maintain that peace and will do so."[121]

British politicians, industrialists and financiers watched Germany's burgeoning economic success with increasing consternation as the quality and output of German products rapidly began to surpass their own. In 1897, for example, German exports to Canada were valued at $6,500,000; and, fifteen years later, trade between the United States and Germany was estimated to be worth approximately $160 million per annum. Between 1902 and 1907 the total value of German trade doubled with an annual increase of $250,000; and whereas, at the start of Wilhelm's reign, the British were producing twice as much steel as the Germans, by 1913, the German output tripled that of Britain.

German manufacturing was so successful that the British government ordered imports to be labelled 'made in Germany' in the hope that patriotic people would boycott those items, but the plan backfired as the public quickly realised that the German products were less expensive but of a far better quality and so actively sought out the labels. Transport, too, was becoming increasingly dependent on German manufacturers as they alone made certain parts for motor cars; and rail companies were placing orders for locomotives in Berlin because the German designs were far more modern and efficient than their own.

The Germans' success was not due solely to the quality of manufacture but also to the care with which they studied the specific needs of their clients, and a system of credit which enabled foreign businesses to pay for their purchases over several months or even years. The English Consul at Rio de Janeiro said, 'The Germans have conquered South America by the peculiar study they have made of its requirements,' and the Consul at Riga said that, 'A German seizes every opportunity of pleasing his customers'."[122]

Beyond Europe, the Kaiser's desire to improve the economy was largely viewed as admirable since he was motivated not by a desire for luxury but rather, as Professor Sanborn of the Vanderbilt University in Tennessee, observed, 'for the sake of [Germany's] higher civilisation and culture'; and this in Sanborn's view was 'a right, not a crime although it caused much resentment in Britain.'[123].

As early as 1905, the Belgian Ambassador in London, Count Lalaing, reported that German efficiency provoked bitterness and hatred in England; and seven years later, an American diplomat based in Germany gave an interview to the Houston *Chronicle,* in which he stated that:

> "Germany is today the most efficient nation, economically on the globe…The German policy is one of peaceful development of domestic and foreign trade. Germany does not seek offense [sic] nor seek occasion to give offense…When the day comes that Germany passes Great Britain in the exportation of manufactured products, British resentment will perhaps precipitate an armed conflict between these two great nations."[124]

In 1907, another American diplomat, Henry White, attended the Second Hague Conference where Britain's former Prime Minister, Arthur Balfour, jokingly told him that the British were fools not to find a reason to go to war with Germany before she built too many ships and took away British trade. When White protested that it was 'politically immoral' to provoke a war 'against a harmless nation which has as good a right to a navy as you have,' Balfour replied that it would be simpler to have a war than to lower the standard of living in Britain and added that it was not a question of right or wrong but rather simply 'a question of keeping our supremacy.'[125]

Seven years later, in 1914, the patriotic British author, H.G. Wells echoed this warning in an article in which he claimed that Germany was ten years ahead of Britain in aviation and other forms of transport; her army was stronger; her welfare provisions more comprehensive; and her universities had replaced those of England as centres of innovation and academic excellence. The success of the 'new' nation had, he stated, created intense bitterness in Britain – a bitterness which was not shared by India, Canada, Australia or any other British dominion.

"We in Britain are intensely jealous of Germany," he wrote, "not only because the Germans outnumber us and have a much larger and more diversified country than ours, and lie in the very heart and body of Europe but because...they have had the energy and humility to develop a splendid system of national education, to toil at science and art and literature, to develop social organisation, to master and better our methods of business and industry, and to clamber above us in the scale of civilization. This has humiliated and irritated rather than chastened us."[126]

In response to the expansion of German markets and the rapid improvements to the Kaiser's navy, other nations began to develop shipbuilding programmes of their own. In 1903, the Japanese produced two all-big-gun battleships; and three years later, as the Germans passed the Third Naval Bill, their plans were thrown into disarray by the launching of Britain's first dreadnought. Tirpitz immediately pressed for the building and upgrading of more German battleships, but the Reichstag insisted that it would be too expensive to upgrade all the vessels to the dreadnought standard, particularly since that would also necessitate widening canals and locks to allow such huge vessels to pass through. Even Wilhelm's brother, Henry, opposed Tirpitz' plans on the grounds of expense, but ultimately Wilhelm and his Chancellor, Bernhard von Bulow, prevailed upon the Reichstag to release sufficient funds to embark on the plan. Over the next seven years, despite a rapid accumulation of debt, the navy continued to expand by approximately two dreadnoughts and one battlecruiser per year.

The Kaiser was, therefore, blamed for precipitating the naval race but while he proudly addressed the Tsar as the Admiral of the Pacific and referred to himself as Admiral of the Atlantic, he firmly believed that the British fears of his success were based on paranoia. At the turn of the century, British sailors outnumbered their Germany counterparts by over five to one; and even at the height of German naval expansion, there were over twice as many naval personnel in England as in Germany. Moreover, with the encouragement of London, the British dominions were not only presenting battleships to England, but were also slowly developing smaller navies of their own.

Nonetheless, the press continued a scaremongering campaign and, in 1908, a series of articles about the Kaiser's evil intentions appeared in British papers. In response, Wilhelm wrote to the First Lord of the Admiralty, joking about the nonsense that was written about him. His letter was brought to the attention of Parliament, and when the press discovered that he had personally contacted the Admiralty, they accused him of attempting to influence the naval budget and to persuade the First Lord to disarm British ships. It was left to Lord Roseberry to dismiss such reports as ridiculous:

> "The German Emperor is not merely a great potentate, but a potentate of remarkable intelligence, born of an English mother, who has paid many visits to this country, and is intimately acquainted with our political Constitution, and I am quite sure that it never would have entered his head, or the head of any educated person outside of a

lunatic asylum in Germany, that by a private communication to my noble friend he could exercise such influence."[127]

The damage to his reputation, though, had already been done, and attacks increased as his naval expansion was taken as evidence of his belligerent intentions. In 1912, Winston Churchill, gave an impassioned speech to the House of Commons, claiming that Britain had every right to maintain 'naval supremacy in the face of the world' because:

> "We are an unarmed people…we cannot menace the independence or the vital interests of any continental state…we cannot invade any continental state…When we consider our naval strength, we are not thinking of our commerce but of our freedom. We are not thinking of our trade but of our lives."[128]

It was a disingenuous statement, designed to frighten people into believing that the Kaiser's Germany posed a direct threat to their lives and freedoms. Considering that Britain ruled approximately one-fifth of the world's surface, and that a quarter of the world's population officially owed allegiance to the Crown, it was ridiculous to claim that the country was so helpless that her very existence depended upon the superiority of her navy.

Nonetheless, the first seeds of fear had been sown and, over the next two years, the scaremongering would intensify, creating the false impression that the German military and naval expansion were signs of the Kaiser's plans to conquer the whole of Europe.

Chapter 10 – 'The Old Peacock'

While Queen Victoria was alive, Wilhelm had every reason to hope for good relations between Britain and Germany, for, notwithstanding the rising tensions over trade, colonies and naval expansion, the loving marriage of the British Queen and the German Prince Albert of Saxe-Coburg-Gotha appeared to symbolise the natural union of the two nations. Queen Victoria often and unashamedly spoke of her affection for Germany in much the same way as Wilhelm expressed his love of England; and, for a man who believed that monarchs had been divinely appointed to their roles, the strength of family ties was all that was necessary to maintain peace.

With the accession of 'Uncle Bertie' – King Edward VII – in 1901, the situation rapidly began to change and, as throughout his nine year reign Anglo-German relations deteriorated, Wilhelm and many of his countrymen believed the King was to blame.

On a personal level, the two men could not have been more dissimilar. While Bertie always 'gave the impression of a polished, suave and finished diplomat'[129], his nephew was brash, impulsive and prone to speaking his mind before thinking through the consequences. Their personality clashes had quickly developed into mutual antipathy, which was, according to Infante Eulalia of Spain:

> "…as frank as the enmity between the nations. Neither monarch made any secret of it when they were together."[130]

Bertie viewed his nephew as too erratic to be relied upon, while Wilhelm saw his uncle as dishonest and lacking in moral calibre. He was not the only one to doubt the King's trustworthiness, for Queen Victoria had often despaired of her eldest son's behaviour. During his childhood and youth, Bertie had caused his father endless disappointment by his apathy and lack of application to his studies, and, despite Prince Albert's best efforts to engage him, he showed no interest in anything other than clothes and pleasure. When, at his own request, he was posted to Ireland with a regiment of guards, he embarked on a liaison with an actress, which so shocked Prince Albert that Queen Victoria believed it contributed to his early death. Concerned about his similarity to her prodigal Hanoverian uncles, and his habit of associating with 'unsuitable' companions, the Queen had so little faith in her son that she refused to allow him to assist in her duties, and although he was heir to the throne, she insisted that he be kept ignorant of sensitive information because, as she told one of her granddaughters, 'he is not to be trusted.'

A serial philanderer, renowned for his numerous infidelities and fondness for gambling, the portly prince's name had been tarnished by several scandals. In the infamous Mordaunt case, the young wife of a Member of Parliament claimed, while suffering from post-natal depression, that the then Prince of Wales might be the father of her child[s]. Two years after Wilhelm's accession, his uncle became embroiled in the Tranby Croft affair – a gambling scandal which resulted in a well-publicised court case and a widespread reprimand for the pleasure-loving prince. As a result of such misdemeanours, and more especially due to his unfaithfulness and neglect of his beautiful wife, Bertie's popularity with the British people had fluctuated dramatically during his early adulthood, but, by the time he ascended the throne in 1901, his charm had endeared him to the masses, and the contrast between his glamourous image and Queen Victoria's semi-seclusion made him a well-loved monarch.

---

[s] The case was taken to court when the M.P. decided to divorce his wife. During the hearing Bertie denied any improper conduct with the unfortunate Harriet, who was committed to a lunatic asylum for the rest of her life, leading the British public to view the whole affair as a cover-up.

To Wilhelm, though, Uncle Bertie – 'the old peacock' – remained the epitome of all he despised. His gluttonous appetites contrasted sharply with the habits of the abstemious Kaiser; and his blatant extramarital affairs and penchant for visiting French brothels, disgusted his nephew, who commented that 'someone ought to tell him that he is a grandfather'. More importantly, like Queen Victoria, Wilhelm did not trust the coterie of cronies with whom Bertie surrounded himself, particularly when he amassed debts which ambitious financiers were happy to settle in return for his friendship. In Wilhelm's eyes, by allowing himself to become beholden to unscrupulous bankers, who placed their own agendas and ambitions above the good of the country, the King was jeopardising international relations – specifically, relations between Germany and England. Wilhelm was not the only one to observe the danger of such friendships. One of Bertie's former mistresses, Lady Warwick, recounted the case of Baron Hirsch, who had:

> "...amassed a vast fortune by curious and unclean methods...I cannot help thinking that the Baron put King Edward VII under certain obligations and it was characteristic of him that he never forgot those who served him....The Kaiser chaffed at his uncle's association with a mushroom financier whose record was only too well known."[131]

Bertie certainly reciprocated Wilhelm's antipathy, not least because he had been close to his sister, Vicky, and had consequently taken at face-value all her criticisms of her son. When he visited Germany soon after Wilhelm's accession, he pointedly snubbed his nephew, who returned the compliment on his first visit to England as German Emperor.

"There will be trouble for England with this man, for he is not a gentleman,"[132] Bertie told Lord Esher in 1888 – a rather ironic statement from the 'gentleman' who had played such an ungallant role in the Mordaunt case, and had abandoned another mistress when she became pregnant!

Undoubtedly, too, Bertie had envied the affection and praise which Queen Victoria showered on her grandson; and it was galling for him to see his young nephew ascend the throne at an early age when he himself did not become King until his sixtieth year. When Wilhelm was still in his twenties, he was free to discuss international relations with Queen Victoria, while the Prince of Wales was refused any meaningful role in affairs of state. The satirist and diplomat, Alfred Kiderlen-Waechter, stated plainly that, 'The Prince of Wales cannot forgive his nephew, eighteen years younger than himself, for making a more brilliant career than has fallen to his lot.'[133]

The Kaiser's bombastic over-exuberance also irked his uncle, who dreaded his annual visit to the Cowes Regatta because he had a habit of 'interfering in everything' to the point where Bertie said the event had once been an enjoyable holiday but 'now that the Kaiser has taken command there, it is nothing but a nuisance.'[134]

In public, uncle and nephew behaved with appropriate decorum but, by the mid-1890s, Bertie spoke so openly of his contempt for the Kaiser that one observer stated bluntly that 'they hated each other'.[135] It was even rumoured that once, when Wilhelm was visiting Windsor, Bertie was so incensed by a comment that he made that he actually struck him. There is no evidence that such an unlikely event ever took place but the fact that the story was widely circulated demonstrates that their mutual antipathy was common knowledge.

Personal animosity apart, Wilhelm soon had a far more serious reason to mistrust his uncle, for, within four years of the King's accession, Britain had formed an entente with her own long-standing rival, and Germany's archenemy, France.

The Entente Cordiale took the Kaiser by surprise for, throughout the 19th century, while other countries were busily securing alliances, British politicians had been so sure of the strength of the Empire that they had shown a distinct disinterest in forming defensive agreements, preferring to remain in 'splendid isolation.' By the 1890s, however, as other trading nations were becoming more prosperous, there was growing concern that Britain could soon be overtaken by competitors; and, by the time of King Edward's accession, politicians, reeling from the losses of the Boer War, realised that isolation was no longer be an option.

Rumours of political intrigues abounded as secret treaties were drawn up, and offers of alliances were made behind closed doors. As early as 1894, Wilhelm had been shocked to learn of the Dual Alliance between Russia and France, finding it impossible to believe that an autocracy could ally itself to a republic which was, in his opinion, the birthplace and seat of socialism. His only explanation was that the French had bought the Russians by providing cheap loans for the construction of railways and the development of industry.

Wilhelm's concern about the Dual Alliance went far beyond differences of political ideology. With the ever-present threat of French retaliation for the losses of the Franco-Prussian War, the prospect of being attacked on two fronts – by France from the west, and Russia from the east – was alarming. With the accession of Tsar Nicholas II[t] in 1894, he felt that he had gained a measure of influence, which might even work to Germany's advantage in keeping the French in check. Over the next twenty years he would frequently plead with the Tsar to be wary of 'those rascals, the French.'

---

[t] See Chapter 11

Up to the turn of the century, the British had had little faith in either France or Russia, and, in 1898, Wilhelm was surprised to hear that his Ambassador in London had been approached by the British Colonial Secretary, Joseph Chamberlain, with an unofficial offer of an Anglo-German alliance. Only the previous year, the British Foreign Secretary had stated that his country had no need of allies, and therefore the Ambassador believed that Chamberlain was acting on his own initiative, without the backing of his government. What was more, at that very time, the Reichstag was debating Tirpitz' Naval Bill, leading to the suspicion that the offer was merely a ploy to discover the details Tirpitz' plans. Consequently, Chamberlain's idea received a cool reception in the Reichstag, and, although Wilhelm remained optimistic about forming stronger ties with Britain, he was not in a position to sway public opinion or to elicit a positive response from his ministers. Soon afterwards, Chamberlain broached the subject again, and, in 1899, while Wilhelm was visiting England, he pressed his point still further. This time he spoke of the possibility a quadruple alliance between Germany, Britain, the United States and Japan, leading Wilhelm to suspect that this was an attempt to curb Russia's interest in the East. Although he was keen to remain on good terms with the Tsar – not least to protect German interests in China – he did not dismiss Chamberlain's proposal outright but responded positively to his ideas during an informal conversation over dinner.

Unfortunately, Chamberlain was so delighted by the Kaiser's encouragement that, a few days later on 30th November, he gave a speech in Leicester in which he implied that negotiations between Britain and Germany were reaching a definite outcome. 'A new Triple Alliance between the Teutonic [German] and the two great branches of the Anglo-Saxon race [Britain and the United States],' he said, 'would be a…potent influence in the future of the world'[136]. Although he emphasised that nothing had officially been signed, his speech was widely reported and distorted by the press, provoking a great furore in France, and leading to such an outcry in Berlin that Chancellor von Bulow was compelled to repudiate publicly all of Chamberlain's claims.

Undeterred, twelve days before Queen Victoria's death, Chamberlain approached a German diplomat, von Eckardstein, and told him that the days of splendid isolation were over and Britain would soon be forced to make an alliance either with Germany or with France and Russia. This time, the Kaiser and most of his ministers believed that Chamberlain was indeed acting on behalf of his government to solicit Germany's support in the Boer War, and ensure that she did not enter the conflict on the side of the Boers. The Head of the German Foreign Office urged caution, warning that a hastily-made alliance could result in Germany being dragged into British disputes and possibly even becoming embroiled in a war with Russia:

> "Hardly any general treaty with England is conceivable for Germany which would not involve the threat of war. And Germany could only expect compensation comparable to the intense risks it was taking if England had a more accurate, that is a more modest, opinion of its own performances."[137]

The Germans were also concerned that, if they agreed to the alliance, a general election in Britain could produce a different government which might overturn any agreement, leaving Germany in a precarious position, having alienated France and Russia, and gained nothing from a rapprochement with Britain.

Moreover, six years prior to Wilhelm's accession, Germany had entered into a Triple Alliance with Austria-Hungary and Italy, and, in a private conversation with Edward VII in August 1901, the Kaiser stated that the Reichstag would never ratify an Anglo-German treaty unless it were extended to include their allies, and came with a guarantee that it would be ratified by the British Parliament. During several similar political discussions, the King assured the Kaiser that he had no desire to take Britain into an alliance with either Russia or France; and the British Naval defence Act of 1899 had been specifically designed to ensure that the Royal Navy was equal to those of the aforementioned countries. Just five months later, Britain entered into an alliance with Japan from which Germany was excluded; and, two years later, to Wilhelm's horror, Britain and France signed the Entente Cordiale.

Notwithstanding Queen Victoria's doubts about his abilities, King Edward was an astute diplomat with a keen eye for furthering British interests and an ability to sway politicians to his way of thinking. In 1903 he embarked on a tour of Europe, the true purpose of which, many Germans believed, was to arrange alliances leading to the isolation of Germany. These suspicions appeared to be justified when he approached the Austro-Hungarian Emperor Franz Josef – Germany's closest ally.

> "It is well known," wrote the Austrian Foreign Minister, "that Edward VII made an attempt to exercise a direct influence on the Emperor Francis Joseph to induce him to secede from the Alliance and join the Powers encircling Germany. It is likewise known that the Emperor Francis Joseph rejected the proposal, and that this decided the fate of Austria-Hungary."[138]

Unlike his mother, whose devotion to Germany was second only to her love for England, Bertie's natural inclinations drew him towards France – a country with which he became enamoured during his first visit to Paris at the age of fourteen. Consequently, when, a year after his European tour, Britain entered into the Entente Cordiale, the Germans were convinced that he had personally arranged the agreement with the intention of isolating

Germany to curb her economic expansion. Even the Kaiser's eldest son, Crown Prince Wilhelm, who was personally fond of King Edward, observed that:

"It was his personality which drew France into the entente cordiale with England…and it was he who attracted the Tsar further and further away from Germany and won him for England…Why do all that? To destroy Germany? Certainly not! But he and his country realized that for some years the curve of Germany's commercial economic-political situation and industrial progress had been such that England was in danger of being outstripped. Here he had to step in."[139]

From then onwards relations between Germany and Britain rapidly deteriorated and, within a year, the Kaiser was accused to attempting to undermine Anglo-French relations.

One of the official purposes of the Entente was to alleviate tensions between French and British interests in North Africa. By the terms of the agreement, Britain would be given free rein in Egypt, and in return France was free to expand unimpeded towards Morocco, which, as the last uncolonised territory in the region, had been guaranteed independence by an international conference in 1880, and which Germany viewed as a potentially lucrative market.

In March 1905, while Wilhelm was preparing for a Mediterranean cruise, Chancellor von Bulow, asked him to visit to Lisbon to pay his respects to the Portuguese King and, shortly before his departure, Bulow suggested he might also detour to Tangier to offer his support to the Moroccan Sultan. Initially, Wilhelm refused to do so, warning that his presence would inflame the French, but he had barely departed on his cruise when he received a message from the Chancellor, telling him that it was his duty to fulfil the wishes of the Reichstag and the German people. "I gave in with a heavy heart," Wilhelm wrote

113

later, and, just as he had predicted, the visit prompted an outcry in Britain and France where he was accused of interfering in foreign affairs. In reality, as one of his strongest critics, the German diplomat, von Eckerstein, asserted:

"The Kaiser was not directly to blame...for the disastrous Morocco policy of 1905...He was involved [in this] by his official advisors against his will and without seeing what fatal effects these aberrations of German diplomacy would have on the peace of the world."[140]

As was expected, while in Tangier, Wilhelm expressed his support for the Sultan, assuring him that, since Germany had many commercial interests in the region, he would abide by the 1880 convention, guaranteeing the country's independence so that 'a free Morocco might be open to the peaceful competition of all nations, without monopoly and without restrictions'[141].

The French reacted angrily to the speech, viewing it as a direct challenge to their activities in the region, and as the Foreign Minister, Declassé, 'tried to rouse the nation to war,'[142] the Belgian Ambassador in London, reported that King Edward VII had actively encouraged him to take such a belligerent stance.

"It can no longer be doubted," he wrote, "that it has been the King of England who, independent of his government, drove M. Declassé into his bellicose policy and who gave him a promise, which he would not have kept, to land 100,000 British soldiers in Holstein."[143]

It was a view reiterated by von Bulow who wrote to an advisor to the German Foreign Office that King Edward VII was encouraging the French to take a strong line against Germany, as Britain was trying to ferment war between the two nations.

Wilhelm, continuing on his cruise, knew nothing of the furore until he arrived at Gibraltar and was 'formally and frigidly received by the English, in marked contrast to my reception the year before.'[144]

With tensions running so high, at the Sultan's request the Germans proposed an international conference to advise him on appropriate domestic reforms and to demand an explanation for the French activities in the region. When Declassé declared that no such meeting was necessary, von Bulow warned that the situation could escalate into war. Edward VII wrote to Wilhelm, offering to mediate between France and Germany, but in view of the Entente agreement it is unsurprising that Wilhelm rejected such a proposal.

Over the next few months, tensions intensified as the French cancelled all military leave and the British assured them that, if necessary, they could land one-hundred-thousand men at Holstein to seize the Kaiser Wilhelm Canal.

Fortunately, thanks largely to the German Ambassador in Paris and the Prince of Monaco – with whom Wilhelm had spoken of his desire to live peacefully with the French – the situation was resolved through negotiation. Declassé was forced to resign, and the conference, which the Germans had requested, was arranged for 1st July. In spite of this apparent success, however, the 'Algeciras Conference' revealed quite how isolated Germany had become. Of the thirteen nations present, only Austria-Hungary supported the Germans, and ultimately, despite a few minor concessions, France maintained much of the control of Morocco. To add insult to injury, the French then conferred the Legion d'Honneur on the German Ambassador, Prince Radolin, for services to France.

Ultimately, the Algeciras agreement did little to ease the tensions in the region and, a year after the conference, an incident occurred which, with hindsight, foreshadowed the events of July 1914 and the outbreak of the First World War.

In August 1907, following the murder of a number of European workmen by a gang of Moroccans, the French hastily dispatched a gunboat to bombard the coast of Casablanca with such ferocity that the Belgian Ambassador in Paris reported that:

> "...the French government have acted even more odiously than the assassins, inasmuch as they bombarded an open town, massacred women and children, and ruined inoffensive merchants at the very time when their delegates were virtuously delivering fine humanitarian speeches in The Hague."[145]

Just over a year later, a group of six deserters, including three Germans, fled the French Foreign Legion and sought the protection of the German consulate. The Consul arranged for them to leave Morocco aboard a German ship but, as they attempted to embark, they were violently seized by the French authorities, leading to a further bitter dispute between the governments of France and Germany. The British Prime Minister, Asquith, assured the French that if the disagreement escalated into war, Britain would stand by her ally, but the issue was finally resolved by a tribunal in The Hague. Although armed conflict had been averted, the situation in North Africa not only continued to thwart Germany's hopes of obtaining a naval base in the region but also strengthened the Entente and paved the way for an Anglo-Russian agreement.

Chapter 11 – 'He Has Invariably Worked for Peace with England'

In November 1894, several months after the introduction of the Dual Alliance between France and Russia, Tsar Alexander III died and his twenty-six-year-old son, Nicholas II, ascended the throne. Less than three weeks later, to the Kaiser's delight, the new Tsar married Princess Alix of Hesse – Wilhelm's first cousin, the youngest surviving child of Queen Victoria's daughter, Princess Alice. As Nicholas was also a distant cousin, Wilhelm was keen to develop their friendship and to use their family ties to secure greater co-operation between their nations.

Over the next two decades, the Kaiser and the Tsar maintained a regular correspondence and, while their letters frequently discussed matters of international importance, they were also filled with affectionate messages for each other's family, and usually concluded, 'ever your affectionate friend, Nicky', or 'your devoted cousin and friend, Wilhelm.' Such was the amity between the two Emperors that the Belgian Ambassador in Paris observed that the natural antipathy between the Russians and the Germans was held in check by the fact that 'the relations between the rulers...have always been better than those between the nations and even between the two governments.'[146]

To fulfil his grandfather's dying request and to prevent the encirclement of Germany, Wilhelm eagerly pursued the possibility of an official alliance with Russia and he had every reason to believe that Nicholas shared his enthusiasm. In 1903, when the Kaiser's son visited St. Petersburg, he was warmly welcomed by the Tsar who gave him the distinct impression that he was eager to form closer ties with Germany but was hindered by two powerful Germanophobes: his cousin, Grand Duke Nikolai

Nikolaicvich, and his mother, the Dowager Empress Marie Feodorovna[u]. At seven-feet tall, the Grand Duke, who was soon to be appointed Commander of the Russian Armed Forces, towered over the more diminutive Nicholas, and was so popular with the army that it was difficult to oppose him. The Danish-born Dowager Empress, to whom Nicholas was devoted, so detested the Prussians for their seizure of Schleswig-Holstein from the Danes thirty years earlier that, according to one member of the Imperial Family, she gasped at least three times a week for twenty-two years, "Germany must be punished! Russia must make an alliance with France!"[147]

As she and her English relations frequently repaired to her family home in Denmark, Copenhagen became a centre of royal gatherings but, to his great distress, Wilhelm was never invited, and he feared that, in such a relaxed atmosphere, King Edward VII might use his influence over the Tsar to turn him against Germany. Nonetheless, his hopes for a Russian alliance were strengthened by the encouragement of the recently appointed Chairman of the Committee of Ministers, Count de Witte, who, twenty years earlier, as Minister of Finance had been instrumental in concluding a commercial treaty with Germany. In 1903 when Crown Prince Wilhelm visited Russia, he and Witte:

> "…had a long talk on the question of a new Russo-German treaty of commerce, in the course of which the politician, with his far-sighted views of finance and political economy, maintained emphatically that, in his opinion, the healthy development of Russia depended closely on her proceeding hand in hand with Germany."[148]

The following year, when war broke out between Russia and Japan, Wilhelm had even more reason to hope for a stronger bond between Germany and Russia for he

---

[u] Sister of Britain's Queen Alexandra, wife of King Edward VII

was quick to offer Nicholas his unfailing support and passed on to him any information he could find regarding Japanese capabilities and troop movements. Russia's official allies, the French, Wilhelm noticed, were particularly unhelpful, leading to 'great disappointment and annoyance in Russia.'[149] When an article appeared in the *Morning Post,* urging Britons to support the Japanese, the Kaiser offered to create a defensive agreement between Germany and Russia and even went so far as to state that France could be included in the arrangement. Nicholas, galled by the British government's arrogant offers to mediate in the conflict, leaned further towards Wilhelm's proposal and agreed with him that the British were simply 'afraid for [their] money and [want] to get Tibet cheaply.'[150] When Nicholas declined the British offer of mediation, Wilhelm promised to approach King Edward to dissuade him from 'harassing you with any more proposals'[151]; and, when the war eventually reached its conclusion, President Roosevelt, who had been instrumental in brokering the subsequent Treaty of Portsmouth, stated categorically that the one man who had been most helpful in drawing up the treaty was Kaiser Wilhelm.

> "From no other nation did I receive any assistance but the Emperor personally and through his Ambassador in St. Petersburg, was of real aid in helping to induce Russia to…come to an agreement with Japan. This was a real help to the cause of international peace, a contribution that outweighed any mere talk about it in the abstract."[152]

In spite of this, the Russian ministers refused to countenance a German alliance, but Wilhelm remained optimistic, assuring Nicholas that he would draw up a treaty which even the most hardened Germanophobes would be powerless to reject. True to his word, throughout out the autumn and winter of 1904, he worked on creating an agreement by which Germany and Russia would come to each other's aid if either were attacked by more than one power. Delighted by his completed work, Wilhelm confidently told Nicholas that, by signing the treaty, they would ensure the peace of the world, but the Tsar, mindful of the Franco-Russian agreement, insisted that his allies must be included in any negotiations.

Wilhelm, mistrusting politicians, believed that their inclusion in the discussions would only hinder the process. The French President, Émile Loubet, and the renowned Germanophobe, Théopile Declassé, were, he told Nicholas, experienced statesmen, but, since they were not princes or emperors, he could not 'place them – in a question of confidence like this one – on the same footing as you, my equal, my cousin and friend.' [153]

Eventually Nicholas agreed to Wilhelm's proposals on condition that the French would be informed as soon as the agreement came into effect. To avoid speculation or outside interference, the Kaiser and the Tsar arranged an apparently informal meeting aboard Wilhelm's yacht, *Hohenzollern,* which would be cruising the waters around Finland when the Tsar was in the area. On a warm Sunday evening, 24th July 1905, in the company of a two diplomats – one German and one Russian – and an Admiral of the Russian fleet, Nicholas and Wilhelm signed the Treaty of Bjorko.

Wilhelm returned home ecstatic about what he had achieved and, two days later, he wrote to Nicholas, thanking him effusively for the pleasure of his company and assuring him that the alliance would:

> '...restore quiet in the minds of people and confidence in the maintenance of Peace in Europe and encourage financial circles in foreign countries to place funds in enterprises in Russia.' [154]

His joy, alas, was short-lived.

As soon as Nicholas presented the treaty to his horrified ministers they told him that, without France's agreement, it could never be ratified and was therefore meaningless. Aghast at the news, Wilhelm, in a moment of rage, told the Tsar that their vows had been made before God and were therefore too sacred to be broken. His rant achieved nothing, but their friendship remained intact, and, in their continuing correspondence, both agreed that they should stand together against the machinations of 'the Arch-intriguer and mischief maker in Europe' – Nicholas' description of King Edward VII.

In view of the failure of his own efforts to broker a treaty with Russia, Wilhelm was predictably dismayed when, in 1907, he was told that Russia and Britain were involved in talks about their interests in Persia, and it was widely rumoured that they were about to enter a formal alliance. The possibility of the formation of a Triple Entente of Britain, Russia and France was deeply disconcerting, since it would lead to a complete encirclement of Germany.

> "The Triple Entente…is being talked of by the whole world as an accomplished fact," the Kaiser wrote anxiously to the Tsar. "English and French papers miss no opportunity of representing this alleged Triple entente as being directed against Germany, and only too often the Russian Press chimes in joining the chorus."[155]

Already Russian officers were attending British military manoeuvres and, within a matter of months, Wilhelm's fears were realised when the agreement was formalised.

Wilhelm, dubbing his uncle, 'Satan', held him totally responsible for the alliance, the sole purpose of which, he believed, was the isolation and encirclement of Germany. Many independent commentators shared this opinion:

> "It can readily be seen what Russia can gain by the friendship of England," wrote one neutral observer,

121

"but it is much less clear what good the Russian friendship could do England. What else can they aim at in London if not making enemies of Germany?"[156]

That year, a captain in the Imperial Navy told a correspondent for the *Observer* that the general feeling was that Britain was weaving a web to surround Germany with enemies. The Belgian Ambassador in France concurred, reporting to Brussels that, 'the King of England is personally pursuing a policy the final aim of which is the isolation of Germany'[157]; and some months later, he added that, 'M. Declassé boasts he has kept the peace of the world thanks to his policy of encirclement which he has pursued against Germany in union with the King of England.'[158]

"Yes," wrote the *Observer's* correspondent in 1907, "there is a crisis between England and Germany, and it would be useless to deny it....The feeling in German military, official and private circles is that England sooner or later intends to make war on Germany, to crush her fleet, destroy her trade, ruin her future and reduce her to penury and Anglo-Saxon vassalage."[159]

The same year, Edward VII met the King of Spain and, once again it was widely reported that the purpose of his visit was to gain another anti-German ally, prompting the Kaiser to ask why his uncle travelled the world attempting to make friends and allies of everyone except the Germans.

By this time, tensions were escalating, too, over the Germans' interest in the Baghdad Railway which would create a direct link from Berlin to the Persian Gulf, and facilitate trade between Germany's African colonies, without the necessity of passing through the French-controlled Suez Canal. The Turkish Sultan had approved the railway in 1899, and the concession for its construction was granted to the German Anatolian Railway Company, funded by the Deutsche Bank with backing from French financiers.

Initially there was little opposition to the project until the British feared it might impact upon their political interests in Egypt and India, and the Russians saw the potential of a threat to their commercial interests in Persia.

In an effort to appease the British, Wilhelm suggested that the terminal part of the railway should become a joint venture between Britain and Germany, the former being allowed complete control of that part of the line on the understanding that it would be permanently available for German trade. Britain's Foreign Secretary, Edward Grey, approved the suggestion in theory but insisted that no agreement could be reached unless the French and Russians were involved in any discussions. In view of the fact that this would leave Germany at the mercy of the Triple Entente, Wilhelm could not accept the stipulation but, three years later, he concluded an amicable arrangement with Russia through a personal meeting with the Tsar.

Nicholas himself had proposed the meeting and, despite his unpopularity in Germany due to the formation of the Triple Entente, he received a warm welcome from the Kaiser on his arrival in Potsdam in November 1910. According to an Australian newspaper 'insulting placards in protest against the Tsar's visit had been posted overnight in various parts of Berlin,'[160] but these were hastily removed by the police before Nicholas saw them, and, after several friendly discussions with Wilhelm, a happy compromise was reached. Russia would withdraw any opposition to the railway on condition that it did not intrude into Armenia or Kurdistan, and, in return, Germany would raise no objections to Russian railway projects in Northern Persia.

The signing of the 'Potsdam Agreement' undermined the strength of the Entente, as the British greatly resented the free hand that the Russians had given to Germany. One Belgian observer noted:

> "For years the English press has advanced the arrogant claim to control and even forbid the completion of the Baghdad Railway, that is to say they wanted to lay their hands on an undertaking which concerns only Turkey, the concessionary company, and indirectly the German government which supported it."[161]

Under pressure, however, the following year, Britain's Foreign Secretary, Edward Grey, was forced to concede that his country had no right to interfere in Germany's plans or any agreements that the Kaiser had made with either the Sultan or the Tsar. For Wilhelm, this admission was a moment of triumph.

Even throughout his uncle's reign, Wilhelm continued to enjoy his visits to England and, in the summer of 1907, while recuperating from a persistent throat complaint, he rented Highcliffe Castle, the Dorset home of a seasoned British soldier, General Stuart-Wortley. During the visit, he and Wortley spoke much of relations between their two nations and, in an informal conversation, Wilhelm expressed his exasperation at Britain's persistent mistrust of his motives. Impressed by his obvious desire for peace, Wortley related the conversation to a journalist named Spender who suggested that, with the Kaiser's permission, it could be written in the form of an interview which the *Daily Telegraph* would print. The completed article was duly sent to Wilhelm for his approval, and before sanctioning its publication, he forwarded it to his Chancellor, von Bulow, who concurred that there was no reason why it shouldn't be printed. When, however, it eventually appeared in the press in November 1908, it raised such a storm of protests in Germany and England that Wilhelm was left prostrate on the verge of a nervous breakdown.

While the English viewed it as insulting, the Germans saw it as a demeaning attempt to appease Britain, but in reality it accurately captured the Kaiser's genuine desire for peace and his exasperation at the growing tensions between the two countries. The English, he had said, were 'mad, mad, mad as March hares' to mistrust him, and, although admitted that there was a good deal of anti-British feeling in Germany, he stressed that he personally was a true 'friend of England'.

"I strive with all my power to improve our relations, and, in spite of all, you persist in viewing me as your archenemy."[162]

Drawing attention to the support he had offered his 'sorrowing grandmother' during the 'black week of December 1899' when British losses were mounting and the rest of the world was condemning her part in the Boer War, he asked, 'Would an enemy of England behave thus?' He explained, too, how he had informed Queen Victoria of the message he had received, inviting him to join France and Russia in humiliating England into the dust. 'Posterity will one day read,' he said, 'the exact terms of the telegram – now in the archives of Windsor Castle – in which I informed the Sovereign of England of the answer I had returned to the Powers which then sought to compass her fall.'

Warning of Japan's economic rise to power and the potential for war in the Pacific, he repeated that his Imperial Navy was necessary for German trade and that, rather than fearing it, the British should be reassured by its strength:

"When the German and British squadrons are fighting side by side, England will rejoice over the fact that Germany had a strong Navy." [163]

In Britain, the Foreign Secretary, Edward Grey, denied the existence of the telegram which Wilhelm had mentioned, and accused him of attempting to create discord between Britain and her allies. To the end of his life, however, Wilhelm adhered to his account of having sent it, and the fact that he even included the episode in his memoirs suggests that he was indeed telling the truth. Moreover, the entire interview was taken from a private conversation which he had not intended to be heard by the public, and therefore he had no reason to lie nor to attempt to sow mistrust between Britain, France and Russia.

While the British both ridiculed and took offence at his statements, the Germans were so outraged that for a while it seemed as though the country were on the verge of revolution. 'All his subjects are now against him,' claimed one member of the Reichstag, as newspapers published lengthy articles, recounting and exaggerating every mistake he had made throughout his twenty year reign. The vitriolic attacks were not confined to his speeches or policies, but went deeper, criticising him personally and portraying him as a figure of fun at whom the whole of Europe was laughing. One socialist speaker went so far as to state that his one success was to achieve national unity since now the entire nation was united against him; and even von Bulow, who had read and agreed to the publication of the interview, distanced himself from the Kaiser by claiming that the transcript which he had received was written illegibly in English and he had not understood its contents. To protect his own reputation and to attempt to ameliorate the situation, von Bulow threatened to resign unless Wilhelm met certain conditions, the chief of which was that in future he would say nothing, even in private conversation, which could be construed as contradicting the policy of his ministers.

The effect on the Kaiser was disastrous. Feeling betrayed and deserted by everyone, he was utterly 'broken down by the catastrophe, which had snatched the ground from beneath his feet; his self-confidence and his trust were shattered."[164] So distraught was he that, according to his eldest son, he never regained sufficient confidence to oppose his ministers who had, by forcing him to accept their conditions, basically seized the authority from his hands.

In February 1909, three months after the *Daily Telegraph* storm, King Edward attempted to smooth relations between Britain and Germany by paying a formal visit to Berlin. Wilhelm desperately hoped that this show of friendship might silence the press and 'have useful results for the Peace of the World'[165], but even in this he was to be thwarted. The meeting began on a sour note when, with typical meticulousness, Wilhelm, having made precise preparations for the visit, waited with his family at the station to meet his uncle's train. At the last moment, however, the King – who was surely aware of the usual protocol – decided to leave from his wife's carriage rather than from his own, leaving the Kaiser and his suite to make an unceremonious dash along the platform. To make matters worse, the horses pulling the landau of Queen Mary and the German Empress refused to move, necessitating a delay and a disruption of the procession; and, since the King was suffering from chronic bronchitis and feeling unwell, he appeared completely uninterested in the formalities, which he attempted to complete as quickly as possible.

Over the next three days, the King and the Kaiser behaved with appropriate courtesy but, as one witness noticed, despite Wilhelm's efforts to 'do all he could to make the visit a success', he was obvious ill-at-ease around his uncle and their conversation, punctuated by forced jokes, was stilted and awkward:

"To my mind, the effect of this visit was nil…and the whole atmosphere when the two were together seemed charged with dangerous electricity."[166]

The following month, at the opening of Parliament, the King referred in passing to the visit, stating he was 'much impressed and gratified by the warmth of the public reception given to the Queen and Myself…by all classes of the community' and adding that he hoped this would strengthen 'amicable feelings between the two countries which are essential to their mutual welfare and to the maintenance of peace.'[167] This show of cordiality, however, was largely superficial, for, in the minds of the majority of Germans, King Edward VII remained the architect of Germany's encirclement and isolation.

Within fifteen months of the meeting with the Kaiser, Edward VII succumbed to bronchitis, dying on 6th May 1910. Wilhelm was one of ten reigning monarchs to attend his funeral, riding beside his cousin, the new King George V, immediately behind the coffin. The *Daily Telegraph* affair was obviously forgotten, as one English newspaper reported that the Kaiser's 'English origin is impressed as it were upon every feature of his character, and…he comes among us again as one of our own English blood'[168].

Still, however, the Kaiser and his people believed that the King had been responsible for the damage done to Anglo-German relations. Four years after his death, on the outbreak of the First World War, a German officer, Rheinhold Wagner, wrote a book entitled *Edward VII, the Greatest Criminal against Humanity in the 20th Century*, in which he claimed:

"It was unquestionably Edward VII who was responsible for this war…The King was deeply annoyed that Germany should develop a Colonial Empire….and he used his 'nefarious journeys' to isolate Germany."[169]

128

It was a view shared by many of his compatriots, one of whom wrote to an English friend in early 1914, 'I am sorry to tell you that in Germany the feeling is strongest against England, and especially against the late King Edward whom we curse in his grave"[170]. Even neutral diplomats viewed the King's influence as dangerous for, as officials at the Belgian Embassy in Berlin observed, 'the peace of Europe was never in such danger as when the King of England concerned himself with maintaining it.'[171]

With the death of his uncle, Wilhelm hoped for an improvement in relations with Britain, and, despite his mistrust of the Triple Entente, he maintained his friendship with the Tsar and with Britain's George V. His efforts did not go unnoticed for, as late as 1913, the British peer, Lord Suffield wrote that:

> "Kaiser Wilhelm is, and always has been, very fond of England and the English, in spite of all that people may say to the contrary. He has invariably worked for peace with England, but, in spite of all his really earnest endeavours and his sincere love of this country, there has always been friction between the two courts...It is certainly not the Emperor's fault."[172]

It was, however, Wilhelm's greatest mistake to believe that family ties could yet preserve 'the peace of the world.'

Chapter 12 – 'I Am Convinced That He Sincerely Loves Peace'

Seven months after his father's death, King George V sent his cousin, the Kaiser, a 'most cordial' invitation to the unveiling of the Victoria Memorial on May 16th 1911 – an event which appeared to portend an improvement in relations between Britain and Germany. After the unveiling, George spoke warmly of the German Emperor's devotion to his grandmother whom he 'always loved and venerated'; and, when Wilhelm had placed a wreath at the foot of the statue, he was loudly applauded by the crowds. Unfortunately this moment of reciprocal appreciation was fleeting, for within a couple of months a second Moroccan crisis again brought the Great Powers to the brink of war.

In April 1911, in the wake of a rebel uprising in Morocco, the Sultan took refuge in his palace in Fez from where he sought French help to restore order. By the end of the month, against the advice of their British allies and in contravention of the Algeciras Agreement of 1905, French troops had occupied the city, creating the suspicion that they had deliberately provoked the uprising in order to gain complete control over the entire region. As Wilhelm was still in England at the time, von Bulow's successor, Theobald von Bethmann-Hollweg, asked him to discover the King's view of the situation. When Wilhelm mentioned that the French move was illegal according to the Algeciras Agreement, George replied that the agreement was no longer valid and that:

> "...the French were fundamentally doing nothing different in Morocco than the English had previously done in Egypt; that therefore England would place no obstacle in the path of the French, but would let them alone."[173]

Realising that this could jeopardise Germany's commercial interests in North Africa, Wilhelm's ministers asked him to authorise a gunboat to sail to the area, ostensibly to protect German nationals. Despite serious misgivings, the Kaiser was prevailed upon to sanction the plan and, on July 1st, the *Panther* arrived at the port of Agadir. As the German press was already baying for war, the presence of the *Panther* attracted widespread attention and the British dispatched battleships to the region and sent a diplomatic note stating that Britain had a right to be involved in any subsequent negotiations.

Then suddenly, three days later, a second German ship arrived in the area and the *Panther* calmly sailed away.

According to a somewhat disreputable double agent, Armgaard Karl Graves, who spied for both Britain and Germany, the *Panther's* withdrawal was due entirely to Wilhelm. Graves claimed that before the ship had reached Agadir, he had been summoned to a secret meeting with the Kaiser at Wilhelmshaven, where he was given a written message for the *Panther's* captain, which he was told to memorise verbatim and then destroy. Following the Kaiser's instructions, Graves set out to intercept the ship before it reached Agadir, in order to deliver the message. By order of the Emperor, he said, no matter what instructions the captain received from the Admiralty, or how much pressure might be placed upon him, 'you are under no account to use any force against France or England.'[174]

The captain, Graves claimed, was dumbfounded since he had been specifically told to make Germany's presence felt:

> "Those previous orders had been to create war, this verbal message was to stop war...The big gun manufacturers, the shell people, the army and navy men...the whole Empire wanted war, but the tired, swarthy-faced man [Wilhelm]...deemed it wise not

to fly in the face of public opinion at that time and countermand the official orders to the *Panther*. So he had done so in the dark, serving the best interest of the Empire."[175]

Whether or not this account is to be believed, the *Panther's* withdrawal did little to resolve the crisis, which Wilhelm insisted was not sufficient cause for armed conflict. Writing directly to King George, he stated that Germany would not go to war over Morocco but, if the French were to gain control of the region, he would expect compensation for Germany's loss of trade and potential naval bases. To that end, he authorised his Foreign Secretary, Alfred von Kiderlen-Wächter, to negotiate with the French Ambassador in Berlin, offering to withdraw any opposition to French activity in Morocco in return for the rights to the French Congo.

Although George did not reply to Wilhelm's letter, the *Times* published an article warning that, if Germany were to achieve all her plans for North Africa, it would pose a serious threat to British interests. On July 21st, Britain's Chancellor of the Exchequer, David Lloyd George, took up the same theme in an inflammatory speech at the Mansion House:

> "...If a situation were to be forced upon us in which peace could only be preserved by the surrender of the great and beneficent position Britain has won by centuries of heroism and achievement, by allowing Britain to be treated where her interests were vitally affected as if she were of no account in the Cabinet of nations, then I say emphatically that peace at that price would be a humiliation intolerable for a great country like ours to endure."[176]

The speech was widely viewed as a direct threat to Germany and had undoubtedly been prepared in advance with the collaboration of the Foreign Secretary, Sir Edward Grey. The German Chancellor, Bethmann-Hollweg, responded in a far more moderate address to the Reichstag, urging his countrymen not to become carried away by arrogance or by despondency, but, in spite of this exhortation, the Belgian Ambassador observed that, 'The Germans who, six months ago, were by no means hostile to England, have become so now.'[177]

For over a month, Franco-German negotiations continued until suddenly, in September, the German stock market crashed and, as the panicking public began exchanging their bank notes for gold, the Kaiser and his ministers were forced to turn their attention from Morocco to their own economy, causing some speculation that the French Finance Minister and his allies had deliberately orchestrated the crash.

Once again, the Moroccan Crisis had demonstrated not only the strength of the Anglo-French Entente, but also the weakness of the Triple Alliance, for, when the Russians vaguely offered France their support, Germany's ally, Austria-Hungary, refused to become involved. Isolated, the Germans had no option but to yield to the decision that Morocco would become a French protectorate, in return for which the Germans received two strips of marshy land in the French Congo.

In the midst of the Moroccan Crisis, Wilhelm was unexpectedly approached by Sir Ernest Cassel, an English merchant banker and close friend of the late Edward VII. He had come, he explained, to deliver directly to the Kaiser a proposal from the British government, and had been instructed to avoid the usual diplomatic channels. Britain, he said, would remain neutral in any future 'warlike complications' involving Germany, if, in return, the Germans agreed to curb their naval programme.

Not a little taken aback by the obvious subterfuge, Wilhelm summoned the Chancellor, Bethmann-Hollweg, and Admiral Tirpitz, both of whom were equally surprised at the unconventional approach. Cassel, however, gave them little time to reflect on its full implications, since he insisted that he had to return to England that evening and needed an immediate response. Wilhelm, therefore, composed a note – in English to avoid any misinterpretation – in which he expressed interest in the idea but asked for more details, including who would represent British interests during any subsequent negotiations. Cassel told him that a negotiator had not yet been chosen but, in the meantime, he needed details of Tirpitz' most recent Naval Bill which was about to be debated in the Reichstag.

When eventually, some days after Cassel's departure, the British negotiator was named, Wilhelm was more surprised to see that he was neither a naval man nor a representative of the Admiralty, but rather Lord Haldane, Britain's Minister of War. According to Wilhelm's own account, he and the Chancellor assumed that Haldane had been selected because he spoke fluent German and had spent some time in Berlin. They accordingly welcomed him when he arrived in Germany, where Wilhelm entertained him as a personal guest. After several hours of amicable negotiations, Haldane professed himself satisfied with all that had been discussed, and returned to England, promising to send a draft agreement within a couple of weeks.

Weeks passed but Wilhelm heard nothing more of the matter, leaving Tirpitz uncertain as to whether or not to proceed with his Naval Bill. Eventually, with the Kaiser's approval, he decided to introduce the bill to the Reichstag as planned, believing that it could be altered if necessary once the British had sent their terms. When at last further messages arrived from England, however, they contained no mention of an agreement but rather requested more intricate details of Germany's naval programme.

"Little by little," wrote Wilhelm, "the suspicion grew in me that the English were not in earnest...since question followed question and details were sought which had nothing directly to do with the agreement. England withdrew more and more from her promises and no draft of the agreement came to hand."[178]

Understandably, he was convinced that the offer was merely an attempt to wreck Tirpitz' plans for the navy – a suspicion that appeared to be justified when, as soon as the bill was passed, he received a note from London telling him that Cassel had had no authority to make such a proposal. Moreover, many years later during his exile, he was told by a Dutchman, who had been in close contact with the British government at the time, that his misgivings were well-founded, for the British had never had any intention of forming or abiding by an agreement.

While this incident heightened Wilhelm's mistrust of politicians, it had little effect on his desire to remain on good terms with his cousins in Britain and Russia. In July that year, while cruising off Finland, he accepted an invitation to join Tsar Nicholas and his family aboard his yacht – a meeting which was, according to Wilhelm, a most enjoyable family gathering, during which he and his entourage received 'a brilliant and uncommonly amicable reception.'

The following year, his daughter's wedding gave Wilhelm the opportunity to repay the Tsar's hospitality and to extend the same warm welcome to Britain's King George.

On the day of George's arrival, Wilhelm, dressed in the uniform of a British Field Marshal, greeted the King at the station and accompanied him back to the palace in a grand procession through streets festooned with flowers and British flags. As Wilhelm intended to repeat the procedure for the Tsar the following day, he was most put out to discover that George insisted on accompanying him to meet Nicholas' train. As a guest, George's decision was decidedly ungracious for it threatened not only to throw Wilhelm's carefully laid plans into disarray but also to undermine his position as host. Nonetheless it was widely reported that the Kaiser's objection to the idea was based solely on his fear that the King and the Tsar would immediately start plotting against him. Although this is clearly preposterous in view of the fact that, during the wedding celebrations, there would be numerous opportunities for George and Nicholas to spend time together, it has frequently been cited as 'evidence' of the Kaiser's paranoia!

In the event, an agreeable compromise was reached when Wilhelm agreed that George should accompany him to the station, and George agreed not to take part in the subsequent procession but to return to the palace by an alternative route in an unmarked car.

Throughout the celebrations there was nothing but goodwill between the cousins, whose obvious amity gave no hint of an impending war. Eight months later, Wilhelm wrote to the Tsar:

> "I am most gratified that you still keep pleasant recollections of the visit you paid us last summer on the occasion of Sissy's wedding, and you may be assured that we all most heartily reciprocate your kind feeling and remembrance."[179]

That summer, despite rising international tensions, peace was being spoken of everywhere. In August, the Peace Palace was officially opened in The Hague; and, in June, as Wilhelm celebrated his Silver Jubilee, he repeatedly stressed that throughout the twenty-five years of his reign he had never spilt human blood and he intended to keep it that way. The American industrialist and philanthropist, Andrew Carnegie, who dined with him, was deeply impressed by his sincerity, believing him to be 'an earnest man, anxious for peace and the progress of the world'[180]. Such was Carnegie's faith in him that he came to the conclusion that the world had little to fear from Germany, since her interests were 'all favourable to peace' and Wilhelm was:

> "...not only an Emperor, but something much higher – a man anxious to improve existing conditions, untiring in his efforts to promote temperance, prevent duelling, and, I believe, to secure International Peace."[181]

Others were equally convinced of his pacific intentions. The recently retired American President, William Howard Taft, concurred that, for the last quarter of a century, the Kaiser had been 'the single greatest force in the practical maintenance of peace in the world'; the French Ambassador, Jules Cambon, reported to the British Foreign Secretary that 'Germany and the Emperor were bent on avoiding war'[182]; and a British newspaper described the Kaiser as a man of great versatility, being an artist, musician, sportsman, 'theologist' and traveller who had seen enough of the world to recognise the horror of battle. Others drew attention to his efforts to promote good relations between nations through academic, artistic and sporting events. He had arranged an exchange of German and foreign professors; he had invited foreign contributors to numerous art exhibitions; and he had organised a variety of international yachting and motor races, convinced that such events would promote greater mutual respect and understanding. In 1902, when the Berlin Yachting Club sent vessels to the Cork races, the Kaiser had written personally to the Lord Lieutenant of Ireland, inviting him to send Irish yachts to similar events at Kiel 'because such manifestations are excellent for the furtherance of goodwill and brotherhood between nations.'[183] Two years later, when starting a race at Cuxhaven, he announced optimistically that:

"Together with our colours, the Union Jack, the Stars and Stripes, and the Tricolour will flutter in the breeze in peaceful contest and partnership....If the merchant, the manufacturer and the farmer are able to progress, they owe it to this solidarity which gives them confidence in the future."[184]

Even in France, he was not without admirers, as the renowned pacifist and editor of *Temps,* Baron d'Estournelles, recorded:

"I am convinced that he sincerely loves peace, and that he believes in his mission to maintain it. A man who, even if he is an Emperor, lives daily in the company of his children, does not love war. He understands better than anyone else its tragic risks."[185]

His detractors, however, continued to portray him as a warlord, pointing out that on several occasions he had spoken of 'a World Empire', suggesting that he viewed himself as a latter-day Caesar, intent on conquering Europe and making Germany the equivalent of a new Roman Empire. This idea was largely based on a speech he had given in 1896, when he spoke of the number of Germans who had settled in various parts of the world:

"Out of the German Empire a world empire has arisen...German riches, German knowledge, German activity find their way across the ocean. The duty devolves on you to help me knit this Greater German Empire close to the home country by helping me to fulfil my duty also to the Germans in foreign parts."[186]

In reality, as Wilhelm often sought to explain, his vision was rather of the European nations working together in 'mutual confidence...striving towards the same ideal.' To that end, he raised no objections to the idea of a federal Europe, telling one Danish newspaper editor, whom he entertained aboard the *Hohenzollern,* that he was happy to support any scheme that might help to promote 'the great cause of peace.'

So it was in the summer of 1913, that two contradictory stories were being told about the Kaiser. On the one hand, he was presented as an aggressor, busily fostering Germany militarism by his bellicose speeches; and, on the other hand, those who met him in person were convinced that his greatest desire was to promote and maintain peace.

Chapter 13 – 'In Favour of an Understanding With Serbia'

Like the Kaiser, Archduke Franz Ferdinand, heir to the Austro-Hungarian Empire, was a man of many contradictions who simultaneously inspired in his contemporaries admiration and antipathy. An obsessive huntsman who prided himself on his collection of trophies, he was also a passionate gardener who, with feminine tenderness, cultivated roses and personally laid out the grounds of his idyllic Bohemian retreat, Konospischt. An avid collector and connoisseur of antiques, he was at the same time a progressive thinker whose ideas for the future of the Empire met with ridicule and apprehension in the traditional court of his uncle, Emperor Franz Josef. His shortness of temper, his indifference to others' opinions of him, and his refusal to be moved by flattery created the impression of aloofness and rigidity, and yet those who knew him well saw him as a loyal friend, a loving father and a devoted husband who was prepared to sacrifice everything for the woman he loved.

"The Archduke," wrote the diplomat, Ottokar Czernin, "lacked the knowledge of how to deal with people. He neither could nor would control himself, and, charming though he could be when his natural heartiness was allowed free scope, just as little could he conceal his anger and ill-humour."[187]

This 'anger and ill-humour' was chiefly directed towards the princes and ministers who surrounded the aged Emperor, who, by 1914, had reigned for sixty-six years. Not only did they dismiss the Archduke's innovative suggestions, but, more infuriatingly, they took every possible opportunity to snub and humiliate his wife.

No Royal Family in Europe was as bound as the Habsburgs were to tradition and the belief in the necessity of preserving the royal bloodline, and when Franz

Ferdinand insisted on marrying Sophie Chotek, a former lady-in-waiting, he was widely and unjustly accused of doing so simply to irk the rest of his family.

But for the intervention of the Pope and persuasive letters from the Kaiser and the Tsar, Emperor Franz Josef might never have granted Franz Ferdinand and Sophie permission to marry at all; and, even when he grudgingly gave his consent, he ensured that no member of the Imperial Family would attend the wedding. To add to the insult, on the morning of the ceremony, the Archduke was compelled to read a public proclamation, declaring that neither his wife nor any children born of their marriage would have the right to inherit his titles or imperial position.

Time did nothing to soften Franz Ferdinand's resentment over this humiliation, nor the court's intransigent opposition to his wife. Denied the right to travel in her husband's carriage in state processions, Sophie was not permitted to share the Imperial Box at the theatre, or even to sit at Franz Ferdinand's table during official banquets. On the rare occasions when she attended court, she was placed in such a lowly position in the order of precedence that infant Archduchesses entered the room before her; and if she arranged a ball or reception, aristocratic ladies organised simultaneous entertainments to ensure that no one of note would accept her invitation.

> "The Archduke suffered most terribly under the conditions resulting from his unequal marriage," Czernin observed. "The sincere and true love he felt for his wife kept alive in him the wish to raise her to his rank and privileges, and the constant obstacles that he encountered at all court ceremonies embittered and angered him inexpressibly."[188]

Unsurprisingly, Franz Ferdinand avoided the Emperor's palaces as far as possible, and, as he gathered around him his own small group of like-minded friends, he was suspected of creating a rival court to that of Franz Josef. Their ideas for the future of Austria-Hungary could hardly have been more disparate, for, while the aged Emperor clung tenaciously to tradition, Franz Ferdinand realised that without a dramatic transformation the Empire, with its numerous ethnicities and cultures, risked coming apart at the seams. Even the three armies were in disarray – each working independently of the others, and consisting of soldiers from such diverse backgrounds that many did not speak the language of their officers and consequently failed to understand their orders. The navy, too, was in desperate need of improvement; and the conflicts in which Austria had engaged over the past century had almost invariably ended in defeat.

Throughout his youth, Franz Ferdinand had travelled widely and seen many different forms of government, some of which he believed could be adapted to suit the needs of Austria-Hungary. The United States in particular attracted his attention as he planned to grant semi-autonomy to various regions of the Empire while maintaining overall cohesion with an Emperor in place of a President.

Few of Franz Josef's ministers and generals shared his ideology, and, despite the internal tensions that were simmering within the Empire, several dreamed of further imperial expansion. Equally, while Franz Ferdinand realised the necessity of focussing on Austria-Hungary's domestic affairs, certain military and political groups fixed their attention on the country's external enemies – particularly neighbouring Serbia.

Since gaining complete independence from the Ottoman (Turkish) Empire in 1877, many Serb nationalists had dreamed of establishing a 'Greater Serbia', involving the assimilation of Albania, Croatia, Bosnia-Herzegovina and various regions of Hungary. The chief obstacle to the achievement of their goal was the Austro-Hungarian

Empire, which controlled many of the regions that they hoped to assimilate. The Austrians had occupied Bosnia-Herzegovina since 1878, ostensibly to protect the native Christians from the Islamic Turks, but thirty years later, in 1908, as Emperor Franz Josef celebrated his Diamond Jubilee, they unexpectedly announced that the region was now part of the Austro-Hungarian Empire.

Franz Ferdinand had firmly opposed the move, warning that it would not only increase the Serbs' antagonism towards Austria-Hungary but also could inflame the Russians, who had assumed the role of protector of the Serbs. The bond between Russia and Serbia was not simply a matter of their sharing the same Slavic origins, for the Tsar was keen to cultivate their friendship in order to maintain access to the Mediterranean via friendly states; and, more importantly, according to the British Envoy to Bulgaria, Sir Henry Bax-Ironside, the Serbs played an important role in bolstering Russia's position as a Great Power. If Russia failed to support the Serbs in times of crisis, her status would be seriously challenged, and, Bax-Ironside claimed, all the former upheavals and social unrest that Russia had endured would be minor in comparison to:

> "...the overwhelming force of a Revolution based on national and Pan-Slav ideals. Were the Emperor and his government suddenly to find themselves in opposition to a movement of this nature, they would most certainly be swept away."[189]

When, therefore, in 1908, the Austrians annexed Bosnia-Herzegovina, the Russians raised such vehement protests that the Serbs began to mobilise in preparation for war.

The situation left Kaiser Wilhelm in an unenviable position, for, irked as he was that the Austrians had failed to forewarn him of their plans, he felt obliged to stand by his ally while desperately trying to avoid antagonising Russia.

> "The annexation of Bosnia and Herzegovina was a genuine surprise for everybody," he wrote to the Tsar, "but particularly so for us, as we were informed about Austria's intention even later than you...The fact is that once Austria had taken this step...hesitation as to the course we had to follow as loyal allies was out of the question...You will be the first to approve of this loyalty of ours."[190]

He assured the Tsar that the Austrians had no intention of attacking Serbia, since Franz Josef was far too 'wise and judicious and such a venerable Gentleman,'[191] but he stressed the importance of Serbia putting 'an end to these warlike preparations' and added that:

> "These small states are an awful nuisance...The slightest encouragement from any quarter makes them frantic."[192]

Privately, though, he was incensed by the Austrians' unilateral decision and, according to Countess Olga Leutrum, he angrily upbraided Franz Ferdinand, 'I will thank you in future not to rattle my sword!'[193] Nonetheless, it was largely thanks to Germany's support that war was avoided, and, as the Russians – somewhat humiliatingly – backed down, the Belgian Ambassador recorded, 'Germany alone imposed peace.'[194]

Since the annexation was viewed as a *fait accompli,* the Russians demanded territorial compensation for the Serbs but, as this was refused, the Serbs' resentment of Austria increased, resulting in the formation of a number of violently anti-Austrian groups. Confident of the Tsar's support, Serb nationalists produced vast quantities of anti-Austrian propaganda while secret groups of insurgents made threats to the Habsburg monarchy. These written attacks were so persistent and aggressive that the British Ambassador in Vienna, Sir Fairfax Leighton-Cartwright, urged the Austrians to launch an invasion 'before anyone can stop you' since 'the end of Serbia will be a blessing for all of Europe.'[195]

The government in Belgrade sought to distance itself from the propaganda and, in March 1909, under international pressure, issued a declaration, assuring the Austrians that henceforth Serbia would raise no more objections to the annexation, and:

> "She undertakes, moreover, to modify the direction of her policy with regard to Austria-Hungary and to live in future on good neighbourly terms with the latter."

Still, though, underground presses continued to produce inflammatory books, pamphlets and posters; and even the daily newspapers contained articles about the impotency of the Habsburgs and the benefits of Austria becoming a republic. While the Serbian ministers claimed to play no part in these publications, they did little to suppress them or to investigate the societies that produced them. The Austrians' inaction in the face of such attacks created an impression of weakness, which served only to bolster the Serbs' rising ambitions.

Over the next couple of years, these ambitions gained a new impetus from the successes in the Balkan Wars. In 1912, with the Tsar's encouragement, Serbia, Greece, Montenegro and Bulgaria formed the Balkan League and declared war on the Turks. Within a few weeks they achieved a resounding victory, as a result of which Serbia gained a part of the Ottoman Sanjak[v] of Novi Pazar. Barely had the conflict concluded, when quarrels broke out between the members of the League, and, in 1913, a Second Balkan War erupted when Serbia and Greece joined forces with their former enemy, Turkey, to combat Bulgaria. Again, the Serbs were triumphant and, by the

---

[v] An administrative region

terms of the Treaty of Bucharest, their territory almost doubled in size, fuelling the nationalists' aspirations for even greater expansion.

The Turks, unhappy with the outcome and refusing to believe that the treaty was binding, feared further incursions into their territory from Russia, and turned to Germany for support. The Austrians, too, were greatly disturbed by the treaty, seeing it as a precursor of the establishment of a Serbian Empire, particularly when in April 1914, rumours spread that Serbia was about to merge with Montenegro. In view of this, many ministers and military officials in Vienna called for a pre-emptive strike against the Serbs, but Wilhelm – failing perhaps to realise the extent of the problem – repeatedly urged them to find a peaceful solution, as his Chancellor, Bethmann, wrote to the Charges d'Affaire in Bucharest, 'The Kaiser, as King Carol [of Romania] is aware, has always intervened at Vienna in favour of an understanding with Serbia.'

When, while holidaying in Corfu, Wilhelm heard of the Austrian's fears about the potential union of Serbia and Montenegro, he wrote immediately to Vienna, warning that any protests would merely damage the prestige of the Austro-Hungarian Empire. Instead he urged them to take a 'sensible view' and adapt to the situation. 'There must be found,' he wrote, 'a *modus vivendi* with the Dual Monarchy which will be attractive to Serbia.'

A month later, however, Emperor Franz Josef stated that Serbia's rising ambitions were making war between the two countries almost inevitable.

Chapter 14 – 'It's Nothing…It's Nothing'

In the winter of 1913, eighty-three-year-old Emperor Franz Josef of Austria-Hungary suffered such a severe bout of bronchitis that, for a while, it was feared that he would not survive. The prospect of his death filled many of his ministers with trepidation, for they knew that, once Franz Ferdinand succeeded to the throne, they would no longer be able to retain their positions. Already the Archduke had drawn up lists of those who would replace them, and so confident was he of his imminent accession that he was rumoured to have already had his coronation portrait painted.

In the midst of the Emperor's health crisis, the Archduke received a letter from the Austrian military governor of Bosnia-Herzegovina, Oskar Potiorek, inviting him to review the troop manoeuvres near Sarajevo the following June. In view of the volatile nature of the region and the Serbs' intense resentment of the Hapsburgs, Franz Ferdinand realised that his presence in Bosnia was liable to inflame an already dangerous situation. What was more, as he told his nephew, the future Emperor Karl, he had come to believe that the Freemasons had passed a resolution to kill him, and, since several Austrian and Hungarian ministers were party to the plot, a visit to Sarajevo might present them with an ideal situation in which to carry out their plan. Rather than dismissing his uncle's fears, Karl recalled that his own wife, Zita, had recounted a rather strange story which seemed to justify Franz Ferdinand's suspicions. Shortly before their wedding in 1911, Zita had had an audience with Pope Pius X, who told her that he was pleased that she was about to marry Franz Josef's heir as he would one day make an excellent Emperor. When Zita pointed out that Karl was second-in-line to the throne and that his uncle would succeed before him, the Pope shook

147

his head vaguely and murmured something to the effect that Franz Ferdinand would not live to be crowned.

In spite of his premonitions of doom, Franz Ferdinand felt that, as Inspector of the Military Forces, it was his duty to attend the Bosnian manoeuvres, which would also give him an opportunity to present his plans for granting greater autonomy to the region once he became Emperor. An even greater incentive came from Potiorek, who had extended the invitation to Sophie. This would give her a rare opportunity to appear in public at her husband's side, and, for the first time in fourteen years of marriage, she would receive the acclamations due to the wife of the heir.

Franz Ferdinand and Sophie might have been treated with disdain in the court of the Emperor Franz Josef but, in that of the German Kaiser, they found only respect and kindness. Although Wilhelm and Franz Ferdinand were in some way quite disparate characters – the former longing for approbation, and the latter careless of others' opinions – on a personal level they had certain aspects in common. In childhood and youth both had endured physical difficulties, which had led to jibes that neither was suited for a throne. While Wilhelm had heard the cruel taunt that 'a one-armed man can never be king', Franz Ferdinand, while suffering from a lung condition from which he was not expected to recover, found himself suddenly discarded by former flatterers and friends.

> "He often spoke…of that time and all that he had gone through, and referred with intense bitterness to the people who were only waiting day by day to put him altogether on one side. As long as he was looked upon as the heir to the throne, and people reckoned on him for the future, he was the centre of all possible attention; but when he fell ill and his case was considered hopeless, the world fluctuated

from hour to hour and paid homage to his younger brother Otto."[196]

Both the Kaiser and the Archduke were hot-headed and prone to impulsive outbursts; and both had reason to doubt the sincerity of some of their ministers. More importantly, they shared a similar vision for the progress of the Central Powers[w], each aiming to improve their country's armies and navies, believing that a powerful military deterrent was the best means of preserving peace. Contrary to a myth that survives to this day, Franz Ferdinand was not a member of the 'war party', but as one who knew him well, recorded,

> "...he had an instinctive feeling that the Monarchy would never be able to bear the terrible test of strength of a war, and the fact is that, instead of working to encourage war, his activities lay all in the opposite direction."[197]

Although reluctant to allow Austria-Hungary to be dominated by German policy, Franz Ferdinand greatly appreciated the Kaiser's friendship and, more particularly, the gentility he showed to his wife. Sophie might have been scorned in Vienna but, during informal and formal dinners in Berlin, she was seated at the right-hand of Wilhelm, who enjoyed her conversation and frequently praised her intelligence. He had even suggested to her that, although her eldest son, Maximilian, was debarred from ever becoming the Austrian Emperor, there was no constitutional reason why he might not eventually succeed his father as King of Hungary. In the meantime, said the Kaiser, he would happily appoint him Governor of Alsace-Lorraine when he came of age.

In October 1913, Franz Ferdinand and Wilhelm met with Emperor Franz Josef to discuss the Balkan situation

---

[w] The Central Powers was the name given to the Quadruple alliance of Germany, Austria-Hungary, Bulgaria and the Ottoman Empire (the Turks).

and the best means of maintaining peace in Europe. Wilhelm agreed with the Archduke that a pre-emptive strike against Serbia would do nothing but aggravate international tensions, and could eventually lead to a large-scale war. He was still more impressed by Franz Ferdinand's desire for better relations between Austria and Russia, and offered to use his ties to the Tsar to that effect.

Such was the rapport between the two men that, in early June 1914, just before Franz Ferdinand's departure for Bosnia, Wilhelm accepted an invitation to spend a weekend at Konopischt Castle, to visit the beautiful gardens and to continue their discussions about foreign affairs. In such an informal setting, their friendship developed and the Kaiser 'undoubtedly grew more attached to the Archduke.'[198] Nonetheless when, on Franz Josef's instructions, Franz Ferdinand asked Wilhelm if Germany would stand by Austria if she deemed it necessary to take military action against Serbia, Wilhelm was non-committal. The best solution, he explained, would be to develop closer ties with Bulgaria, to balance Russian influence in the Balkans, and, despite his personal dislike of the self-styled *Tsar* Ferdinand of Bulgaria, he favoured drawing him into the Triple Alliance. More importantly, before returning home, he agreed to approach Tsar Nicholas II directly to tell him of Franz Ferdinand's eagerness for greater co-operation, and the Archduke's hopes of reviving the League of the Three Emperors, by which Russia, Germany and Austria-Hungary had formed an alliance which lasted from 1873 until a year before Wilhelm's accession. 'The Archduke,' Wilhelm wrote later, 'was Russia's best friend.'

Within days of the Kaiser's visit, Franz Ferdinand apprehensively left Vienna for Bosnia. A thunderstorm erupted as he boarded the train, and, on entering the carriage, he commented ominously that it was as dark as a tomb. In spite of these unpropitious beginnings, the tour was far more enjoyable than he had anticipated, for the manoeuvres were impressive and, as Sophie commented to an aide, everywhere they travelled they were met with warmth and kindness. On 28th June, they arrived in Sarajevo, where cheering crowds lined the streets that were decorated with Imperials flags and portraits of the couple. By chance or design, the date was highly significant, being not only Franz Ferdinand and Sophie's fourteenth wedding anniversary, but also the Feast of St Vitus – a national holiday for the Serbs in celebration of the heroes of the fourteenth century Battle of Kosovo, which had come to symbolise all their dreams of a united Yugoslavia.

The couple was driven in an open phaeton through the crowded streets of Sarajevo with no military escort, and their only protection was a row of policeman standing at intervals along the route. This lackadaisical approach to security is startling in view of the volatility of the region, and it stands in stark contrast to the precautions taken at other royal events at that time. When, for example, a German princess married a Russian Grand Duke, weeks of preparation went into the security arrangements for her arrival in Russia, including the temporary holding of suspected trouble-causers, the hiring of shops along the route from the station to the palace, incognito policemen mingling with the crowds, and the stationing of armed officers on roofs tops and other vantage points. In 1910, when Emperor Franz Josef visited Sarajevo, a line of soldiers had been present on the street to keep the crowds at a reasonable distance from his car; but, for Franz Ferdinand and Sophie, there was minimal protection in a town which was known to be riddled with anti-Austrian insurgents.

As the motorcade moved slowly through the streets, a sudden crack like the sound of a tyre blowing, caused the driver to halt for a second and then to accelerate at full speed towards the destination. On arriving at the City Hall, an aide ran back along the route to discover what had happened, returning soon afterwards to report that a grenade had been thrown, injuring thirteen by-standers and some members of the Archduke's suite.

The attacker was quickly apprehended and, in view of the likelihood that he had accomplices in the town, it was deemed wise to cancel the rest of the day's activities. Franz Ferdinand, however, insisted on visiting the injured before leaving Sarajevo, and it was agreed that that afternoon, he and Sophie would be taken to the hospital via a circuitous route avoiding predictable thoroughfares. After lunch, notwithstanding the potential for a second attack, the couple and Potiorek were again driven in open-roofed car with neither a military escort nor any extra security other than one bodyguard, Count Franz von Harrach, who rode on the running board of the phaeton. Even more remarkably, their driver was not told of the change of route until he missed a turning, prompting Potiorek to order him to stop and reverse. As he did so, a young Bosnian Serb, Gavrilo Princip, stepped onto the pavement and fired point blank into the car. Sophie was shot in the stomach and, as she slumped to the floor, Franz Ferdinand begged her not to die but to 'live for the children'.

He also had been fatally wounded by a bullet lodged in his neck.

"It's nothing…it's nothing…" he managed to murmur but, by the time the phaeton reached the hospital, he, too, was dead.

The nineteen-year-old assassin was set upon by the crowd and immediately arrested. Within a matter of hours, it was reported that he had admitted to being a member of the Black Hand – a fiercely anti-Austrian terrorist group, said to comprise top military personnel and Serbian politicians. No one thought to ask why such a group would appoint a tubercular youth who had only recently learned to fire a gun, for such an important mission as the assassination of the heir to the throne of Austria-Hungary;

and there was no explanation as to why there were no recorded atrocities committed by the Black Hand since 1903 when they claimed responsibility for the murder of the Serbian Royal Family. It would, however, prove highly convenient for the Austrian War Party to lay the blame for the killings on the Serbs; and there were many in Vienna who stood to gain from the Archduke's murder, and many who stood to lose had he succeeded his uncle as Emperor.

It is interesting that Franz Ferdinand received the invitation to Bosnia at a time when the Emperor was sick and feared to be dying; and it is equally interesting that the visit to Sarajevo should be arranged on a date of such significance to the Serbs. That the couple were driven in an open car with no security; that the driver had not been told of the change of route; that Sophie, too, was murdered at point-blank range but neither the bodyguard nor Potiorek was hurt; and that Franz Ferdinand himself had stated openly that the Freemasons were planning to kill him, all give rise to the suspicion that the murders were actually planned from Vienna[x], or at least that the Archduke was deliberately placed in a position which would facilitate his assassination. That day, the British Foreign Secretary, Edward Grey, received a confidential telegram from a diplomat in Rome, reporting that:

> "I heard from two bankers here that at Trieste when the news was received Hungarian stock rose from 72 to 80."[199]

Even in death, Franz Ferdinand's enemies continued to treat him and Sophie with disdain. As their bodies were returned to Austria, respectful crowds gathered at every station along the route, but the ministers arranged for the funeral train to arrive in Vienna in the middle of the

---

[x] This idea would later prove a convenient justification for the Entente Powers to condemn Austrian reprisals against Serbia.

night so that the majority of the Viennese were not even aware of the final homecoming. Only one member of the Imperial Family stood on the station platform – Franz Ferdinand's nephew, Archduke Karl, whom a British diplomat referred to as 'a mere boy' – and when the coffins were taken to the chapel of the Hofburg Palace, Sophie's was placed several feet lower than that of her husband, and was crowned with a fan to signify her lowly status as a lady-in-waiting.

The bodies lay in state for so short a time that the majority of those who wished to pay their respects were turned away, and the Cardinal Archbishop who performed the requiem was ordered to make the service as brief as possible. Foreign princes and kings were discouraged from attending – Wilhelm being told that the Viennese had received word that a band of twelve insurgents were waiting in Vienna to kill him; and King Carol of Romania being unceremoniously turned back at the border. As the cortege made its way from the chapel to the station from which the couple would be taken to their last resting place, Artstetten, the crowds were held back to prevent them forming a procession behind the coffins until Archduke Karl, appalled by such a blatant lack of respect for his late uncle, broke through the cordons and invited the public to follow. It was customary for a reception to be held after a state funeral, but in Franz Ferdinand's case, foreign princes had been specifically asked not to attend, and so, once the rite was over, the day continued as though nothing extraordinary had happened.

Chapter 15 – 'An Invention of Malevolent Persons'

In the aftermath of the assassinations, messages of condolence poured into Vienna from around the world. Fellow sovereigns wrote personal letters to Franz Josef and ordered periods of mourning; and the United States' Ambassadors to Austria and Turkey expressed their 'abhorrence and that of [their] nation for the deed, and our sympathy with the aged emperor.'[200]

Almost invariably the expressions of sympathy were combined with condemnation of the Serbs who appeared to be making little effort to root out the assassin's accomplices or, despite their pledges of 1909, to suppress the widespread anti-Austrian propaganda.

> "Be convinced," the British Ambassador, Maurice de Bunsen, told the Austrian ministers, "that the whole English nation condemns the criminals of Sarajevo. No Englishman has any sympathy left for Serbia...There is no Englishman who does not wish heartily that Serbia should receive a sound and lasting lesson."[201]

In view of the general criticism, the Serbs claimed that, three weeks before the Archduke set out for Sarajevo, their Prime Minister, Nikola Pasic, informed the Austrian Ambassador in Belgrade that he had received intelligence that plans were afoot to assassinate him. A fortnight later, realising that his warning had been ignored, Pasic was said to have sent an envoy to the Austrian Civil Governor of Bosnia to repeat the message and to tell him that he had given orders that all suspected terrorists were to be arrested if they attempted to cross the border. The Austrians denied ever receiving such a report, and, according to the London *Times* on 7th July, 'there is no foundation for the reports that information of the existence of a plot against the Archduke was given to the Austro-Hungarian Government

155

by the Serbian Minister in Vienna.' Moreover, when the Austrian government accused the Serbs of being aware of a conspiracy prior to the assassination, Pasic stated that he had known nothing about it, and gave an official statement denying he had attempted to forewarn Vienna.

In Sarajevo, meanwhile, pro-Austrian demonstrators destroyed Serbian shops and houses causing damage costing up to ten million krona, and it was rumoured that Southern Slavs were about to be ejected from Bosnia. Delighted by such widespread anti-Serb sentiments, the bellicose Austrian Chief of Staff, Conrad von Hőtzendorf, who had long been urging the Emperor to allow him to crush the Serbs, realised that there would never be a more opportune time to take action. Although he had had little affection for Franz Ferdinand, who had once publicly upbraided him for leading a chaotic series of military manoeuvres in a manner more suited to an eighteenth century cavalry charge than to twentieth century warfare, Hőtzendorf saw in his death the ideal excuse to declare war.

The Hungarian Prime Minister, Tisza, however, favoured a more cautious approach. The Tsar's Ambassador in Belgrade, Nicholas Hartwig, was openly assuring the Serbs that any military action on Austria's part would meet with an immediate response from Russia, and Tisza knew that a war with Russia would end in disaster for Austria-Hungary. There were, though, many influential men in Vienna who did not share his pessimism and were so eager to take on the Russians that they viewed an invasion of Serbia as merely a stepping-stone to a much grander conflict. In 1913, Countess Leutram had been told by a former minister, '...whether Germany helps us now or not, we are ready and quite strong enough to attack Russia by ourselves, and even without Germany we are sure to beat her with the left hind leg [meaning with the utmost ease]'[202]. Articles in Viennese newspapers actively encouraged such sentiments, claiming that the Russians had instigated the Archduke's assassination, and they were the real 'black hand' behind the Serbian atrocities and anti-Austrian propaganda.

Initially, the Austrian Foreign Minister, Leopold von Berchtold, shared Tisza's view and proposed a more moderate response to the Serbs. Within a matter of days, however, he came round to the idea of an invasion on condition that Austria could rely on German support. Purporting to believe that the Russians were not ready for war[y], he dispatched his adjutant and Chef de Staff, Count von Hoyos, to Berlin with specific instructions to obtain the Kaiser's backing for a military strike. Von Hoyos was to take with him a moderate letter from Franz Josef, which, on Berchtold's instructions, he was to present in an as aggressive a light as possible.

In June 1914, the Kaiser had been happily entertaining British and American guests at the Kiel Regatta when news reached him of the events in Sarajevo. Appalled by the murder of his friends, and angered at what he saw as a blow to monarchies in general, he returned at once to Berlin stating, with typical impetuosity, that the killer and his fellow conspirators must be brought swiftly to justice. Reprimanding his Ambassador in Vienna, Heinrich von Tcshirschky, for attempting to dissuade Berchtold from acting too hastily, Wilhelm made it clear that, although it was for the Austrians to decide what to do, he *expected* a severe response to put a permanent end to their problems with the 'band of brigands' – the Serbs. This reaction echoed that of the British Ambassador and yet it would later be used as evidence that the Kaiser urged his allies to

---

[y] If Berchtold truly believed this, he would not have needed the assurance of German support, for the Austro-Hungarian army was superior to that of Serbia and victory would have been an almost foregone conclusion.

make war. In reality, he did *not* encourage the Austrians to launch an invasion nor is there any evidence that he expected an armed response. Until now, the Austrians had appeared patient to the point of weakness, and Wilhelm, desirous of having a strong ally, was keen to ensure that this time they stood their ground by sending to the Serbs a series of harsh demands with which, under international pressure, they would be forced to comply.

Surprised that he and his brother, Henry, had been asked not to attend Franz Ferdinand's funeral, the Kaiser waited a week for the arrival of von Hoyos and the Austrian Ambassador, Szogyeny, to explain exactly what was happening in Vienna. On reading Franz Josef's letter, he observed that the greater part of its contents concerned forming a closer union with Bulgaria – an idea which Wilhelm himself had already mooted and with which he immediately concurred. There was no direct reference to an invasion or any form of military intervention, although Hoyos, on Berchtold's instructions, insisted that the majority of Austro-Hungarian ministers realised that there was no alternative but to soundly defeat the Serbs.

Wilhelm believed that there was little likelihood of Russian intervention, since Russia was not ready for war and, more importantly, Tsar Nicholas, whose own grandfather had been murdered by anarchists, would appreciate the necessity of dealing harshly with regicides. Moreover, as Szogyeny and Hoyos assured him that the Austrians had no plans for territorial gain since their sole purpose was to put an end to the anti-Austrian aggression, he insisted that this was essentially a private matter between Vienna and Belgrade. When pressed by Hoyos, however, he gave his word that he would not abandon his ally, and Austria had his full support for whatever action they chose to take.

The following day, Wilhelm was due to depart for his annual Scandinavian cruise but, due to the crisis, he thought it better to remain in Berlin. His Chancellor and Chiefs of Staff, however, feared that if he cancelled his holiday, it would lead to speculation that Germany was preparing for war, and so, after much discussion, he agreed to continue with his plans.

On July 5th, before leaving Germany, he held a series of meetings with his ministers, which would later be misrepresented as 'the Potsdam Council', during which he was alleged to have met with all his Ambassadors, ministers and Chiefs of Staff to prepare Germany for war. In 1919, during the Treaty of Versailles negotiations[z], this fictitious meeting was used as evidence that he and his country were entirely responsible for the war. Writing later, Wilhelm vehemently denied that such a council ever took place, stating that it was:

> "...an invention of malevolent persons. Naturally, before my departure, I received, as was my custom, some of the Ministers individually, in order to hear from them reports concerning their departments. Neither was there any council of Ministers and there was no talk about war preparations at a single one of the conferences."[203]

There is plenty of evidence to support Wilhelm's claim, including the fact that the majority of his Chiefs of Staff and ministers were away on holiday and nowhere near Potsdam on July 5th. The ambassadors, who were alleged to have attended this meeting, were still in position in Vienna, London and Paris; Moltke, the Chief of Staff, who was ill, was taking a cure in Baden-Baden; Tirpitz was holidaying in Switzerland; and the recently-married Foreign Secretary, Jagow, was away on honeymoon until after the Kaiser had set off on his cruise.

Moreover, when the Minister of War, Falkenhayn, asked whether he should make precautionary military

---

[z] See Chapter 24

preparations during the Kaiser's absence, Wilhelm replied that such measures were unnecessary as the crisis would undoubtedly be resolved before his return. He advised informing the Chiefs of Staff of what was happening, but added that there was no need for them to cut short their holidays. That afternoon, Falkenhayn wrote to Moltke and stressed that, following his meeting with Hoyos and Szogyeny, the Kaiser had not expected any 'warlike issue' but rather 'some energetic political steps, which seemed to indicate for example the making of a treaty with Bulgaria, for which [the Austrians] wished to be assured of the support of the German Empire.'[204]

On July 6th, when the Kaiser had left Berlin, Bethmann sent an official telegram to Vienna, stating that:

"...as far as concerns Serbia, His Majesty, of course, cannot interfere in the dispute now going on between Austria-Hungary and that country, as it is a matter not within his competence. The Emperor Franz Joseph may, however, rest assured that His Majesty will faithfully stand by Austria-Hungary, as is required by the obligations of his alliance and of his ancient friendship."[205]

Although there was still no mention of military intervention, and, according to Falkenhayn's letter, Wilhelm clearly thought he had assented simply to a treaty with Bulgaria, Berchtold and his fellow ministers saw this as the 'blank cheque' for which they had been hoping – a written guarantee of German backing for their invasion. That afternoon, when the Austrian Council of Ministers met in Vienna, Hoyos delivered a false statement, claiming that the Kaiser was urging them to exploit the situation, and that he had assured him of German support in the case of 'a warlike complication' with Serbia. With almost unanimous backing for an immediate invasion of Serbia, Berchtold insisted that it was necessary to create a semblance of diplomacy while buying time to make the necessary preparations. He offered to draw up a 'Note' to Belgrade, comprising a series of demands which, if met, would avoid the necessity of war. In reality, however, the demands would be so severe that it would be impossible for the Serbs to comply with them without compromising their autonomy.

As the French President, Poincaré, was due to make a State Visit to Russia, it was deemed wise to postpone sending the Note until after his return to France, to prevent him from swaying the 'peace-loving Tsar' into flying to the Serbs' defence. In the meantime, military preparations would continue in secret, while, on Berchtold's advice, Hőtzendorf and the Minister of War, Krobatin, would take their annual holidays to create the impression that nothing untoward was happening – a ploy which Wilhelm later described as 'childish'.

On July 14th, eight days after the Kaiser's departure, the German Ambassador in Vienna, Tcshirschky informed Bethmann that 'the note is being composed so that the possibility of its acceptance is *practically* excluded' and, soon afterwards, he misinformed the Reichstag that it would be delivered to Belgrade on July 25th. Bethmann would later claim that he had no prior knowledge of the contents of the Note, but the Ambassador's message reveals that, although he had not read the actual wording, he was well aware of Berchtold's intentions.

On his yacht in Scandinavian waters, the Kaiser received few detailed communications about what was transpiring in his absence, and, as he later recorded, he was left to glean what he could from the Norwegian newspapers. Likewise, Emperor Franz Josef, who had retired to his summer estate, Bad Ischl, after the murders, was deliberately misled about what his ministers were doing; and, when Tisza, writing to him daily, attempted to warn him that an attack on Serbia could lead to a full

European war, Berchtold ensured that the letters were intercepted so that he would not receive them.

In spite of these clandestine undertakings, Serbian suspicions were mounting, and when, three days after the meeting of the Austrian Council of Ministers, the Russian Ambassador, Hartwig, died suddenly of a heart attack while visiting the Austrian Embassy, it was widely believed that he had been poisoned to silence his promises of Russian support for the Serbs. As rumours spread, the British Ambassador to Vienna, Maurice de Bunsen, and his French counterpart, Alfred Dumaine, approached the Austrian Foreign Ministry seeking an assurance that any demands made of the Serbs would be reasonable enough to be met. Both were told that this was the case but neither was informed that the Note was virtually completed and ready to be presented.

In Berlin, as the Austrian Ambassador reported to Berchtold, the government was becoming 'nervous', and the Foreign Minister, Jagow, advised the Austrians to assemble sufficient proof of the Serbs' complicity in the assassinations or evidence that the Serbian government posed a real threat to the Dual Monarchy, before proceeding with the demands. Berchtold ignored this advice and when, on July 13th, he received a full report of the Austrian investigation into the murders in Sarajevo, which concluded that there was no evidence of the Serbian government's involvement in either the plot or in anti-Austrian propaganda, he did not reveal the outcome either to Franz Josef or to his German allies. Instead, a week later, he showed a draft of the Note to his Emperor; and, on 20th July, sent it to Giesl, the Austrian Ambassador in Belgrade – with instructions that he was to present it to the Serbs on 23rd – and to the Austrian Ambassadors in all the major European countries, with instructions to present it on the 24th.

Szogyeny felt it was his duty to inform Austria's allies of the details at once, and on 22nd July, he handed the Note to the German Chancellor. Despite having been forewarned of its severity, Bethmann, was aghast at the extent of the demands and condemned the Austrians' duplicity for hoodwinking the Kaiser and for their pretence at diplomacy. The Foreign Minister, Jagow, and the Secretary of State for Foreign Affairs, Zimmermann, concurred that it would be impossible for the Serbs to comply with all the stipulations – an opinion shared by the shocked German Ambassador to Paris.

"It was an absolute surprise even to me," he wrote. "As recently as on the day on which the Note was forwarded, my Austro-Hungarian colleague had told me that, according to his information, it would be so worded that the Serbia could agree to all the demands, and this would practically settle the matter."[206]

By then, it was too late for the Germans to suggest any alterations, as, the following day, Giesl, delivered the Note to the Serbian government. In the absence of the Prime Minister, Giesl handed the Note to the Minister of Finance, who protested that he was not authorised to receive it. In response, Giesl threw it onto a desk and told him he could do what he liked with it, before returning to Embassy and, on Berchtold's instructions, preparing to depart for Vienna as soon as a reply was received.

The Note, to which the Serbs had only forty-eight hours to reply, was immediately forwarded to the Serbian Regent, Prince Alexander, who, reeling in horror, urgently sought the advice and protection of the Tsar. Among various points demanding the suppression of anti-Austrian propaganda and the arrest of known insurgents, including certain leading figures in the army and civil service, the Austrians insisted that their agents should be allowed to operate in Serbia to exact justice on all who had participated in, or supported, the murder of Archduke Franz Ferdinand.

On July 24th, the Austrian Ambassadors handed copies of the Note to the governments of the Great Powers, and, in an attempt to garner international support, the Serbs released copies to the international press. Like Jagow and Bethmann, all agreed that this was basically an ultimatum rather than a simple series of demands. The British Foreign Secretary, Edward Grey, accepted that some of the statements were justified but, for the first time, observed that the situation was now 'very grave', as, 'I have never before seen one state address to another independent state a document of so formidable a character.' One French commentator claimed that acceptance would basically turn Serbia into an Austro-Hungarian vassal; and the Russian Foreign Minister, Sazonov, was even more explicit, gasping, 'This means a European war!'

Not everyone, however, believed the Note to be unjust or extreme, for, as the Austrians claimed, the demand to be allowed to participate in the investigation and trial of the perpetrators was perfectly reasonable in the light of the Serbs' failure to adhere to the promises they had made in their declaration of March 1909. Moreover, there had been a precedent for such intervention, for, in 1868, when a Serbian prince was murdered, the Serbs asked permission to carry out their investigations in Hungary where the assassins were believed to be living. The Hungarians agreed to this request and there was no international outcry about foreign investigators acting in an independent country.

One contemporary American circuit judge, Peter Stenger Grosscup, examined the Note and concluded that it was perfectly reasonable since the Serbs had failed to root out the anti-Austrian 'firebrands', and therefore the Austrians had every right to do so.

"We went to war with Spain," he wrote, "for less than Austria was suffering at the hands of Serbia. England declared war on the republic of Paul Kruger for less. And in each case the war closed with territory detached from the vanquished and taken by the victor from the vanquished...Why then should any outside Power say nay to Austria, especially if no territory was to be taken?"[207]

The *Manchester Guardian* was equally supportive, stating that any country, believing the heir to the throne had been assassinated in a plot hatched by army officers of another country, would respond with equal vehemence; the widely-circulated newspaper, *John Bull,* concurred that there was no reason for the peace of Europe to be disturbed by Austria's 'just demands'; and the *Telegraph* declared that the British had no sympathy whatsoever with the Serbs.

The Kaiser, to his great chagrin, had not been informed of what was taking place and only discovered the contents of the Note when an officer aboard his yacht read the details in a Norwegian newspaper. According to his companion and cousin, the English-born Prince Albert of Schleswig-Holstein, Wilhelm was 'terribly upset' and sought to calm his nerves by inviting Albert to join him in bathing the dogs before ordering an immediate return to Potsdam.

On hearing that the Kaiser was racing home, his ministers attempted to dissuade him, repeating their former argument that his presence would cause undue 'speculation and excitement', which, as one American writer observed:

"...suggests the possibility that the German Foreign Office, which had already made substantial progress in precipitating the crisis, did not wish the Kaiser's return for fear that he might...exert his great influence in the interests of peace."[208]

In London, Paris and St Petersburg, meanwhile, it was reported that the Austrians would never have dared to send such inflammatory demands without German backing, and it was therefore assumed that the Note had been dictated by Berlin. Quick to deny this suggestion, the Foreign Minister, Jagow, wrote to all the Great Powers, insisting that Germany knew nothing of the details prior to 22nd July, and emphasising the necessity of non-interference in the Austro-Serbian dispute lest a local conflict should escalate into a major European war. Sir Edward Grey, having received from the British Embassy in Berlin a telegram to this effect, confirmed that the contents of the Note had been kept from Berlin until the last minute; and the Russian Foreign Minister, Sazanov also concurred that the Germans had not been informed in advance of the complete set of demands.

Chapter 16 – 'The Most Sorrowful Man in the World'

On receiving Prince Alexander's desperate request for advice and support, Tsar Nicholas urged him to proceed with great caution and to ask for an extension of the forty-eight hour limit so that there might be time to negotiate or to take the matter to the International Court of Arbitration in The Hague. The German Ambassador in Vienna also suggested allowing more time for discussion but the Austrians summarily dismissed the idea, drawing attention to a clause in the various arbitration treaties which stated that the International Court could not consider questions dealing with the independence, vital interests or national honour of any country.

In order to buy more time, the Tsar, therefore, urged the Serbs to write a placatory reply, agreeing to as many points as possible without sacrificing their autonomy. Similar advice reached Belgrade from Paris, and it was widely hoped that a show of goodwill would demonstrate the Serbian government's willingness to accept responsibility for its failure to suppress anti-Austrian propaganda, and its determination to prevent any future atrocities.

The Serbs followed the Tsar's advice and sent a conciliatory response five minutes before the expiry of the time limit, excusing the lateness of the reply by explaining that they could not find a typist with sufficient linguistic skills to translate the letter into French. In the meantime, however, they also began a complete mobilisation, suggesting that, despite the conciliatory tone of their reply, they did not expect to satisfy Austria and were readying themselves for war.

By this time, the Kaiser had reached Kiel, and, on seeing the Serbs' response, he expressed his relief that the dispute appeared to have been settled.

"That is more than one could expect," he said. "A great moral victory for Vienna but with it disappears every reason for war."[209]

This was not what the Austrian ministers and Generals wanted to hear; nor, indeed, did the Austrian people, who had been bombarded by newspaper headlines insisting that it was time to crush the Serbs once and for all. On hearing that the Note had been accepted, there was, according to the British Ambassador, 'a moment of keen disappointment' in Vienna, but Berchtold and his fellow ministers were not prepared to let the opportunity slip through their hands. Little more than an hour after receiving the response, they approached Franz Josef at Bad Ischl with a mobilisation order and a draft declaration of war. The speed with which the documents were presented was evidence that they had been prepared in advance and there had never been any intention of accepting a favourable response from the Serbs.

When Franz Josef expressed his reluctance to authorise the mobilisation, Berchtold told him truthfully that the Serbs, in a panic, had already mobilised but he falsely added that they were shelling Austrian positions. With a heavy heart, Franz Josef signed the order, still stressing that he was not in favour of military action and, as late as July 27th, when his ministers had already prepared a fuller declaration, he stated categorically, 'we are not yet at war, and if I can, I shall prevent it.'

At once, according to the British Ambassador:

"Vienna burst into a frenzy of delight, vast crowds parading the streets and singing patriotic songs till the small hours of the morning."[210]

The Viennese were not the only ones eager for a conflict. As the Emperors were desperately searching for a peaceful solution, newspapers across the continent were stirring up jingoistic feelings in the cities of all the Great

Powers. Just two weeks after Franz Ferdinand's murder, an article in the Russian press bragged that:

> "We are now able, thanks to the support of the British Fleet and to our own now completely prepared army, to demand that Berlin put an end to that political system which is neither in keeping with our dignity nor our international position."[211]

Popular sentiment in Russia was reaching such proportions that it was clear even to the Kaiser that, in the event of an invasion of Serbia, it would be difficult for the Tsar to withstand his people's demands for a declaration of war. Already, pressed by his ministers, Nicholas had given an order to prepare for a partial mobilisation – a movement of troops towards the Austrian border – and the fortification of towns along the border with Germany; and, by July 24th, all Russian roubles had been withdrawn from German banks.

Tsar Nicholas himself, however, had absolute faith in the Kaiser, dismissing his ministers' arguments that Wilhelm's speeches were evidence of his belligerence.

> "I can't believe the Emperor wants war," Nicholas told the French Ambassador. "If you knew him as I do! If you knew how much theatricality there is in his posing!"[212]

The French, though, thought differently, if not of the Kaiser himself, at least of his country. While the public saw little reason to go to war with Austria over the death of 'an unnecessary Archduke', there was a general feeling, stoked by the press, that Germany was behind the increasing international tensions. One British author and journalist who happened to be in Paris observed that:

> "During the last days of July and the first days of August Paris was stunned by the shock of this menace, which was approaching swiftly and terribly. War! But why?...Germany was behind the business, Germany was forcing the pace,

exasperating Russia, presenting a grim face to France and rattling the sword in its scabbard so that it resounded through Europe."[213]

Such was the intensity of the perceived menace that in France, soldiers' leave was cancelled and the army was placed on standby in preparation for mobilisation.

As a full-scale European war became more likely, the Russians were desperate to ensure that they could count on the support of their allies. The French Ambassador, without hesitation, assured the Russians that this was the case, but, initially, the British were vague and non-committal. The Tsar's Foreign Minister, Sazonov, sent a message to his British counterpart, Edward Grey, advising him that if Britain failed to support her ally, she could no longer count on Russian support for her interests in the Persian Gulf. Grey consequently asked the German Ambassador to urge his government to use its influence to dissuade Austria from launching an attack, and, in response, on the instructions of the Chancellor, the Ambassador asked Grey to perform a similar service in St. Petersburg – a request with which Grey failed to comply.

The German Ambassador in Russia suggested a direct conference between St. Petersburg and Vienna, and the idea was taken up by – and later claimed to have been instigated by – Edward Grey. The plan, however, was vetoed by the French President Poincaré, who bizarrely insisted that any discussions between Russia and Austria would be 'very dangerous' unless the British and French were involved.

In view of the failure of this proposal, Grey suggested a 'four-power' mediation, whereby Britain, France, Italy and Germany would seek a solution that would be acceptable to the Austrians, the Russians and the Serbs. After the war, the Germans were portrayed as having rejected this suggestion outright, but in reality the German Ambassador, on behalf of his government, immediately expressed support for the plan in the event that all attempts to confine the dispute the Austria and Serbia should fail. Wilhelm himself was less than enthusiastic, insisting that there was no need for outside intervention as this was a local dispute, but the Ambassador did not relate the Kaiser's personal views to the British. The Russian Ambassador, however, told Grey that the proposal implied that Russia was not in accord with the other members of the Entente; and the French also insisted that Russia should be involved in any discussions.

On 25th July, the Austrians broke off all diplomatic relations with Serbia and openly began mobilisation. Grey then proposed an idea, initially put forward by Sazonov, of holding in London a conference of the Ambassadors of Germany, Italy, Britain and France. The Germans, aware that the Russians were already preparing to mobilise, feared that this was simply a ploy to buy time to allow them to complete their preparations, and, what was more the idea seemed to suggest some form of tribunal which would put Austria – the innocent party – on trial. Still hoping to confine the dispute to Austria and Serbia, the Germans preferred the idea of direct conversation between Vienna and Belgrade; and the Austrians objected to Grey's proposal since, due to a series of disputes with Italy, they believed the Italians would not present their case fairly.

On 27th July, Wilhelm 'with a careworn expression', finally reached Potsdam. Aghast at what had been allowed to happen during his absence, and convinced that he had been duped by the Austrians, he vented his anger on Bethmann, demanding to know why he had not recalled him to Berlin and how he could have let the situation deteriorate so rapidly. When the Chancellor, realising the precariousness of his position, offered his resignation, Wilhelm refused to accept it, telling him, "You have cooked this broth and now you will stay and eat it!"

His temper was not soothed by the atmosphere of animosity between the Foreign Office and the Chiefs of Staff, the former believing that peace would be maintained as long as the Kaiser did not order his troops to mobilise, and the latter insisting that war was now inevitable and Germany needed to make urgent military preparations.

From the moment that he arrived back in Potsdam, Wilhelm worked frantically to avoid a full European war. As different ministerial departments presented him with conflicting opinions and advice, he was forced to admit, 'I never knew whom to believe. People would tell me so-and-so was the case and yet I could never be sure that I was being told the truth.'[214]

Unsurprisingly, therefore, he turned to those whom he trusted most deeply – his cousins in Britain and Russia. Somewhat naively believing that everything could be settled through agreements between monarchs, he assured both King George and Tsar Nicholas that he would do everything in his power to keep the peace. As his brother, Henry, was holidaying in England, Wilhelm asked him to discover 'Cousin Georgie's' opinion of the situation and to find out what stance Britain would take if Russia entered the conflict. After dining with the King, Henry blithely reported that Britain would remain neutral, and added that Britain's neutrality was evinced by the dispersal of the Royal Navy following the summer manoeuvres off Spithead. That very evening, however, the First Lord of the Admiralty, Winston Churchill, sent orders to halt the dispersal[aa] and, in response to the Russians' complaints that

---

[aa] In 1915, Sir Henry Lucy, gave an interview to the New York *Sun*, in which he quoted a letter from Admiral Fisher, boasting of Winston Churchill's brilliance in secretly mobilising the Royal Navy before war had been declared, 'on the innocent pretext of an expected visit from the King' so that the fleet would be ready to take command of the North Sea and to seal the Imperial Navy in German harbours.

172

the German ministers were convinced that Britain would not enter the conflict, Grey told Sazonov:

> "This impression will be dispelled by the orders which we have given to the First Fleet, which is concentrated as it happens in Portland, not to disperse for manoeuvre leave."[215]

Despite increasing consternation in Berlin, Wilhelm remained optimistic and devised a plan which he believed would be acceptable to all parties. He ordered Bethmann to deliver a message to the German Ambassador in Vienna, telling him to advise the Austrians to agree to a temporary occupation of Belgrade until the Serbs had fulfilled all their promises. That way, war could be avoided; the Austrians would have shown a firm hand; there would be time for further negotiation; and the Russians could remain out of the conflict without abandoning her ally or appearing dishonourable. For some reason, Bethmann waited twelve hours before transmitting the Kaiser's order and, during that time, the Austrians unexpectedly declared war on Serbia. When the message finally reached the Ambassador, the Chiefs of Staff claimed it would be too expensive to halt the invasion.

The declaration of war, which was due to be sent on August 12th, was delivered by telegram to Belgrade at eleven o'clock in the morning of 28th July, and was so unexpected that the Serbs initially believed it to be a hoax. They were quickly disillusioned when the Austrians began firing shells across the Danube, prompting the anxious Serbs to blow up the main bridge across the river to prevent the invading army from reaching Belgrade.

On hearing that Austria had launched an attack, the Russian press roused the people to demand retribution for the 'ignoble war' against a 'weaker and smaller' country, and the Tsar ordered a partial mobilisation against Austria. In spite of their antipathy towards Austria-Hungary, the Russians were largely unmoved by the headlines that attempted to turn them against Germany, and, according to one witness, the people of St Petersburg generally believed that the Kaiser would eventually prove successful in his attempts to resolve the situation peacefully.

> "Everyone firmly believed in Kaiser Wilhelm's peaceful intentions, and the efficacy of his powerful mediation, and were convinced that he would intervene in the last moment. The Kaiser's vaunted love of peace seemed a guarantee."[216]

Wilhelm, realising that the situation was rapidly escalating out of control, urgently telegraphed Nicholas, asking him to halt the mobilisation, and offering further mediation while promising to 'induce Austria-Hungary to seek a frank and satisfactory understanding with Russia.' True to his word, he repeatedly sent emissaries to Vienna, exhorting the Austrians to show restraint and to agree to some form of compromise but his suggestions were rejected as Franz Josef's ministers and Chiefs of Staff insisted that there could be no compromise without a complete acceptance of their demands.

Over the next forty-eight hours, telegrams flew back and forth between St Petersburg and Berlin as the Kaiser and the Tsar pleaded with each other to do everything possible to avoid war.

'I beg you in the name of our old friendship to do what you can to stop your allies from going too far...' wrote Nicholas, to which Wilhelm responded by reminding him of their 'sacred' friendship which he had always treasured. War, he said, could still be averted, 'if Russia will agree to stop the military measures which must threaten Germany and Austro-Hungary.'

Although Nicholas stated that it was not possible to stop the preparations since Austria had already mobilised, he insisted that this did not mean there would be war and he assured Wilhelm that, as long as he continued to mediate, Russia would take no *provocative* action. Wilhelm again sent emissaries to Vienna urging restraint, and he asked the Austrian Ambassador in Russia to try to persuade the Foreign Minister, Sazonov to maintain neutrality. With the bombing of Belgrade, however, the Tsar gave orders for a general mobilisation – an order which he subsequently agreed to rescind in response to yet another urgent telegram from the Kaiser.

On 29th July, under intense pressure from Sazonov and the public, the Tsar was compelled to change his mind again. This time he signed the order for a partial mobilisation against Austria, which came into immediate effect, and for a general mobilisation against Germany, which would come into effect if Germany took up arms in support of the Austrians.

On 30th July, Wilhelm's brother, Henry, received a further message from King George, stating that he was 'so pleased to hear of William's efforts to concert with Nicky [the Tsar] to maintain peace'; and the following day, George wrote directly to Wilhelm, suggesting – as Wilhelm himself had suggested – that the Austrians might temporarily occupy Belgrade.

> "Your proposal coincides with my ideas," Wilhelm promptly replied, "and with the statements I got this night from Vienna and which I have forwarded to London."[217]

Even as he was writing, however, news arrived of the Russians' general mobilisation and, as he told George, 'strong Russian troops are already amassing on my eastern borders.'

On receipt of the Kaiser's letter, and hearing that Germany had mobilised, George wrote to his cousin, the Tsar, offering to mediate and trusting that Nicholas would 'leave the door open' to negotiation, since 'some misunderstanding must have produced this deadlock'. He was, he said:

"...most anxious not to miss any possibility of avoiding the terrible calamity which at present threatens the whole world."[218]

That morning, however, German newspapers, which were widely circulated in Russia, erroneously reported that the Kaiser had ordered a full mobilisation and Germany was in the throes of 'extensive war preparations'. That evening, as all mediation attempts appeared to have failed, Nicholas signed the order for the full mobilisation to begin the next morning.

Wilhelm was later informed by a Cossack Commander, Prince Tundutoff, an aide-de-camp to the Commander-in-Chief, Grand Duke Nicholas Nikolaivich, that he had been present at the Russian General Headquarters when the Kaiser and Tsar were exchanging telegrams. He testified that, when Nicholas received a further telegram from Wilhelm, he decided once again to halt the general mobilisation and telephoned his Chief of the General Staff, Januskevitch, telling him to cancel the previous order. Rather than obeying the command, Januskevitch contacted Sazonov for advice, and was told that 'the Tsar's order was nonsense,' and that it should be ignored. Januskevitch consequently lied to Nicholas, telling him that it was too late to rescind the order as the troops were already on the move.

"Therefore," wrote Wilhelm, "[Nicholas] wished to stop the war machine, the murder of entire peoples...This would have been possible and peace might have been preserved if Sazonov had not frustrated his wish."[219]

This was no figment of the Kaiser's imagination. The British Ambassador to St Petersburg, George Buchanan, was also present at the time and reported that, on receiving a telegram from Wilhelm, Nicholas telephoned the Chief of Staff and the Minister of War, ordering them to halt the mobilisation. Although they objected that this was not possible as it was already underway:

> "The Emperor...insisted, but, in spite of his categorical orders, the military authorities allowed the general mobilisation to proceed without his knowledge."[220]

It was two o'clock in the morning when Pourtalès, the German Ambassador in St Petersburg, realised what was happening, and, on the Kaiser's orders, he set out at once to the Foreign Office to plead with Sazonov to halt the mobilisation. By then, though, as Sazonov told the Tsar, the Austrians were bombarding Belgrade and every effort to restrain them had proved futile.

The Russians' general mobilisation was a decisive factor in precipitating a full scale war, and the Germans were not alone in viewing it as too hasty an action. In London, the *Daily Graphic* reported that, with the Tsar's troops approaching his border, the Kaiser would have no option but to ready his armies.

> "We confess, we are unable to understand the action of Russia....The mobilisation goes far beyond the limits of necessary precaution...as the matter stands it is inexplicable and is calculated to cast doubts on the loyalty and straightforwardness of the Russian government."[221]

Wilhelm was horrified when his Chief of Staff, Moltke, informed him that Russian troops were moving towards East Prussia, and, in view of the Russians' alliance with France, there was every possibility that, unless he acted quickly, Germany would be encircled. On the afternoon of July 31st, German troops were, for the first time, put on alert in preparation for a potential mobilisation, and, that evening, an approach was made to France to discover her intentions. As a guarantee of French neutrality, the Germans naively requested permission to occupy the border towns of Toul and Verdun until the end of the conflict. The French responded vaguely – neither agreeing to remain neutral nor giving any assurances that they would stand by their ally, Russia. To Sazonov and the Tsar, however, the French Ambassador had already pledged his country's support and, early in the evening of 31st July, France authorised a full mobilisation.

Wilhelm's desperate efforts had been in vain, and even the former French Empress, who had no personal liking for the Kaiser, saw him as a latter-day King Canute, fruitlessly trying to hold back the tide. 'When the river reaches the waterfall,' she said, 'no earthly power can stop it.'[222] For days, Wilhelm had been bombarded by conflicting information: telegrams assuring him of the Tsar's desire for peace, followed by reports of the Russians' movements towards East Prussia; Bethmann's professed belief that war was avoidable, followed by Moltke's insistence that unless Germany began immediate preparations she would find herself encircled.

"Kaiser Wilhelm did everything in his power for peace," an American correspondent in St Petersburg telegraphed to Washington. "Despite the protests of von Moltke, he delayed the mobilisation decree."[223]

On the evening of 31st July, Wilhelm addressed the crowds who had gathered beneath the balcony of his Berlin palace:

"Envious rivals everywhere force us to legitimate defence. The sword has been forced into our hands. I hope that in the event that my efforts to the very last moment do not succeed in bringing our opponents to reason and in preserving peace, we may use the sword, with the help of God, so that we may sheathe it again with honour. War will demand enormous sacrifices by the German people, but we shall show the enemy what it means to attack Germany. And so I commend you to God. Go forth into the churches, kneel down before God, and implore his help for our brave army."[224]

With his usual theatrical aplomb he played the role of a mighty General rousing his troops for battle, but, later that evening, after he had dined with his brother and son, his anxiety and desperation were apparent. Walking up and down in the garden, he expressed his hope that there yet might be a way to avoid the impending catastrophe but, pressed and harassed by his General Staff and increasingly panicking ministers, he was finally forced to sign an ultimatum. 'They have forced my hand,' he said, 'I cannot do otherwise.' Unless the Russian military preparations ceased within twelve hours, Russia and Germany would be in a state of war.

It was left to the desperate Ambassador Pourtalès to deliver the ultimatum to Sazonov at eleven o'clock at night, Russian time. According to the French Ambassador, Pourtalès stated that the ultimatum would expire at midday on August 1st. Then:

> "...he continued in a trembling, hurried voice: 'Agree to demobilize! Agree to demobilize! Agree to demobilize!'
>
> "Sazonov, quite unruffled, replied: 'I could only confirm what His Majesty the Emperor has told you. As long as the conversations with Austria continue, as long as there's any chance of averting the war, we shall not attack. But it's technically impossible for us to demobilize without dislocating our entire military organization. It is a point the soundness of which your General Staff itself could not deny.'
>
> "Pourtalès went out, scared out of his wits."[225]

Even then, the Tsar hoped that the situation might yet be resolved, writing to Wilhelm that he understood why he had felt compelled to mobilise but trusting that 'these measures do not mean war and we shall continue to negotiate', but, by noon the following day, no response had been received to the ultimatum, and the worst fears of both Emperors materialised.

"A burst of patriotic enthusiasm shook the whole country to the foundations," wrote on observer in St Petersburg. "...It was a general intoxication which had exalted all classes...Never during the twenty years of his reign had the Emperor been so beloved, so respected, so popular in the eyes of his subjects as at that moment."[226]

On the same day, the British-born Lady Bentinck was travelling by train across Germany en route to England, and everywhere, she heard the same story, 'The Kaiser is the peace-Kaiser. He does not want war.'[227] It was a view reiterated by the American industrialist, Andrew Carnegie, who recorded that, 'The Kaiser was the most sorrowful man in the world when he realized that war could not be averted.'[228]

For Wilhelm, war with Russia was all the more distressing because he had genuinely enjoyed Nicholas' friendship, and was also acutely aware of the promise he had made at his grandfather's deathbed. Worse, though, was yet to come, for, within three days, he would find himself, too, at war with his beloved grandmother's England.

Chapter 17 – 'A Sentimental Subterfuge'

In all his correspondence with his cousins, Britain's King George V repeatedly emphasised his desire for peace but, in July 2014, an article appeared in the *Daily Telegraph* which calls into question his sincerity. According to recently discovered evidence, including a personal letter from Buckingham Palace, on August 2nd 1914, the King summoned the Foreign Secretary, Edward Grey, and told him directly that Britain must participate in the war to prevent Germany from becoming the most dominant force in Europe. When Grey observed that there was no justifiable reason for Britain to do so, the King told him he must find one.

Throughout the crisis, Grey had remained ambiguous in response to questions from Germany, Russia and France as to what role Britain would play in the event of a European war. When Sazonov pressed the British and French Ambassadors to stand by their Russian allies, the French Ambassador, Maurice Paléologue, had responded affirmatively without hesitation but the British Ambassador, George Buchanan, explained:

> "I could not hold out any hope of [Britain] making a declaration of solidarity that would involve unconditional engagement to support France and Russia by force of arms on behalf of a country like Serbia where no British interests were involved."[229]

When informed of this conversation, Grey commented that this was the correct response, but Buchanan was already eagerly trying to persuade his government to back the Russians and he promised Sazanov that he would 'make strong representations…in favour of the policy of resistance to Germanic arrogance.'[230] He was equally keen to ensure that Germany should take the blame for the subsequent conflict, telling Paléologue, on 28th July:

"The German Government must be saddled with all the responsibility and all the initiative. English opinion will accept the idea of intervening in the war only if Germany is indubitably the aggressor...Please talk to Sazonov to that effect."[231]

The Germans in general, and Wilhelm in particular, were desperate for an assurance of British neutrality, and several approaches had been made to Grey to ascertain his position and to discover under what conditions Britain might feel it was necessary to take up arms. In view of the Anglo-French Entente, Bethmann asked whether Britain would remain neutral if the Germans did not invade France, but since this did not preclude an attack on French colonies, the British refused to accept it.

On 1st August, however, the Kaiser received a message from Prince Linchowsky, his Ambassador in London, stating that Grey had told him that Britain would remain out of the conflict providing France was not attacked. Wilhelm was so overjoyed that, without informing his Chief of Staff, he immediately ordered a halt to the German advance towards Luxembourg, and sent a message to his cousin, George, assuring him of his willingness to accept the proposal. To his horror, however, George replied – in almost identical terms to those in which he had written to Nicholas following the Russian mobilisation – that there 'must have been some misunderstanding' as the discussion between Grey and Linchowsky was merely an informal and hypothetical conversation and had no significance.

On the same day, Linchowsky again asked Grey if the British would remain impassive provided that the Germans did not invade neutral Belgium. Grey refused to give that assurance, stating that Belgium *might* be 'an important *but not a decisive* factor.' On behalf of the Kaiser, the German government then asked on what terms Britain *would* remain neutral, but, as the British Member of

Parliament, James Ramsey-McDonald, stated openly in the House of Commons:

> "Sir Edward Grey declined to discuss the matter. This fact was suppressed by Mr Asquith and Sir Edward Grey in their speeches to Parliament. When Sir Edward Grey failed to secure peace between Germany and Russia, he worked deliberately to involve us in the war, using Belgium as his chief excuse."[232]

Three days after stating that the invasion would not be a decisive factor, Britain went to war in defence of 'plucky little Belgium.'

Since the conclusion of the Franco-Prussian War, the German Chiefs of Staff had anticipated that eventually the French would seek to reclaim the territories of Alsace-Lorraine; and, with the formation of the Franco-Russian Alliance, followed by the Triple Entente, that threat was magnified by the possibility of Germany being encircled and attacked on two fronts. In 1905, the then Chief of Staff, Alfred von Schlieffen, drew up a defensive plan which his successor, Moltke, modified the following year. Due to the vastness of the Tsar's Empire, Moltke estimated that it would take at least six weeks for the Russians to mobilise, which would give the Germans time to crush the French before turning their attention to the east. The difficulty lay in the fact that, since 1871, the French had heavily fortified the towns along the Franco-German border, making a swift advance into France virtually impossible. Moltke's solution was to take an alternative route through Belgium, after which, he claimed, the Germans would take Paris within forty days.

Since the 1839 Treaty of London, however, Belgian neutrality had been guaranteed by all the Great Powers including Prussia and the German Confederation. To the Kaiser, as to King Albert of the Belgians, neutrality included denying access to foreign armies, and therefore, from the start Wilhelm opposed an invasion. Nonetheless, despite the Kaiser's objections, on August 2nd, a formal request was sent to King Albert seeking permission for German troops to pass through his country on the promise that they would pay in cash for all their provisions and an indemnity for any damage which they caused. In spite of these apparently friendly offerings, the request concluded with the rather ominous threat that, should the Belgians make difficulties, Germany would be forced to view them as enemies.

Unsurprisingly, King Albert refused, declaring, 'I rule a Kingdom, not a road'; and warning that, if this refusal were not accepted, 'the Belgian Government are firmly resolved to repel, by all the means in their power, every attack upon their rights.'

The British Ambassador, anticipating that the Germans would ignore the refusal, approached the Belgian Foreign Minister to find out what his government would do in the event of a German invasion. The Foreign Minister replied that he had no reason to suspect that the Germans would violate Belgian neutrality, and his colleagues had not considered appealing to the other Powers if that should occur. More importantly, he insisted that his government did not want foreign armies intervening, as *'they* [the Belgians] *would rely on their own armed force as sufficient to resist aggression from whatever quarter it might come.'*[233]

Clearly the Belgians believed that they had as much to fear from the French as from the Germans; and within a matter of days, these fears appeared to be justified. According to the Kaiser, before the Germans had even sent their request to King Albert, 'a large number of French aeroplanes came flying into [Germany] across the neutral territory of Belgium and Luxembourg without a word of warning on the part of the Belgian government.'[234] This claim was corroborated by the British Ambassador in

184

Berlin, who reported to Edward Grey on 2nd August that 'the French had already commenced hostilities by dropping bombs from an airship in the vicinity of Nuremberg'[235].

On the same day, Edward Grey informed the British Ambassador in Paris that he had received a report from the German Ambassador that:

"This morning eighty French officers in Prussian uniforms attempted to cross the German frontier at Walbeck, west of Geldern [in the Netherlands]. This constitutes most serious violation of neutrality on the part of France."[236]

The French denied this accusation but said little in response to reports that a patrol of French cavalry officers had crossed into Alsace and opened fire on the Germans; and two French officers were shot while attempting to blow up a German railway tunnel.

Still, the Kaiser strongly objected to an invasion of Belgium because 'he did not wish Germany to break her word...and he knew that it would bring [Britain] into the war'[237], but his Chiefs of Staff saw no feasible alternative, and on August 4th ordered the troops across the border. The following day, they began bombarding the fortified city of Liège.

No sooner had the Germans set foot on Belgian soil than King Albert sent an urgent message to Britain requesting '*diplomatic* intervention to safeguard the integrity' of his country. The British government, disregarding the mention of diplomacy, responded at once, urging the Belgians to offer armed resistance and assuring them of military support. The Belgian Foreign Minister replied that 'there is no question that Belgium will fire on the Germans immediately'[238]; and, on the same day, in response to a French offer of military assistance, his government stated:

"...in actual circumstances we are not appealing to...the Powers. The Belgian Government will determine later on action which it may be necessary to take."[239]

Nonetheless, that evening, the British issued an ultimatum: unless the Kaiser's troops withdrew from Belgium with immediate effect, Britain would declare war on Germany.

When the British Ambassador, Sir Edward Goschen delivered the ultimatum, the German Foreign Minister, Jagow, expressed deep sorrow, claiming that he had always hoped to form closer ties with Britain and, through those ties, to ameliorate Germany's relationship with France. Chancellor Bethmann was even more distressed, asking why Britain was prepared to sacrifice her friendship with 'a kindred nation' all for 'a scrap of paper'[bb]. Both men insisted that passing through Belgium was their only means of protecting themselves from encirclement and, by international law, every nation had a right to self-preservation. It was a view shared by the renowned playwright and pacifist, George Bernard Shaw:

> "Germany with hostile France on one side, and hostile Russia on the other is in a position so dangerous that we in our secure island can form no conception of its intolerable tension...Is it to be wondered that Germany...made a wild attempt to cut its way out."[240]

None, however, was as devastated as Wilhelm when he heard that Britain had declared war.

> "His shock and surprise were genuine when he realized what England was doing," wrote Princess Evelyn Blucher. "He had not thought it possible. To his friends standing near him he said, 'To think that Nicholas and Georgie should have played me false! If my grandmother had been alive, she never would have allowed it.'"[241]

[bb] Meaning the treaty which had assured Belgian neutrality

Princess Blucher's view was supported by a German socialist, Anton Friedrich, who met Wilhelm shortly after the outbreak of war:

> "My strongest impression was that the German Kaiser had been desirous of preserving peace down to the last moment. And my second impression was his disillusion concerning his relatives in England and Russia who failed him in the hour of danger."[242]

That day, as he addressed the Reichstag, observers noted that his voice and careworn expression betrayed the great strain that he was under and his obvious distress and disappointment at the way in which events had unfolded. Now, though, as Emperor and Supreme War Leader, he knew that his first duty was to support his armies and to maintain the morale of his people. His theatrical orations repeatedly returned to the theme that this was a war engineered and precipitated by Germany's enemies, and the Imperial troops were fighting for Germany's very existence. The sentiments expressed in these speeches were completely sincere, for he, like many of his countrymen viewed the British indignation at the invasion of Belgium as utterly hypocritical and merely an excuse to put an end to Germany's economic successes.

The American consul in Munich recorded that for twenty years he had paid scant attention to the frequent conversations he had heard in Britain about the need to destroy Germany in the interests of British trade.

> "Little did I dream at the time," he wrote, "of the conspiracy that England had woven to mobilize the world against the Germanic people and how she would succeed in using the blood and treasure of other nations to accomplish her criminal ambitions."[243]

The Consul was unexpectedly recalled to Washington and asked to resign.

Another American Consul in Aix-La-Chapelle – a man of English descent with no personal ties to Germany – shared this opinion, reporting to the State Department that English statesmen realised that the only hope of retaining the British position as 'manufacturer and banker for the world' was to check 'German progress in the arts of peace.'

"...the violation of Belgian neutrality as the reason for England's declaration of war," he wrote, "is a sentimental subterfuge, sounding well for English chivalry before the world, but meaning from the beginning suicide and death to poor Belgium. The whole Belgian situation has proved fortuitous for England."[244]

Wilhelm found plenty of evidence to justify his claim of hypocrisy, for Britain and her allies were equally guilty of violating other nations' neutrality. The British had passed through Portuguese territory to fight the Boers; and the Japanese marched through neutral China to seize the Germany colony of Kiao-Chau. 'It is alright for the allies to do these things,' the Kaiser observed bitterly, 'but when Germany does them, England rises up in righteous indignation.'[245] Later, when the British bombarded neutral Greece in an attempt to compel the country to join the Allies, he was even more incensed:

"The way they have treated my poor sister, the Queen of Greece, is a shame and a disgrace. They talk of our invasion of Belgium but their acts in Greece are infinitely worse....The English...try to cover all their acts with religion and talk of the benefits to civilization and humanity but, hypocrites that they are, they continue to grab all they can get their hands on just the same."[246]

To Wilhelm it seemed patently obviously that Britain had never intended to remain neutral but rather had been preparing for war for some time. He discovered that in April 1914, as Germany continued to export gold and grain,

British banks began to accumulate vast reserves of gold as though preparing for a conflict. Moreover, the British had gone to great lengths to examine Germany's financial situation, resulting in a report from the British Consul in Frankfurt, sent to Edward Grey on 29th July, detailing virtually every aspect of Germany's economy and concluding that 'the situation of the German money market has never been stronger than today.'[247] What was more, it was alleged that during a Cabinet meeting on the same day – before the question of Belgium had even been raised – Grey threatened to resign if Britain remained neutral.

Still more galling for Wilhelm and his staff was the belief that Belgian neutrality had been violated long before the Germans crossed the border. As the Kaiser's troops advanced through the country, they discovered stores of British uniforms, phrase books and military maps which, according to Wilhelm, 'had been established by England with the permission of the French and Belgian governments *before* the war.'[248] These findings led to the conclusion that the French and British had already planned to march through Belgium to reach Germany's borders; and, what was more, their troops had been active in the country before the German invasion. Baroness von Bissing, wife of Germany's Governor of Belgium, told an American visitor that:

> "It is a pleasant little joke of theirs about our invading Belgium first, but I know that the English and French were there before us...I have seen in Antwerp a house, seven-storeys high, which was so filled with English hospital supplies that we haven't yet used them all up."[249]

When the invading armies reached Brussels, they found incriminating documents which proved that as far back as 1906, the military attaché at the British Legation had discussed with General Ducalme, the Belgian Chief of the General Staff, plans to send British troops to the

189

country in the event of war. In return, Ducalme had furnished the British officer with top secret details of 'the military circumstances and the situation' of Belgium's 'Eastern neighbour' – Germany. Six years later, a similar conversation took place, during which the British attaché informed the Belgian Chief of Staff that, whether or not the Belgians sought their help, one-hundred-and-sixty-thousand troops were readied for immediate dispatch to the continent in the event of a war with Germany. When the Chief of Staff protested that, if the British troops landed without Belgian consent they would be violating the country's neutrality, the attaché replied:

> "...he knew that but, as we were not in a position to prevent the Germans from passing through our territory, Great Britain would have landed her troops in any event."[250]

This claim was verified by Lord Roberts in an article for the *Military Review* in 1913, where he stated that in 1911 'our Expeditionary Force was held in readiness to embark for Flanders to do its share in maintaining the balance of power in Europe.'

When these findings were made public in Germany, neither Britain nor Belgium denied that the discussions had taken place, but the Belgian ministers claimed that it was within their rights to ensure their own defence in view of a series of recently constructed German railways which could be used to transport troops to the Belgian border. In 1915, Edward Grey confirmed the story, again referring to the danger posed by the German railways but, as even Germany's greatest critics were forced to concede, the railways were necessary to facilitate the successful trade between Germany and the United States, via the city of Antwerp. Ironically, too, there were only four direct lines between Germany and Belgium, whereas between the latter and France there were twenty-two. Naturally, then, the Kaiser asked why the Belgians had fortified the towns along the German border but had taken no similar precautions against a potential invasion by the French. Even Baron Grendl, the Belgian Minister Plenipotentiary based in Berlin, had questioned his government's neutrality and had warned Brussels that:

"From the French side, danger threatens...us on our entire frontier. We are not reduced to conjectures for this assertion. We have positive evidence of it."[251]

In 1912, Lieutenant-Colonel Bridges sent a confidential report to the Foreign Office in London, recounting a conversation he had had with the Belgian Minister of War. Expressing his fears that, since joining the Entente, Britain was no longer viewed as an impartial protector, the Minister asked how London would respond if the French violated Belgian neutrality. Bridges dismissed that possibility, leaving the Minister convinced that the British would only act in their own interests or those of their allies, which, he said, meant that henceforth 'Great Britain...was a potential enemy and as such had to be watched and could no longer be regarded as the Power to which Belgium could confidently appeal for help.'

When Bridges responded by stressing that Belgium had more to fear from Germany than from France, the Minister replied that the recent concentrations of French troops along the border suggested that the French were already 'envisaging an offensive movement' through Belgium. In his report to the Foreign Office, Bridges added tellingly that it was necessary to allay the Minister's fears since:

"It is highly desirable that the Belgian Government should be disposed to, and on the side of, the Entente in a war with Germany."[252]

In Germany, further questions were raised as to why a neutral country had recently introduced a series of expensive military reforms and, three months before the outbreak of war, had obtained a large loan from London to facilitate compulsory national service, and increased the size of the army to half a million men.

To many Germans, it appeared that Belgium had secretly allied herself to Britain and France long before the invasion, and had therefore already compromised her own neutrality; while to others it seemed that the Allies had used Belgium, without her consent, to their own ends. A study of French war plans, obtained by Germany some months before the outbreak of hostilities, contained a description of how the French armies would unite with those of Britain and Belgium, and, 'after passing through Belgium', would oppose 'the German forces advancing from northern Germany.' More damning still for the Entente, were the affidavits of captured French soldiers, who swore that they had entered the country with their regiments as early as July 27th – six days before the German invasion, and eight days before Britain declared war on Germany for violating Belgian neutrality.

All these facts consolidated Wilhelm's overriding belief that Belgium was merely an excuse for the British to implement their plans to put an end to Germany's economic success; and in the months that followed the outbreak of war, events appeared to validate his suspicion.

Within hours of the commencement of hostilities, the British Admiralty ordered a blockade of several German ports to prevent supplies from reaching the enemy. Officers were issued with a list of contraband items and authorised to stop and search neutral vessels for armaments, field glasses, military bridles, saddles and horseshoes, chemicals used in the manufacture of munitions, and a variety of other potential implements of war. Repeatedly over subsequent months, the list was revised and extended to include cotton, clothing, agricultural fertilizers and even vital food supplies. In November 1914, the Allies declared the North Sea a warzone to deter neutral ships from carrying cargoes to the

Central Powers; and embargos were placed on exports to Scandinavia to prevent supplies from being transported overland. In 1915, an article appeared in a British Sunday newspaper, showing a photograph of desperate Austrian peasant women in Galicia, queuing for a meagre hand-out of bread and black salt, and a quotation from David Lloyd George, stating openly that the British would win the war not through valour but through starving out peasant women such as these.

Apart from a half-hearted objection from America's President Woodrow Wilson, German protestations about the illegality of the blockade went largely unheeded. British politicians excused their actions by claiming that the invasion of Belgium nullified all previous agreements and, as Arthur Balfour disingenuously stated, even if the blockade contravened international law, it was morally justifiable, being 'a reply to an attack which is not only illegal but also immoral.'

Contrary to international law, the purpose of the blockade was to lower morale and starve the civilian population into submission, but Wilhelm saw in it, too, the equally sinister purpose of disrupting Germany's commercial success and stealing German trade with neutral countries. This was done so openly that several London newspapers gloated about it. The *Financier* reported:

> "Germany is about to lose...not only the great markets of Russia, France and Belgium, but those of all the English-speaking race. German foreign trade has suddenly ceased and it is for us to see that it never revives. What Germany has won by long and painful toil is suddenly given into our hands....Provided we make full use of the opportunity, the complaint of German commercial competition will not be heard again."[253]

In August 1914, the *Daily Mail* printed a long list of British industries which would profit from a ban on

German imports, prompting one prominent German lady to observe that 'England is in this war solely for money,'[254] and a German intellectual to claim that for England it was 'a commercial war with a view to her own enrichment and the annihilation of her chief rival.'[255]

Lord Northcliffe, the fiercely anti-German proprietor of both the *Daily Mail* and the *Times,* published an even more striking article, stating that:

> "We are fighting this war because Germany intends to take our trade and colonies and to reduce us to third-rate Powers under the heel of the Kaiser and his swashbuckling Generals."[256]

No mention whatsoever was made of the violation of Belgium.

Chapter 18 – The Defamation of Kaiser Wilhelm

For Queen Victoria's grandchildren, war was a personal tragedy as well as an international catastrophe. Siblings and cousins, who had played together as children and had attended each other's christenings, weddings and funerals, were suddenly on opposing sides, compelled to disregard family feeling for the sake of their countries. Life would become particularly difficult for princesses who had married into foreign courts, for, no matter how faithfully they served their adopted lands, they soon became objects of suspicion and hatred. Wilhelm's cousin, the German-born Tsarina Alexandra, and her sister, Grand Duchess Elizaveta Feodorovna, were wrongly accused of spying for the Germans; and it was falsely rumoured that his sister, Queen Sophie of the Hellenes, had a private telephone line to Berlin by which she conveyed secret messages to the Kaiser.

English princes serving in the German army were vilified in Britain and accused of treachery. Wilhelm's cousins, Charles Edward, Duke of Coburg, and Albert of Schleswig-Holstein, both of whom had been raised in England and whose families still resided there, were condemned as traitors by the British press and Members of Parliament. Questions were asked in the House of Commons as to why they had not been detained, since both had been visiting their families in England in the summer of 1914, and one newspaper went so far as to ask why, since Prince Albert was 'fighting in the field against Great Britain':

> "...was he not taken prisoner and interned at the concentration camp in Olympia or elsewhere? Is it not true that Prince Albert was a mischief-maker between the Imperial Court of Germany and the British Court during King Edward's reign?"[257]

Both allegations were blatantly untrue, for the Prince had always been a popular member of the British Royal Family and, when he returned to his Prussian regiment in August 1914, he specifically stated that he could not take up arms against his native land. The Kaiser accommodated his wishes and arranged for him to join the staff of the half-English General Loewenfeldr in charge of the Berlin defences. The Duke of Coburg was also disparaged in Britain, although he, too, had been so reluctant to fight against his native country that he asked to be posted instead to the Eastern Front.

The sudden hostility of his British relations was particularly difficult for Wilhelm to accept, for, like Queen Victoria, he mentally separated his role as a monarch from that of a member of the extended family. The day after war broke out he sent a message to King George via the departing British Ambassador in Berlin, telling him:

"...that he has been proud of the titles of British Admiral and British Field Marshal but that in consequence of what has now occurred he must divest himself of those titles."[258]

He was, nonetheless, deeply wounded to hear that he had been stripped of the Order of the Garter, which his grandmother had conferred on him, and that his crest had been removed from St. George's Chapel in Windsor. He was equally distraught that the British public, who had once welcomed and praised him, now despised him thanks largely to the efforts of the British Propaganda Bureau, established in September 1914 under the auspices of the Chancellor of the Exchequer, David Lloyd George.

So secretive was the Bureau that even many Members of Parliament were unaware of its existence, but, from its offices in Wellington House it worked tirelessly to create an entirely false impression of the Kaiser. Posters portrayed him as a vicious monster devouring the world, while encouraging his bestial troops to slaughter innocent women and babies. So disconcerting were the caricatures that, in December 1914, Wilhelm shortened his moustache to distance himself from the grotesque figure presented on the posters.

> "I wish," wrote a German émigré, who had often met him, "I could make [people] see William II not as that vulgar brutal caricature with which *Life* has poisoned the imagination, but as he really appears, man to man…The absurd caricature has done much to create that widespread feeling against the leader of the Fatherland…How much better everybody would understand the man…if all had heard his hearty laugh and had looked into those wonderful eyes!"[259]

Supported by the British Propaganda Bureau, countless books and pamphlets were published, criticising, distorting and mocking virtually every aspect of the Kaiser's life and personality. Repeatedly stories were told of his alleged cruel treatment of his widowed mother; and, the well-known affection between him and Queen Victoria was explained away by stating that he had had 'a mesmeric influence' over her, and had 'played his part so cunningly'[260] that the usually astute Queen was greatly misled!

> His artistic, musical, military and literary talents were mercilessly ridiculed and even his religious beliefs were used to portray him as a deluded warlord. It had been reported that he had once told a pastor that he often studied the Bible, which he kept on his bedside table, '…and I love to read it every night…I find the most beautiful thoughts expressed in it.' With greater cunning than that of which the Kaiser had been accused, one anonymous British author sought to reconcile the image of the devout Emperor with that of a ferocious megalomaniac by pointing out that Wilhelm read the Lutheran version of the Bible, which unlike that of 'our own glorious English Bible, which was translated by peaceful scholars', was 'the work of a fighter

and the grandest renderings it contains of the original are the warlike books of the Old Testament.'[261]

Most difficult of all to explain away was the belief, which had persisted right up to the declaration of war, that Wilhelm was essentially 'the peace-Kaiser', whose country had not been engaged in conflict throughout his twenty-six year reign, and whom Carnegie had recently described as 'the Apostle of Peace'. Again, with rather ludicrous machinations, the propaganda machine sought to dismiss this long-held view by stating that he, whom they simultaneously portrayed as a complete buffoon, had successfully hoodwinked the world for almost three decades, talking of peace while secretly plotting war. One author, who claimed to have been a lifelong friend of the Kaiser, wrote under a pseudonym that he met him during the July Crisis and was horrified to see him in his true colours for the first time. According to this 'friend', Wilhelm's face suddenly became distorted like Stevenson's *Dr Jeckyll and Mr Hyde,* as, in language worthy of a Shakespearean villain, he calmly explained that for decades he and his country had silently endured criticism and abuse from all sides but throughout all that time, despite his impassive appearance, he had been silently preparing his plan to dominate the whole of Europe and bring his enemies into subjugation.

"It has taken me twenty-five years," he is alleged to have said, "to have established on a solid basis the attempt I am going to make at present, but never for a single day have I forgotten the mission which lies before me...Every one of these insults and provocations has seared into my soul like a red hot iron. I have felt it eating into my rest, driving sleep from my eyes but I remained impassive because I knew that the hour of reckoning was at hand when [Tsar Nicholas and King George V] would crawl in the dust at my feet...and would have to recognise that Germany is the most powerful nation in the whole world and her Emperor the one potentate whom no one dared to thwart in any way."[262]

Considering that 'William the Sudden' was, throughout his reign, mocked for his impulsiveness and habit of speaking before thinking of the consequences of his words, it is remarkable that so many people willingly believed that such a man could remain silent in the face of insults for over a quarter of a century, patiently plotting his revenge!

Less dramatic writers concluded that the Kaiser had indeed originally wanted peace but he had been forced into war by a Pan-German[cc] military clique, which threatened to dethrone him unless he acquiesced to their wishes. Much was made of the Pan-Germanists' influence but, as one German apologist explained, 'had [the Kaiser] acted according to the desires of the Pan-Germanists, peace could scarcely have been preserved so long', and their views were in direct contrast to those of the Emperor whose twenty-five year reign gave proof of his 'steadfast desire to preserve peace.'[263]

Nonetheless, in Britain, the books continued to describe how the Kaiser had sent his spies into Britain in the years prior to the war, as he secretly plotted the country's downfall, vowing that he would never rest until his enemies were destroyed.

'The head of the assassin, William the Kaiser, should be hung from the highest tree in Potsdam as just retribution for cold-blooded murders,'[264] cried a British Member of Parliament, Admiral Charles Beresford; while the Earl of Halsbury described him as a 'dirty thief' who ought to be hanged.

[cc] Pan-Germanism was a political ideology which aimed to unite all German speaking peoples in Europe into one united 'Greater Germany'.

Several writers who had formerly extolled the progress of Germany, now turned their pens to vicious criticism of the enemy. In a remarkable about-turn, H.G. Wells, who had so recently described the Germans' many achievements, now joined a group of fellow-writers, including John Galsworthy, Thomas Hardy, Rudyard Kipling and Arthur Conan-Doyle, to decry the invasion of Belgium with horrific stories of atrocities committed by the invaders. The implication was that, unless the Germans were stopped, they would soon land in Britain and carry out similar horrors there. In May 1915, to inspire loathing and fear of the Germans, the Bureau arranged for the 'Report of the Committee on Alleged German Outrages in Belgium' to be published and translated into virtually every European language. The campaign was so successful that thousands of well-meaning and courageous young men enlisted in the army to protect their children and families from the supposed hordes of marauding Huns.

In truth, many terrible atrocities *were* committed by the German troops in Belgium but the difficulty for the majority of correspondents was that they were kept far behind the lines and, having no first-hand experiences of events, felt obliged to invent stories to fill the newspaper columns. These fabricated accounts formed such persistent myths that many are still believed to this day. A Canadian – or variously a French – soldier was said to have been crucified; babies were supposedly being bayonetted and beheaded; and Roman Catholic nuns had been violated in a convent near Ypres – although, in reality, the only Benedictine convent in the area was completely untouched, and the troops in the region at the time were predominantly Catholic Bavarians. Repeatedly, claims were made about drunken German soldiers raping innocent women and young girls and, even more barbarically, mutilating their bodies. According to one widely-publicised story, the intoxicated Huns cut off the breasts of a nurse, but little newspaper coverage was given to the fact that, shortly afterwards, a woman in Edinburgh was arrested and tried for inventing the tale and encouraging the press to publish it. While headlines cried out about the Germans' cruelty, there were very few reports of the Belgian Burgomaster of Solre-Sur-Sambre, who voluntarily came forward to denounce the stories of atrocities committed in the region; or of the German field hospital, attacked by Belgian civilians, who shot the wounded and dying soldiers as they lay in their beds.

The American Consul at Aix-La-Chapelle undertook a serious investigation into many of the alleged war crimes, and reported to the Secretary of State in Washington that, while there were occasional exceptions, German soldiers as a rule did not get drunk and there were strict penalties for those found drinking and those who supplied them with intoxicating liquors. He observed orderly German soldiers, speaking respectfully to the Belgians and paying for their purchases; and he noted that the reports of the desecration of French and Belgian churches were far from accurate. For the most part, he stated, churches were only attacked when their spires and towers were being used as vantage points from which civilians shot at the troops below. Moreover, he said, 'I have photographed German soldiers kneeling at prayer in these same churches, and witnessed the Kaiser participating in the services.'[265] Wilhelm himself appointed art historians and scholars to travel with the troops to record and protect works of art with the definite intention of returning them to their owners after the war. When, in November 1914, the American Consul was instructed by his superiors to abandon his investigations, he resigned in protest, realising that he was being gagged for revealing the truth.

Another American, the journalist, Irvin Cobb, was one of the few pressmen who actually travelled with the Kaiser's army and was able to gain more accurate information than that which was presented by many British war correspondents. Cobb found plenty of evidence to support the Consul's accounts, and, while he did not deny that atrocities took place, he discovered that they were committed neither by ordinary soldiers of their own volition nor on the orders of the High Command, but rather on the whim of a certain officers, who viciously ordered the shooting of innocent civilians and razing of whole villages to the ground. Consequently, Cobb concluded that neither the Kaiser nor his government had encouraged or even sanctioned such behaviour which was rather the result of the cruelty of individuals.

> "I saw," he wrote, "German soldiers marching through the ravished countryside, singing their German songs about the home place, the Christmas tree, the Rhine maiden – creatures so full of sentiment that they had no room in their souls for empathy. And by the same token, I saw German soldiers dividing their rations with the hungry Belgians. They divided their rations with those famished ones because it was not *verboten* – because there was no order to the contrary."[266]

On returning to the United States, Cobb and four fellow journalists signed a statement that:

> "...when travelling with or immediately behind the German columns upwards of a hundred miles through Belgian territory, we had been unable to discover evidence of a single one of these alleged atrocities."[267]

The General Manager of Associated Press refuted the popular belief that the Germans were cutting the hands of little children by drawing attention to the fact that such injuries would almost invariably be fatal and that, among the numerous Belgian refugees with whom he had spoken, he had not seen one who had been mutilated or had personally witnessed any such atrocities. Moreover, an

202

American doctor, Joseph Blake, working at the American hospital in Paris reported that after the retreat from the Aisne, the French wounded were found to have had their injuries dressed by German doctors, and were left with food supplies tucked into their belts to prevent them from starving before their countrymen arrived to take them to safety.

Such reports were rarely seen in Britain due to the success of the British Propaganda Bureau's strict censorship laws, which prevented any articles from being printed which contradicted the portrayal of the Germans as sadistic barbarians acting on the whims of a tyrannical Kaiser. It paid journalists, therefore, to write only the stories which the government wanted the people to read, and, when actual atrocities did take place, they were ready to ensure that every detail was described and exaggerated to extremes. Nonetheless, as it became better known that many of the tales were merely invention, the propagandists' twisted the situation to their own advantage by claiming that the Germans themselves had spread the exaggerated stories, knowing that they could be disproved and, as a result, few would believe the factual accounts of atrocities which had actually been committed.

One event which captured the British imagination and strengthened the belief in the heartlessness of the Kaiser's Germany, was the execution of the British nurse[dd], Edith Cavell, in October 1915. Since the beginning of the war, Miss Cavell had taken charge of the Red Cross Hospital in Brussels where she diligently tended British, Belgian, French and German casualties while secretly helping Allied soldiers *and spies* to escape to England. The Germans had long suspected her operation and gave her two warnings without taking any action until August 1915,

---

[dd] According to the German report, she was not a nurse but rather a manager of the Red Cross Hospital.

when a French collaborator informed the authorities of her clandestine undertaking and she was arrested along with three companions. For three weeks, Miss Cavell was held in solitary confinement as more evidence was gathered against her, until news of her arrest eventually reached her family, prompting an outcry in both Britain and the United States. Urgent messages were sent to Berlin demanding her release but the German authorities in Belgium insisted that she must stand trial on the charges of 'conducting soldiers to the enemy' and 'helping the hostile Power' in the time of war. During the secret hearing, Miss Cavell pleaded guilty, boldly asserting that she had assisted the British soldiers to escape because:

"If I had not done so they would have been shot. I thought I was only doing my duty in saving their lives."[268]

When Wilhelm heard that she had been sentenced to death by firing squad, he used his prerogative of mercy and ordered her immediate release, reminding the Governor of Belgium that he had already issued a statement that no woman could be shot without his express permission – permission which he most definitely had not given. Unfortunately, his message arrived in Brussels half-an-hour too late to save Miss Cavell, who was executed on 11th October 1915.

Later, Wilhelm claimed that the execution had been carried out on the orders of a drunken general, but he did not let the matter drop, for he ordered an immediate pardon for Edith's companions, Princess Marie de Croy, who had been sentenced to ten years' imprisonment; and the Comtesse de Belleville and Mademoiselle Thulier, both of whom had received a death sentence. He sent specific instructions, too, to the German Governor, Baron von Bissing, telling him that he must temper his summary justice with greater mercy.

The Kaiser's attempts to intervene were barely mentioned when the British and French press seized on the execution to further promote the idea that the Germans were merciless butchers led by a brutal Emperor with an insatiable lust for power. Presenting Miss Cavell as a pious and dutiful nurse who had merely been doing her duty, they succeeded in portraying her executioners as men who thought nothing of murdering innocent women – a useful argument in inspiring more young men to enrol in the army to protect their own families. A member of the Bureau of Propaganda, the writer G.K. Chesterton, used the episode to damn all Prussians and to denigrate anyone who dared to speak of making peace. Writing in the *Illustrated London News* he seemed almost to gloat in the execution, claiming that:

> "The thing was not done to protect the Prussian power. It was done to satisfy a Prussian appetite. The mad disproportion between the possible need of restraining their enemy and the frantic needlessness of killing her is simply the measure of the distance by which the distorted Prussian psychology has departed from the moral instincts of mankind...Wherever he goes, and whatever success he gains, he will always make it an occasion for sanguinary pantomimes of this kind. And awful as is the individual loss, it is well that now, at the very moment when men, wily or weak, are beginning to talk of conciliatory possibilities in this incurable criminal, he should himself have provided us with this appalling reply."[269]

While the case of Edith Cavell is widely known, little has been written of two German women, Margaret Schmidt and Otille Moss, who were charged with similar crimes and executed by the French in 1915. In February 1917, the Dutch dancer and courtesan, Mata Hari, was arrested in Paris, accused of spying for the Germans. She was kept in solitary confinement in a filthy cell before facing an unfair trial during which her defence lawyer was not permitted to cross-examine witnesses. Although there was little evidence against her and she denied all charges, she was found guilty of espionage and executed by a French firing squad on 15th October – almost two years to the day since the execution of Edith Cavell had caused such an outcry in the Allied countries.

> "In Germany," wrote a German clergyman, "none of these executions has been made the cause of slandering the people of those hostile countries. Miss Cavell and all the other women…died as heroines. And the German way is to honour and respect heroines."[270]

While the Germans' killing of innocent victims in Belgium is inexcusable, the much-publicised cruelty of the Kaisers' troops was no greater than that of the soldiers of the Entente. The atrocities committed by the British during the Boer War equalled, if not exceeded, those committed by the Germans in Belgium; and, at the time, Winston Churchill had written an article for the *Morning Post* stating that:

> "There is but one way in which the opposition of the Boers can be broken and that is by the most severe measures of repression – we must kill the parents in order that their children may have respect for us."[271]

Unsurprisingly, several leading figures sought to expose the injustice of the anti-German propaganda and recognised that its chief purpose was to inflame hatred. The British Labour Party leader, Ramsay Macdonald, strongly objected to the excessive use of the words 'cruelty' and 'atrocity' whenever the Germans' activities were reported. He did not deny that the Germans *had* committed some terrible crimes in Belgium, and expressed deepest sympathy for all that the civilians had suffered, but, he wrote:

"To use these things, which are inseparably connected with war, and which have been reported of every army operating in the field, as a means of stirring up hate and prolonging the conflict, is devilish and must be condemned by every right-thinking man."[272]

It was a view shared by a correspondent of the New York *Evening Post,* who condemned the 'infamous inventions' which had stirred up such 'blind fury' that innocent Germans in Britain and the United States became the target for the most horrendous reprisals.

Lord Roberts, the former Commander-in-Chief of the Forces, who had repeatedly warned against Germany's military expansion and the eventual inevitability of war, also objected to the continuous descriptions of the Germans as 'barbarous Huns', viewing the whole propaganda campaign as unchivalrous and hypocritical, and reminding his hearers that they should not forget:

"...our concentration camps and raids of fire in South Africa and what the world said about that. We have only to fight the Germans in such a way that, win or lose, when it is over, they respect us."[273]

Emily Hobhouse, who had written of her experiences of British atrocities in the Boer War, travelled through Belgium in 1915 and was surprised to discover that the reports of the country's devastation, which she had read in the British press, were wildly inaccurate and nothing she saw was comparable to what she had witnessed of British atrocities in South Africa.

In 1919, a report was published of the crimes committed by the British in Egypt, including numerous accounts of flagellation, the burning of homes, the stripping naked of prisoners, and, most shockingly of all, the gang-rape and killing of a ten-year-old girl, who was tortured in front of witnesses, who, 'through fear, did not dare to intercede.' According to the report, an autopsy of the dead girl 'qualifies this crime as one of abominable barbarism.'[274] Contrary to the Hague convention, hundreds of German prisoners-of-war were also shot by French and British troop on direct orders from their commanding officers; and, as one British soldier, who refused to be taken in by the 'propagandist poison', observed:

> "...it is safe to say that [the average British soldier] seldom oversteps the mark of barbaric propriety in France, save occasionally to kill prisoners he cannot be bothered to escort back to his lines."[275]

The Russians were equally guilty of plundering, raping and looting in Galicia and East Prussia, where it was alleged that many hundreds of civilians, including women and children, had been executed.

Clearly, Wilhelm's armies behaved no more inhumanely than those of their enemies but, for the most part, Britain controlled the news that was broadcast around the world. The single cable that linked Germany to the United States, was cut by the British as soon as war broke out, and, from then onwards, telegraph messages between the two countries had to pass through England where they could be monitored and censored. Moreover, at the Front, there were only twelve official correspondents of the Central Powers compared to seventy-five for the Allies, and as one German lady explained to an American visitor in 1916:

> "When you are prone to judge us harshly, remember we have had the English censor to deal with for two years...Add to this the fact that England controls the cable service of the world and shows an insatiable curiosity concerning other people's mail."[276]

It was a view shared by Arthur Moore, writing in the *New York American* four months after the outbreak of war, 'England has controlled the news of the world for more than a century. It has been her greatest diplomatic weapon.'[277]

Unlike King George, Tsar Nicholas and President Poincaré, the Kaiser was almost invariably held responsible for the atrocities of his troops.

"'How can people's minds invent such horrors," he gasped, "or think I would instigate or conceive them?'[278]

He was, however, well-acquainted with the power of the press to sway public opinion. He had known of Bismarck's successful campaign to the turn the Prussians against his mother; and he himself had often been the victim of biased journalists. He undoubtedly recalled the manner in which he had been vilified by the French press as his father lay dying; and in Germany he had been frequently attacked for his pro-British feelings. Soon after Queen Victoria's funeral, the Grand Duke of Baden made an impassioned speech, warning of the damage caused by the constant criticism of the Kaiser; and the 1908 *Daily Telegraph* 'interview' prompted a backlash from the German press which was as damaging to his reputation as the articles that were printed about him in England.

> "He was always being criticised by the German press, more than any other sovereign in the world. If it were known he liked a new opera or piece of art, it was mercilessly criticised as rubbish – he was always sneered at."[279]

More sinister than these personal attacks was the way in which certain newspaper proprietors appeared to be working to an agenda to create international tensions and deliberately stir up war. As early as 1895, Wilhelm had warned the Tsar about the dangers posed by scaremongering journalists; and in 1909, Lord Northcliffe, owner of the *Daily Mail,* printed a series of articles that were so extreme that a journalist for a rival paper, observed that Northcliffe 'had done more than any living man to bring about war.'

'Germany,' claimed the *Daily Mail* in 1909, 'is deliberately preparing to destroy the British Empire...The danger is very great and very near.'[280] Northcliffe made no attempt to disguise his purpose in such scaremongering, for he stated openly that he detested the Germans and would not allow anything to be published in his newspapers which might be 'agreeable to' them. His influence was not confined to Britain, since he was also the head of a syndicate which owned no fewer than eighteen American newspapers, each of which could be used to promote anti-German sentiments.

> "There is no such thing as an independent press in America," one renowned American journalist announced at a conference shortly before the war. "It is the duty of a New York journalist to lie, to distort, to revile, to toady at the feet of Mammon, and to sell his country for what amounts to his daily bread – his salary. We are the tools and vassals of the men behind the scenes. We are marionettes. These men pull the strings and we dance."[281]

In 1912, the neutral Belgian Ambassador observed that the British press was making every effort to prevent a peaceful solution to the Moroccan Crisis, preferring to whip up hatred and mistrust; and, the following year, the same Ambassador observed that, 'the English press of course, wishes to lay on Germany the responsibility for the new tensions which arise out of its projects.'[282] A year later, the celebrated playwright, George Bernard Shaw, noted that, from the time that the Kaiser had begun improvements to the Imperial Navy, 'the anti-German agitation [in British publications] became openly aggressive.'[283]

The German press was equally guilty of jingoistic rabble-rousing, particularly during the Boer War when King Albert of Saxony warned that the newspaper campaign against England was highly provocative and served no purpose other than spreading unnecessary discord. The erroneous press reports of a full German mobilisation in July 1914 undoubtedly played a part in hastening the conflict with Russia; and, as Sir Douglas Hague wrote, 'To make armies go on killing one another, it is necessary to invent lies about the enemy.'

Unsurprisingly, Wilhelm had little faith in the press, and he noted with consternation that some proprietors held enormous sway not only over the public but also over politicians. In 1916, he commented that Northcliffe had been instrumental in bringing down Asquith's government, and raising David Lloyd George to the position of Prime Minister, in return for which Lloyd George offered him a government position, which he declined in favour of becoming the Director of Propaganda – a formal title for the role which he had clearly been performing since 1909.

"Lloyd George is ruining England." Wilhelm wrote, "He is...the agent and spokesman of Lord Northcliffe, who is the real ruler of England today. Lloyd George...thinks he's a second Cromwell."

Interestingly, before the war, Asquith himself had warned the Kaiser that the German press was owned by one or two families whose connections extended across the globe and who had the power to sway public opinion even to the point of creating war. Their close connections to bankers and arms manufacturers, he observed, meant that they stood to make fortunes out of the carnage – a view shared by the American Congressman, Oscar Callaway, who vociferously opposed the United States' entry into the war[ee]. In 1917, Callaway accused the banker, J.P. Morgan, and a syndicate of steel and railway magnates, of gathering a group of twelve influential pressmen who would gradually take over one-hundred-and-seventy-nine American newspapers to ensure that the public would only read articles supporting policies which would best suit the financial interests of the syndicate.

[ee] See Chapter 21

It gradually dawned on Wilhelm that, since neither he nor the Tsar had wanted war, the entire conflict had been carefully engineered by 'internationalists' who wished to bring down the monarchies of Austria-Hungary, Germany and Russia, in order to create a 'world government' of socialists and financiers, whose agendas were cleverly concealed behind a façade of pacifism and philanthropy.

Chapter 19 – 'America is More Indebted to Germany than to Any Other Nation'

In his youth and early adulthood, the Kaiser had studied the United States' form of government and had found American culture so interesting that he frequently expressed a desire to tour the country. At the time of his accession, this enthusiasm endeared him to the American people and, four years later, he made an even more favourable impression by being the only European monarch to send a congratulatory telegram to the President for the Columbus Day celebrations.

Throughout the 1890s, however, developing economic rivalry between the two nations threatened their mutual goodwill. Wilhelm became increasingly irked by the President's adherence to the 'Monroe Doctrine' – a unilateral policy adopted by the American government in 1823, declaring that the United States would not interfere in European domestic or colonial affairs but, if the Europeans attempted to influence or colonise any part of the Americas, it would be viewed as act of aggression and could incur an armed response. Wilhelm was not alone in viewing the doctrine as primarily an agreement between the United States and Britain, for, as the American author and journalist, William Morton Fullerton, observed in 1916, that it was 'in reality an alliance with Great Britain for the defence of the common security of the United States.'[284]

During the 1880s and 1890s, the number of German settlers in Brazil, Argentina and Chile had rapidly increased, and, with the support of Berlin, they had established their own schools and churches, and even played a major role in the development of the Chilean army. To some American senators this appeared to be a clandestine form of colonisation, and when, in a desperate search for naval bases, the Germans looked towards Latin America and the Caribbean, the United States made a point of thwarting them at every turn. So frustrated were the Chiefs of the German Naval Staff that they drew up several hare-brained schemes to confront the United States' fleet, and a still more ambitious and totally impracticable plot to invade New York.

By the turn of the century, such fantasies had been abandoned and, in 1901, Wilhelm sent a message to the newly-elected President Roosevelt, assuring him that Germany had no plans to acquire territory in South America. To Roosevelt, this assurance sounded hollow, however, due to the presence of British and German warships, blockading several Venezuelan ports. As Wilhelm sought to impress upon the President, the purpose of the blockade was to compel the Venezuelans to settle their extensive European debts, but, since it was clear to Roosevelt that they lacked the resources to pay what was owed, he suspected that the Germans would demand territory in compensation. Citing the Monroe Doctrine, he warned that if the Europeans landed in Venezuela, the United States would view it as an act of aggression and declare war. The British immediately reneged on their pact with Germany and agreed to settle the dispute through arbitration, leaving the Germans no option but to adopt the same policy.

In the midst of these tensions, Wilhelm, desirous of maintaining co-operation, sent his brother, Henry, to tour the United States as a gesture of amity and goodwill. Thanks largely to Henry's natural charm and Wilhelm's understanding of American culture, the visit proved a great success.

> "The Kaiser," wrote a contemporary commentator, "had come to understand that the government of the United States is a government of the people, by the people and for the people, and that public opinion counts for everything in American diplomacy as in American legislation."[285]

214

He had, therefore, arranged for Henry to meet as many ordinary people as possible, and everywhere he travelled he was received with warmth and kindness.

The British, however, vying with the Germans for American friendship, watched the Prince's progress with consternation, and letters appeared in the press warning the United States not to be taken in by Henry's 'courtly platitudes'. Wilhelm responded good-humouredly, laughing that his brother's visit was causing 'a great toothache at the other side of the Channel.'[286]

Over the next decade, he continued to strengthen the bonds between Germany and the United States by arranging sporting events and international yachting competitions, and providing the solid gold Kaiser's Cup for the winner of a race between Sandy Hook in New Jersey and the Lizard Peninsular in England. He frequently invited American businessmen to participate in the Kiel Regatta, and when, a year after retiring from office, Roosevelt visited Berlin, the Kaiser 'overwhelmed him with kindness.' For a while he considered sending one of his sons to Harvard University and would have done so had the prince not married at an early age; and he personally provided a collection of Germanic casts for the university museum.

There was much, Wilhelm said, that the Germans could learn from the American people, 'above all, their optimism, their almost naïve enthusiasm and unquenchable energy'[287]; and, as German educational methods began to be adopted in the United States, he arranged an exchange of professors and students, making a particular point of attending the lectures given by the visitors. At a large gathering in New York, the President of Harvard University, Charles William Eliot, spoke of the benefits of this arrangement, stating that:

> "It is impossible to imagine or even describe what an immense intellectual gift this has been from

Germany to America...America is more indebted to Germany than to any other nation because the range of German research has been wider and deeper [and] the Teutonic peoples set a higher value on truth, speech and action than any other peoples."[288]

In April 1914, during the Mexican reprisals for the United States' seizure of Veracruz, hundreds of Americans fled to Tampico, anticipating the arrival of a battleship to take them to safety. Through some oversight, no American ship had been sent but, as the desperate refugees waited, an angry mob surrounded the hotel, threatening to lynch them. Hearing of their plight, Captain von Koehler of the German cruiser, *Dresden,* led his men into the city and ordered the crowds to disperse before rescuing the terrified Americans. His actions won the praise and gratitude of the American government, and those whom he had rescued sent a personal message to the Kaiser:

> "To your officers and men we owe our lives and pledge our lifetime gratitude. We salute you and the noble men of your Empire."[289]

At the outbreak of war, the majority of Americans saw no reason to become involve in a European conflict but opinion was divided as to which side they most favoured. In view of their common language and the idea of England as their motherland, the majority felt they owed a natural allegiance to the Allies, and the reports of atrocities committed by the German in Belgium added to the belief that the Central Powers were the aggressors.

Between 1829 and 1912, however, five-a-half-million German immigrants had settled in the United States, and although the number of émigrés had rapidly dwindled during Wilhelm's reign, families of German descent comprised approximately eight per cent of the American population. These German-Americans often retained an affinity to their forebears' homeland and, as areas known as 'Little Germany' developed in several major cities, many adapted German customs and traditions to their American lifestyle. Four-and-a-half million Irish émigrés had also settled in the United States, few of whom had any great liking for England; while Russian Jews who had fled famine and the Tsarist pogroms had little reason to want an Allied victory. Thousands of working people too, particularly in the Southern States, felt increasingly resentful of Britain when the naval blockade put an end to their exports to Germany, resulting in severe hardship and loss of earnings.

Trade between Germany and the United States had flourished throughout Wilhelm's reign, and, as previously stated, by 1914 it was estimated to be worth approximately $160 million per annum. In the twelve months prior to the outbreak of war, the Southern States had sold over two-and-a-half million bales of cotton to the Central Powers but, as their markets were cut off, they were compelled to sell their products to Britain at a vastly reduced rate. Manufacturers of agricultural implements were equally badly affected; and, since food stuffs and grain were added to the list of contraband items, it was claimed that 'starving out the Austrians and Germans will cost the farmers of the United States no less than $40,000,000 per year.'[290]

Throughout the July Crisis, the majority of American newspapers printed accurate accounts of events in Europe, and agreed that, while Russia and France appeared to be the most eager for war, 'Emperor William, called with picturesque inappropriateness 'the War-Lord of Europe' is trying to maintain harmony.'[291]

The editor and humourist, Irvin Cobb, observed that at that time, crowds of Americans attended the numerous peace demonstrations, but, once war broke out, these gatherings became pro-German, and 'Persons who hissed at our President behaved with respectful decorum when mention was made of a certain Kaiser.'[292]

217

Many of the Americans who had settled in Germany decided to return to the United States when war erupted, and, while – thanks to Northcliffe's propaganda – articles appeared in the press on both sides of the Atlantic, about the way in which they were treated by the Germans, the New York *World* published an article based on actual interviews with Americans returning home via Rotterdam. It stated that not one had a complaint to make but all were effusive in their praise of the treatment they had received and the welcome they had been given in the Kaiser's country.

When, in 1916, a German merchant submarine *Deutschland,* succeeded in passing through the blockade to carry a cargo of dyes to the United States, the crewmen were greeted with cheers when they docked in Norfolk, Virginia. The captain, Paul Koenig, stressed that his vessel was unarmed and his intention was to restore a mail link between the United States and Germany and to maintain the friendly relations between the two countries in the hope that 'freedom of the oceans and equal rights to all nations on the oceans will be guaranteed'[293].

Surprisingly, however, President Woodrow Wilson raised only a few feeble objections to the blockade, giving rise to the suspicion that his 'benevolent neutrality' was 'conveniently flexible' and strongly biased towards the Entente. In response to a personal telegram from the Kaiser, telling him that the blockade contravened the Hague Convention, Wilson replied curtly that 'the day for deciding the merits of your protest will come when the war is finished.' Simultaneously, in response to a letter from the French President, Wilson wrote effusively of their 'cordial and spontaneous friendship', and his 'warmest sympathy for the citizens of the great French Republic.' The suspicions of the insincerity of his neutrality mounted as he made no effort to prevent arms manufacturers from supplying munitions to the Allies, or bankers from forwarding loans to France, Russia and 'heroic little Serbia.'.

The arms being shipped to the Allies were unlike any produced in Europe, being made of steel rather than cast iron. 'These steel casings were a diabolical invention: they were ribbed and grooved, and when the shell exploded the casing burst into thousands of small pieces and came down with terrific force upon its victim.'[294]

In order to produce them, the American factories needed to be adapted but initially the banks refused the industrialists' requests for loans to make the necessary adjustment, for fear that there would not be sufficient demand to cover their investments. In order to overcome this, the Allies offered to purchase vast quantities of munitions, paying up front with credits deposited in American banks. Soon, as a result of this,

"...both large and small banks were treading on each other's heels in their anxiety to advance money on Allied contracts, and a munition industry was in being which had veritably shot up overnight."[295]

Within six months of the outbreak of war, one Connecticut factory received an order for twenty-five-million dollars' worth of cartridges, while another received an order for three million rifles and ten million horse shoes for the Allies. Horses, too, were shipped to France and Britain in their thousands, and the billions of dollars gained from exports to Europe almost quadrupled between 1915 and 1918, until the United States – which was viewed as debtor nation at the outbreak of war – was, by the time of the Armistice, a major international creditor.

"America values dollars more than she values German lives!" Wilhelm gasped in exasperation. "She thinks it right to shoot down my people!"[296]

It was an opinion shared by many Americans who condemned Wilson's 'fictitious neutrality', complaining that the sale of arms to one of the belligerents was a flagrant breach of the country's impartiality.

"Sordid profit for a comparatively few self-seeking and murderous industries," one American commentator wrote, "is deemed more important than the true statesmanlike policy of stopping the war by withholding the means for its continuance."[297] The same year, 1915, a fellow-American observed: "Before the war, the United States owed something like four thousand millions of dollars. By the end of the war she will have paid a good deal of that in munitions of war and provisions in corn and cotton, all sold at a very high price. In other words, the United States is paying her debt with great rapidity."[298]

In the autumn of 1914, Secretary of State, William Jennings Bryan, asked President Wilson whether he would have any objections to the banker, J.P. Morgan, forwarding a loan to France and Russia. Wilson replied that those who loaned money to belligerent nations were no different from those who enlisted in foreign armies as mercenaries, and both groups should be denied the protection of American citizenship. Section 5218 of the New York State Penal Code contained a clause stating that any citizen of the United States who assists a Prince, State, colony, district or people at war against a Prince, State, colony, district or people with whom the United States is not at war, 'shall be deemed guilty of high misdemeanour and shall be fined not more than $2000 and imprisoned for not more than three years.' Two months after refusing to authorise the loan, however, Wilson privately accepted that there was a distinction between loans and credit and, insisting that his name be kept out of any official record, secretly authorised Morgan to forward twelve million dollars to the Russians. The following year, the President gave his tacit agreement to a loan of fifty million dollars to the French; and Morgan was appointed the official purchasing and banking agent for the British, empowered to purchase weapons and other provisions of their behalf.

> "In consequence of the Canadian and American markets," Lloyd George told the House of Commons in June 1915, "I have asked Mr A.D. Thomas to go over and assist in developing that line of work...He will co-operate with Messrs. Morgan and Co, the accredited agents of the British Government."[299]

Throughout the remaining years of the war, Morgan formed a syndicate with fellow bankers which would float over five-hundred-million dollars to the Allies, and by 1918 his company was estimated to have loaned two-and-a-half billion dollars to the Entente, making huge profits in the process.

With so much profit to be made, there were many who suspected that certain industrialists and bankers were not only benefitting from the carnage but were even eager to prolong the war by bringing the United States into the conflict. As early as 1915, it was noted that the munitions factories, built specifically to supply arms to the Allies, were not temporary structures, as would have been the case had the war been expected to be of brief duration, but, as the *Wall Street Journal* reported:

> "They are building modern and permanent structures of brick or concrete and steel. If the war continues or is followed by others, the munitions makers would be in a position to reap enormous profits as a result of having the plants ready."[300]

To Wilhelm it seemed that, just as the British had used the invasion of Belgium as an excuse to participate in the conflict, so, too, would Wilson find an equally convenient opportunity to bring the United States into the war. That opportunity arose in 1917 with Germany's adoption of unrestricted submarine warfare.

Chapter 20 – 'Proof Against the Theory of Barbarity and Cruelty'

Despite the rapid expansion of the German Navy, Wilhelm knew that the Imperial Fleet could never compete with Britain's Royal Navy, and, not wanting to risk his beloved ships in what he thought would be a brief conflict, he was reluctant to allow them to engage in sea battles, keeping them largely confined to the harbours at Kiel and Wilhelmshaven. Due partly to his foresight, however, the navy had developed an effective fleet of submarines – U-boats – which sprang into action as early as August 1914, sinking several British warships.

Two months later, following the establishment of the 'starvation blockade', Admiral Tirpitz and his fellow commanders saw no alternative but to retaliate in kind by preventing supply ships from carrying goods to Britain. U-boat captains were ordered to stop and search British merchant vessels, and, after giving due warning to enable to crews to escape into lifeboats, to sink them with torpedoes. Initially, this was carried out in a genteel fashion, for, as one American commentator wrote:

> "The submarines…not only gave time to lower boats but frequently took them in tow and brought them to safety. When the German auxiliary cruisers took aboard the crews and passengers of vessels, they treated them with kindness and humanity. This is proof against the theory of barbarity and cruelty attaching itself to her maritime warfare."[301]

Britain's First Lord of the Admiralty, unhappy with this gentlemanly arrangement, which allowed for the loss of so many merchant ships, issued orders that the crews were not permitted to abandon their vessels, but rather should ram the flimsy submarines or – since much of the merchant fleet had been secretly armed – should open fire upon them. This policy made it impossible for the U-boat commanders to continue to assist the enemy crews without risking the lives of their own men, leaving them no alternative but to sink without warning any British ship that they encountered.

Churchill then issued another illegal order that the merchant marines should paint over the names of their vessels and fly the flags of neutral countries to avoid torpedo attacks. Moreover, he manned some of the merchant fleet with Royal Naval officers disguised as foreign fishermen or civilian sailors, so that, whenever a submarine surfaced, the seemingly innocent trading boat was instantly transformed into a lethal warship.

Due to this deceit, and contrary to his own wishes, in February 1915 the Kaiser was persuaded to sign an order declaring unrestricted submarine warfare, meaning that any vessel sailing in British waters, including the English Channel, would be deemed a legitimate target for the U-boat commanders. Wilhelm's reluctance to authorise this policy stemmed partly 'from feelings of humanity'[302], and partly from his fear that it would alienate neutral countries – particularly the United States.

As soon as unrestricted submarine warfare was declared, President Wilson sent a firm message to Berlin, warning that Germany would be held responsible for any damage caused to American vessels, but, despite continuing appeals from the Kaiser, he refused to take such a firm stand against the British starvation blockade. When the Kaiser complained of this to the United States Ambassador James Gerard, he simply replied that, 'it is not our business.'[303]

Within a month of Wilson's admonition, the German U-28 spotted a British merchant ship, *Falaba,* off the Irish coast. Surfacing, the U-boat captain, Forstner, gave three distinct warnings to the crew to evacuate, but these were ignored and, when a Royal Navy warship appeared on the scene, Forstner launched a torpedo. The

Falaba, which was reported to have been carrying thirteen tonnes of ammunition for the Allies, sank within twenty minutes, causing the deaths of over a hundred people including an American mining engineer, Leon Thresher.

Wilson protested strongly, accusing the Germans of piracy, but, while the Germans apologised for Thresher's death, they again questioned the President's neutrality, asking why he had failed to respond so vehemently when the Allies a seized the *Wilhelmina* and the *Dacia* – two German-American ships which had been transporting food and cotton to the Central Powers on the assurance that these products would not be used for the army.

Little over a month later, two British patrol vessels stopped an American tanker, the *Gulflight,* suspecting that it was transporting fuel for the Central Powers. In fact, the tanker was delivering vast quantities of petroleum and lubricating oil to the French, but the British insisted on escorting it into port for a full search. En route, they were confronted by a U-boat which ordered the ships to halt, but, when the patrol vessels attempted to ram the submarine, the German commander opened fire. As the *Gulflight* received a direct hit, the American crew abandoned ship, two of their members drowning in the process, and their captain dying of a heart attack shortly afterwards.

Again, the incident led to a strong diplomatic protest from the United States, which was met with another apology from Berlin, but, as the Kaiser privately commented, it was only to be expected that American ships would be sunk if they insisted on supplying the enemy with arms. 'Would they,' he asked, 'expect my armies to stop firing if they wandered through a battlefield? Then why do they send their ships through a war zone?'[304]

In Britain, meanwhile, Winston Churchill, like many of his colleagues, were desperately courting the Americans in the hope of persuading them to enter the conflict on the side of the Allies. Well-aware of the power of public opinion, Churchill openly stated that it would be beneficial to draw more neutral – meaning American – shipping into British waters in the hope that a torpedo attack would create such outrage that the United States would be propelled into the war[ff]. Since, however, the U-boat commanders avoided firing at American vessels, Churchill hoped in vain, but he commented that the effect would be same if American civilians should be killed aboard a British liner.

In April 1915, the luxurious British Cunard *Lusitania* prepared to depart from New York to Liverpool – a voyage which necessarily involved passing directly through U-boat patrolled waters. Foreseeing the dangers, and wondering why the United States' government had issued no warning to the passengers, the German Ambassador in Washington arranged for a notice to be printed in over fifty American newspapers:

> "Travellers intending to embark on the Atlantic voyage are reminded that a state of war exists between Germany and her allies and Great Britain and her allies; that the zone of war includes the waters adjacent to the British Isles; that, in accordance with formal notice given by the Imperial German Government, vessels flying the flag of Great Britain, or any of her allies, are liable to destruction in those waters and that travellers

---

[ff] Ironically, in 1936, Churchill gave an interview to the New York Inquirer in which he stated that America should have 'minded her own business and stayed out of the World War. If you hadn't entered the war, the Allies would have made peace with Germany in the spring of 1917. Had we made peace then, there would have been no collapse of Russia, followed by Communism, no breakdown in Italy, followed by Fascism, and Germany would not have signed the Versailles Treaty which has enthroned Nazism in Germany…If England had made peace early in 1917 it would have saved over one million British, French, American and other lives.' (Quoted in *Uncovering the Forces of War*)

sailing in the war zone on the ships of Great Britain or her allies do so at their own risk."

Few of the passengers reacted to the notice although several prominent figures received anonymous telegrams advising them to cancel their voyages, and, consequently when the *Lusitania* set sail on May 1st there were almost three thousand people on board. Few of the passengers were aware that the ship had been built with subsidies from the British government on condition that she could easily be converted into a gunboat in time of war; and fewer still would have known that, in 1912, *Lusitania* docked in Liverpool to be secretly fitted with armaments; or that emigrant German dockyard workers claimed to have witnessed munitions being loaded onto the ship before the departure from New York.

By chance or design, Colonel Edward House, a friend, advisor and, some would claim, puppet-master of Woodrow Wilson, had travelled to England on the *Lusitania* four months earlier, and was still in the country when the liner began her final voyage. On the evening of May 6th, as the ship neared the Irish Sea, House met with the British Foreign Secretary, Edward Grey to whom he confided that, if a passenger ship were sunk, the wave of indignation that would sweep America would almost certainly bring his country into the war. Even more ominously, later that evening, when House and Grey visited the King, George said, 'suppose they should sink the *Lusitania* with American passengers on board...'[305]

Early the following morning, the ship's captain, William Turner, received vague reports from the British Admiralty that U-boats were operating in the vicinity, but he was perplexed to realise that customary naval escort had not been provided. In fact, the battle cruiser, *Juno,* had been dispatched to protect the liner on the final stretch of the voyage but was inexplicably recalled to port, leaving the *Lusitania* completely unguarded. Moreover, Captain Turner received orders to reduce his speed rather than to adopt the usual practice of moving quickly to outrace submarines, and he did not engage in the typical zig-zag manoeuvres by which larger ships sought to dodge torpedoes.

In the early afternoon of May 7th, Captain Walter Schweiger of the German U-20 spotted the vessel within view of the Irish coast. Convinced that the number of lifeboats, the proximity to shore, and the time it would take for the liner to sink, would allow the passengers to escape to safety, he gave orders to launch a torpedo. Moments after the first strike, a second explosion was heard and – unlike *Titanic* which remained afloat for two hours after hitting the iceberg – *Lusitania* sank in approximately eighteen minutes. As soon as word of the disaster reached Queenstown, a Royal Navy vessel was dispatched to rescue survivors but, remarkably, it was suddenly recalled without completing its mission. Almost two thousand people lost their lives in the sinking, one-hundred-and-twenty of whom were American citizens.

When the Kaiser and his family were told of what had happened, they were aghast, one princess describing the attack as 'piratical and barbarous'; and when Schwieger eventually arrived home, he met a very cool and stony reception. Nonetheless, the British and American press reported that the Kaiser was rejoicing and Schwieger had received a hero's welcome in Berlin.

During the subsequent British inquiry, Captain Turner was severely criticised by the Admiralty, but, in the interests of national security, he was forbidden from explaining his own position or repeating any orders that he had received from the very men who now condemned him. The inquiry concluded that Schwieger had launched two – or even three – torpedoes, which, it was claimed accounted for the second explosion.

Back in Germany, Schwieger insisted that he had only fired one torpedo, and it was widely believed that the second explosion signified that the ship was secretly carrying munitions. Although various other theories have been put forward to explain the second explosion, it has been proved that – in contravention of American law – the passenger liner had a cargo of at least 4,200 cases of cartridges, barrels of gunpowder and 5,500 barrels of ammunition. In view of this fact, an American Admiral openly stated that, had he spotted a ship carrying weapons which would take American lives, he would not only have felt justified in firing the torpedo, but would have considered a failure to do so a dereliction of duty. Moreover, he said, since the ship had previously sailed under a false flag, and was listed as an auxiliary cruiser of the Royal Navy, Schwieger had every right and duty to sink it. Interestingly, too, in 1923, the descendants of Alfred Vanderbilt, who had died in the tragedy, put forward an insurance claim on his life, but their case was dismissed, as the American High Tribunal deemed that he had been killed by 'a *justifiable* act of war.'

The recalling of the escort, the failure of the American or British governments to warn the passengers of the risk their were taking, and the words of Churchill, Grey, House and the King all suggest that the *Lusitania* had been deliberately placed in harm's way to rouse the American people to support entry into the war. As an aside, the disaster served also to distract the British public from Churchill's disastrous Gallipoli Campaign[gg].

Barely had the news of the sinking reached London, when Colonel House told Wilson that, '[we] can no longer remain neutral spectators,' and predicted that within a

---

[gg] Churchill had developed an ambitious plan for the Allied troops to take over Constantinople via the Dardanelles, in order to force Turkey out of the war. Before even reaching Gallipoli, several British and French ships were sunk, and the first landing on April 25th proved equally disastrous as the Turks had anticipated the attack and had heavily armed troops guarding the beaches.

month the United States would be at war. House, however, misread the mood of the American public, for, despite their horror at the loss of over a hundred of their compatriots, the majority still saw little reason to engage in the European war. Wilson, therefore, wrote a moderate and restrained note of protest to Berlin, flattering the German sense of justice and their typically 'humane and enlightened' attitude, while urging them to abandon unrestricted submarine warfare.

In response to this, at the Kaiser's insistence, the Germans agreed to halt their 'shoot without warning' policy, but they also pointed out that they had been driven to such measures by the British practice of ramming the U-boats, arming merchant vessels and flying false flags. Moreover, they again reminded Wilson of the illegality of the British blockade and the devastating effect it could have on the civilian population, adding that, while the Central Powers were being starved, America was prolonging the war by supplying munitions to the Allies.

"If the *Lusitania* had been spared," wrote a member of the German High Command, "thousands of cases of munitions would have been sent to Germany's enemies and thereby thousands of German mothers and children robbed of breadwinners."[306]

This time Wilson responded more firmly, dismissing the Germans' claims as irrelevant, and writing in so provocative a tone that his Secretary of State, William Jennings Bryan, who had supported him through his presidential campaign but had frequently questioned his neutrality, handed in his resignation in protest. Bryan asked why Wilson objected so strongly to the Germans' assertion that the waters around Britain were a war zone when he had raised few protests when the British declared the same of the North Sea; and he wondered how Wilson could claim neutrality when he was aware that American arms manufacturers were supplying vast quantities of munitions to the Allies. He also asked why there had been no official public warnings about the dangers of travelling into U-boat patrolled waters; and was convinced that if the United States agreed to stop supplying the Allies with arms, the Germans would abandon their U-boat policy. Some days after his resignation, he made an impassioned speech to a crowd of thousands in Madison Square Gardens, where, according to an eye-witness, he:

> "...denounced bitterly those who insisted on crossing the ocean on belligerent munition-carrying steamers; he shouted that it is their recklessness which endangers the peace between Germany and America."[307]

Bryan was not alone in expressing these concerns. William Stone, the Chairman of the Senate Foreign Relations Committee, was similarly alarmed by Wilson's lack of neutrality, and stated that it would be monstrous for the United States to enter the war because of the 'foolhardiness of our people...recklessly risking their lives on armed belligerent ships.'[308] Senator Thomas Gore, who had also urged the President to warn of the dangers of travelling on armed vessels under foreign flags, claimed that Wilson had actually stated that war against Germany 'might not be an evil'; and Jennings' replacement, Robert Lansing was reputed to have said, "We must educate the public gradually – draw it along to the point where it will be willing to go into this war."

Three months after the sinking of the *Lusitania*, as the Germans had abandoned unrestricted submarine warfare and resumed their stop and search policy, the U27 halted a British steamer, the *Nicosian*, in the Irish Sea. As the steamer was found to be carrying a cargo of munitions bound for France, the U-boat commander allowed the crew to escape into lifeboats before preparing to sink the vessel. As this was happening, a disguised Royal Navy auxiliary cruiser, the *Baralong* approached, flying the American flag and signalling to the German commander that it had come to rescue the crew from the lifeboats. The commander acknowledged the signal and ceased fire at which point the *Baralong's* American flag was lowered and in its place the Royal Navy ensign was raised. Concealed gun ports suddenly opened, and, as the U-boat came under heavy fire, the crew leaped into the sea. Rather than assisting the drowning men, the captain of the *Baralong* ordered his officers to line up against the rails of the ship and fire at them in the water. The few who managed to escape onto the *Nicosian* were hunted down and shot dead, prompting the U-boat commander to leap back into the water. He swam towards the *Baralong,* but:

> "The English seamen on board the *Nicosian* immediately fired on him, although, in a manner visible to all, he raised his hands as a sign that he wished to surrender, and continued to fire after a shot had struck him in the mouth. Eventually he was killed by a shot in the neck."[309]

Following this episode, the captain of the *Baralong* wrote to the captain of the *Nicosian,* warning him to say nothing of what had happened and to advise any Americans who had witnessed the events to keep the matter secret. Nonetheless, several Americans spoke out, compiling reports to the both the State Department and to the President himself, who responded by complaining to the British of the misuse of the American flag. Since these actions contravened all the conventions of warfare, the German government immediately called for the captain and crew of the *Baralong* to be tried for murder. Notwithstanding the numerous witness statements from Americans as well as his own countrymen, Edward Grey dismissed the request, stating coldly that the British government did not believe the events had taken places as described and, even if the witnesses' accounts were true, the guilt of the crew of the *Baralong* was 'negligible

232

compared with the crimes which have been committed by German officers, both on land and at sea.'[310]

In view of this, several of Wilhelm's senior naval officers urged him to allow them to resume unrestricted submarine warfare, but, he firmly refused on the grounds that he could not risk the lives of more innocent women and children.

> "The Kaiser's most glaring fault," stated an exasperated German critic, "is that of trying to fight Great Britain with one foot in the grave of chivalry."[311]

Chapter 21 – 'The American People Do Not Desire It'

Although the sinking of the *Lusitania* did not lead to calls for a declaration of war, the tragedy, combined with reports of atrocities, had a seriously detrimental effect on the Americans' perception of Germany. The image of barbarous butchers, intent on world domination, was fostered by a sudden proliferation of propaganda in the form of books, pamphlets and newspaper articles warning of an imminent German invasion.

"About this time," wrote one German Naval Intelligence Officer, "…everybody in Germany was raging. Large packets of newspapers had been received from America, and there was not a word of truth in the reports that were being made about the military situation. We were particularly indignant at the numerous stories of 'atrocities' which had found their way into the American papers. With this kind of journalism it was inevitable that not only the mass of newspaper readers, but gradually also official circles in America, would assume an anti-German attitude."[312]

Regardless of the fact that the Kaiser's navy was safely ensconced in the harbours at Kiel and Wilhelmshaven, and that, in 1914, an American Admiral had stated that, even were the Germans to send their entire fleet across the Atlantic, the U.S. Navy was strong enough to prevent one single soldier from landing on American soil, some authors claimed that a single German battleship could land sufficient troops to take over the whole of New York.

While this scaremongering had a limited effect, a far more plausible cause for alarm was promoted by several propagandists who claimed that Americans of German descent were arming themselves to ferment revolution in preparation for a German take-over:

> "Germany…already has here an army that could not be carried across the ocean in twelve months if she employed every vessel in her navy and merchant fleet combined...These aliens have their officers; they have, or can secure, at a moment's notice weapons of precision of a uniform type and standardized ammunition."[313]

There was sufficient evidence to make this idea credible, as, in response to the sale of munitions to the Allies, a number of German-American and Austro-American cells had been formed with the backing of the Austrian and German governments to sabotage ships, factories and docks from which armaments were shipped to Europe. The most dramatic and widely-publicised event occurred in July 1915, when approximately one thousand tons of explosives bound for France and Britain were detonated on 'Black Tom Island' in New York Harbour with a loss of $20,000,000. Immediately, German saboteurs were accused of the crime although later suspects included anti-British Indian independence groups, and supporters of Irish Home Rule[hh].

As a result of these activities combined with anti-German propaganda, the public mood swung rapidly into support of the Allies. Further fictitious accounts of atrocities in Belgium appeared in the press, this time claiming that the Germans cut off the ears of children and fed tuberculosis germs to unsuspecting Americans. Much was made, too, of Germany's use of poisonous gasses but, while it was true that they had developed and employed the most horrific phosgene, they were not the first to make use

---

[hh] Two months earlier, following the Easter Rising in support of Irish Home Rule, fourteen leaders of the uprising had been executed, and, two weeks after the Black Tom explosion, a fifteenth, Roger Casement was hanged in Pentonville Prison.

of chemical weapons. The British had use gas during the capture of Colenso in the Boer War; and, in September 1914 – before the Germans adopted the practice – the French were using 'turpinite' in the trenches. That month, a British chemist, writing in the *Pall Mall Gazette,* explained that the death of a regiment of German soldiers, who were found bolt upright in their trenches with their hands still gripping their rifles, was due to an attack of the 'hell product', turpinite, which 'brings death to everything within its reach' by 'producing complete paralysis of certain organs in the body.'[314]

Evidence was also produced about the mistreatment of Allied prisoners-of-war, but a British socialist, Harold Picton, produced countless letters from Allied captives and reports from independent inspectors, asserting that the conditions were very good and the prisoners were generally treated with respect and even kindness[ii]. The chief complaint of the prisoners-of-war was the scarcity of food, but this was due to the Allied blockade rather than any deliberate harshness on the part of their captors.

> "The food question," wrote the American Ambassador in Berlin, "is of course a difficult one in a country where the whole population is put upon a bread ration. Most of the rumours current in England are without foundation or very exaggerated."[315]

When, however, the American Consul in Munich sought permission to make an inspection of the prisoner-of-war camps in Britain, he was actively discouraged from so doing by the American Ambassador to England.

[ii] A soldier of a Lancashire regiment, known personally to this author, was wounded and captured in France and taken to Germany as a prisoner-of-war. He repeatedly spoke of the kindness with which he was treated and stated that on three separate occasions during his captivity, the German doctors saved his life.

Nonetheless, the newspaper editors continued to produce articles condemning the Germans as barbaric. The editor of the New York *Herald* suggested that every 'Hessian' – meaning German – should be hung from a lamp post; while another wrote unashamedly that Germans were not fully human, but rather an inferior species driven by primitive instincts!

"Today," wrote a German immigrant, "the Americans with sincere enthusiasm look on England, France and Russia as the countries which stand for freedom in the world. The suggestion of the pro-Ally propaganda has completely extinguished the memory of all which the history of the last few centuries has taught."[316]

During his exile in Holland, as Wilhelm looked back on this time, he became convinced that Wilson was 'was resolved, probably from the start, certainly from 1915, to range...against Germany...under the influence of powerful financial groups.'[317] Evidence to support this surmisal can be found in an the writings of the French Foreign Minister, Gabriel Hanotaux, who stated that shortly before the Battle of the Marne in 1914, events were going so badly for the French that they were considering approaching Germany with an offer of peace.

"Three American Ambassadors then presented themselves to the government...and implored the government not to give up, promising that America would enter the war."[318]

In October the following year, with Wilson's permission, Colonel Edward House wrote to Sir Edward Grey, telling him that whenever he thought the time was propitious for American intervention in the war, he would propose it to the President. In the meantime, he said, he would meet with the British Government before travelling to Berlin with a concocted peace proposal to 'tell them it was the President's purpose to intervene and stop this destructive war.'

> "I would not let Berlin know, of course," he wrote, "of any understanding I had with the Allies but would rather lead them to think our proposal would be rejected by the Allies. This might lead Berlin to accept the proposal but, if they did not do so, it would nevertheless be the purpose to intervene."[319]

House added that this information was to be kept in the strictest confidence.

It was not the first time that House had attempted to dupe the Kaiser. Shortly before the outbreak of war he had tried to persuade him to disarm by playing on his fears of the Japanese. In order to combat the threat from the East, House claimed, the countries of Europe must stand together in a league of nations, and, in order to do so, it was necessary to overcome their differences, which could only be achieved if Germany reduced her military capability. Wilhelm was not deceived. He asked House whether the United States intended to disarm and 'render herself defenceless against Japan', and on receiving a negative reply, he asked how then Germany could be expected to do so when 'every nation in Europe has its bayonets pointed at Germany.'

> "The last thing we want is a war," he said. "We are getting to be a great rich commercial country…We don't want a war to interfere with our progress…But…we are ready."[320]

Shortly before the outbreak of war, House had written to Wilson that peace was dependent upon England and Germany reaching an understanding about naval armaments, but, he added, 'there is some disadvantage to us by these two getting too close.'[321]

By autumn 1915, House's intentions were becoming more obvious. He was driven by neither a simple desire to halt the U-boat campaign, nor even to bring an end to the war, because, as he wrote, it was 'impossible to maintain cordial relations with Germany [because] her system of government was different in its conception from ours.' From this time forwards, it gradually became apparent that both House and Wilson viewed their mission as a complete overhaul of Germany's internal affairs and ultimately the destruction of the Hohenzollern dynasty. Repeatedly, Wilson's speeches stressed that the United States had no argument with the German people, whom, he claimed, had been misled by their leaders.

In November 1916, Wilson was re-elected with a narrow majority, having campaigned on the slogan, 'he kept us out of the war and will continue to do so.' Even when, two months later, under intense pressure from his Chiefs of Staff, Wilhelm was finally reluctantly compelled to agree to the resumption of unrestricted submarine warfare, Wilson told Congress that the United States could not enter the conflict because 'the American people do not desire it'. In a dramatic speech in January 1917, he nonetheless emphasised the importance of the United States' intervention in the peace process, claiming that the belligerents would be unable to broker peace in a way that was satisfactory to all parties, and insisting that any agreements must be based on the principle that 'governments derive all their just powers from the consent of the people and that no right anywhere exists to hand people about from sovereignty to sovereignty as if they were property.'[322] While the address was hailed as a masterpiece by several New York newspapers, others were less impressed. The *Toronto Globe* observed that 'President Wilson had not aided the cause of peace by intervention at this stage'; while the *Boston Transcript* remarked scathingly that:

> "He seems to have been forced...to the solemn conclusion that he is not only the keeper of the

conscience of the world but also the exclusive if not the ordained moral spokesman of mankind."[323]

His critics observed, too, a certain incongruity between his professed pacifism and the arrangements he had made to enlarge the army through the National Defense Act of 1916, which resulted in greater expenditure on the armed forces than Germany had spent on the same in 1914. An even more obvious signal of his intention to lead the country to war was the effort he put into gaining support for the Armed Ship Bill, which, due to the resumption of unrestricted submarine warfare, would allocate a million dollars to arm and man merchant vessels against German submarines.

It was with immense reluctance that Wilhelm had been obliged to agree to the resumption of unrestricted submarine warfare, and the decision was met with a storm of protests from the United States. Wilson accused the Germans of breaking the promise they had made nine months earlier, in May 1916, while Secretary of State Robert Lansing claimed that this perfidious action was sufficient reason for the United States to enter the war.

As one American commentator pointed out, however, the Germans had not reneged on a promise, since the note to the President in which they agreed to respect neutral shipping and to give due warning before firing torpedoes, also urged the United States government to bring the same pressure to bear on England regarding the starvation blockade and the Royal Navy's impounding of neutral vessels bound for the Central Powers. If this were not done, the Foreign Minister, Jagow, concluded, the German Government would retain the right to alter the decision.

The Germans waited nine months for a reply from the United States but none was forthcoming, and, as the British blockade continued unimpeded, the Imperial Admiralty warned the Kaiser that, unless he agreed to lift the restrictions on his submarine fleet, there was a very real danger that Germany would lose the war.

On the same day as Wilson urged Congress to accept the Armed Ships Bill, the press printed a copy of the Zimmerman telegram – a coded note from Germany's Foreign Secretary, Arthur Zimmerman, to the German Ambassador in Mexico. Zimmerman instructed the Ambassador to approach the Mexican President with a view to forming a military alliance *if America should enter the war*. Although the note was never delivered, and the proposed alliance would only come into effect if the United States took up arms against Germany, the telegram was cited as evidence of the Kaiser's plans to make war on America and the consequent need for greater expenditure on armaments.

Congress, however, was largely unmoved by this argument, and again several senators questioned Wilson's impartiality.

> "Why," asked Senator George Norris, "have we kept our ships out of the North Sea? Simply because it is altogether more dangerous to go through a mine field than it is to go through a submarine field. Mining the high seas is incomparably more inhumane and ruthless than warfare by means of submarines."[324]

Other senators suggested that the President's plan was merely a method of entering the conflict without a declaration of war.

When the Armed Ship Bill was defeated, Wilson was not prepared to abide by his statement that rulers must govern by the consent of the people, for he used his prerogative as Commander-in-Chief to overrule Congress and force it into law. The press immediately condemned as traitors those senators who had opposed the Bill, prompting Senator La Follette from Wisconsin to argue that he had always believed that members of Congress voted according

241

to their conscience and the will of the people but now, 'another doctrine has been promulgated by certain newspapers, which unfortunately seems to have found considerable support elsewhere, and that is the doctrine of "standing back of the President" without inquiring whether the President is right or wrong.'[325]

On 2nd April – less than six weeks after stating that the American people did not wish to enter the conflict – although there had been no escalation of U-boat activity nor any specific atrocity committed by Germany, Wilson again approached Congress, this time asking for a declaration of war. The request was met by vociferous opposition, one senator producing fifteen thousand letters and telegrams from forty states, all of which expressed a desire to remain neutral.

Nonetheless, on 6th April 1917, Wilson declared war on Germany, conveniently forgetting that only the previous year he had stated that:

> "This war was brought on by rulers, not by the people, and I thank God there is no man in America who has the authority to bring on war without the consent of the people."[326]

"All my efforts to show my friendship for America...all for nothing!" gasped the Kaiser; while an American commentator questioned what could possibly have changed between Wilson's initial statement and his dramatic about-turn just a few weeks later. To the commentator, as to the Kaiser, it seemed that, despite his campaign slogan and his frequent reiterations of his desire for peace, the President had, for over two years, been planning to participate in the conflict.

Perhaps it is significant that the United States' entry into the conflict came within three weeks of the Russian Revolution and the enforced abdication of the Tsar. When calling Congress to support his declaration, Wilson expressed delight at the upheavals in Russia, stating that 'the wonderful and heartening things that have been happening' there, had 'added to our hope for future peace of the world.'

Russia, he somewhat bizarrely claimed, had always been democratic at heart, and:

> "The autocracy…long as it had stood and terrible as was the reality of its power, was not in fact Russian in character, origin, or purpose; and now it has been shaken off the great, generous Russian people have been added in all the naïve majesty and might to the forces that are fighting for freedom in the world, for justice and for peace."[327]

This was not how the Kaiser viewed the overthrow of the Tsar, for despite the fact that he and Nicholas were officially enemies, he expressed nothing but sorrow for the fate which had befallen his former friend. On hearing that his cousin, George V, had offered the Tsar safe haven in England, Wilhelm ordered his brother, Henry, to allow free passage through the Baltic to any ship flying the Tsar's ensign, and he secretly arranged for a train to be made available to carry the Imperial Family safely through Germany.

Wilson, however, made it clear that he viewed Nicholas' downfall as a precursor to that of the Kaiser, and, while urging the governments of the world to accept the Monroe Doctrine of non-interference in the domestic affairs of other nations, he insisted that this was no longer a war about international disputes, but rather one which must bring about the termination of the Hohenzollern monarchy. Where once he had argued for 'Peace without victory', he now spoke of the United States' war aims as 'making the world safe for democracy', and, stressing that the Americans were true friends of the German people, he repeatedly stated that the Kaiser had led them into war without their consent:

"It was a war determined upon as wars used to be determined upon in the old, unhappy days when peoples were nowhere consulted by their rulers and wars were provoked and waged in the interest of dynasties or of little groups of ambitious men who were accustomed to use their fellow men as pawns and tools."

The irony of his statement was not lost on many Americans, who observed that Wilson had been re-elected on the promise of keeping America out of the war, but this attack on the dynasty was one to which he would return over subsequent months as pamphleteers, journalists and authors went to great lengths to describe the Hohenzollerns as the cause of virtually every conflict that had taken place in Europe for the past two hundred years. Psychologists wrote books about the Kaiser's supposed mental illness, attributing to him excessive egocentricity, religious mania and a variety of bizarre phobias, concluding that, 'the Kaiser and the House of Hohenzollern, and all they stand for have become Civilization's World-Problem.'[328]

In 1917, the influential American journalist, Carol Ackerman, promoted the idea of the necessity of overthrowing the Kaiser in his book, '*Germany the Next Republic*', in which he claimed that as long as the Kaiser remained in power the world would continue to face 'the same terrorism that it has had to bear during the war.' To emphasise this point, Ackerman falsely claimed that the Kaiser had defied his own Foreign Office in encouraging Tirpitz to engage in unrestricted submarine warfare, and had overseen the sinking of the *Lusitania* in order to terrorise neutral shipping. Why, Ackerman asked, could the German people not think for themselves rather than heeding the Kaiser, whom he accused of 'juggling his people's nerves', but, he patronisingly added, 'people are *beginning* to think.'

"American intervention can put a stop to the Kaiser's juggling with people's minds," he concluded. "…Only a big military defeat will shake the confidence of the Germans in the Kaiser."[329]

Clearly, Ackerman, viewed the primary purpose of the United States' entry into the war as the overthrow of the Kaiser.

In various newspapers, Wilhelm was described as 'the beast of Berlin', 'the incarnation of brutality' and 'the most dastardly foe of culture and civilization'; and even those who conceded that he had never wanted war, condemned him quite simply for being a descendent of Frederick the Great, who, despite having been one of the most enlightened sovereigns of his era, was described as 'having done great evil'.

'The Kaiser forced this war on the world,' wrote a Professor of History at Colombia University in 1917, adding that he – not the British blockade – was responsible for bringing his country to the point of starvation.

"What will happen," he asked, "when the day of disillusionment comes to the German people, when they realise that this war was not thrust upon them by wicked enemies but that their Kaiser and his military ring engaged in it for selfish and dynastic ends?...Sooner or later they will rise against the Hohenzollern Dynasty which has…seduced them into a terrible war…and brought them to the brink of ruin."[330]

By holding the Kaiser personally responsible for the war, his opponents gained an excuse to press for his ousting from the throne. The idea was rapidly echoed in Britain, where David Lloyd George spoke of the greatness of the German people who had been duped by the King of Prussia; and on 4th April 1917, one Member of Parliament told the House of Commons that:

"...we realise just as much as the American people do, that there is a profound difference between the Kaiser and the Hohenzollerns and the people of Germany, and that so long as they are there we have no security that the people of Germany will revert to the position of good friends and neighbours that they were before this outburst of insanity came upon the nation."[331]

In 1918, Winston Churchill wrote even more bluntly that, since Germany sought 'world domination', the Allies would never negotiate but would accept only a complete German surrender, for 'there can be no arrangement, no agreement, no parley or confidence in these modern scions of darkness – the Hohenzollerns' and 'a victory for the Allies must mean a democratic Germany.'[332]

The notion of the Kaiser having compelled his reluctant people to engage in the war was a wild distortion of the truth by any reckoning. Apart from the fact that Wilhelm had done everything possible to maintain peace, once the country was embroiled in the conflict, the people 'stood as one' behind him.

"Even the wildest enemy of Germany," one commentator wrote, "be he in a belligerent or neutral country, knows that the Emperor and nation were of one will in the hour of crisis."[333]

An English lady in Berlin also observed on 9th August 1914 that:

"The Kaiser is the most adored man at the moment...Certainly he has the whole nation behind him this time and, if he has been criticised in the past, this war cry is making him the most popular man in Germany."[334]

In 1914, young men in virtually all the belligerent nations had returned to their regiments or flocked to recruitment offices in a state of near euphoria, eager to play their part in what they saw as a righteous war. In the twelve months from April 1917 – when the United States entered the conflict – only one-hundred-and-thirty-three-thousand volunteers came forward from eleven American states. Clearly, the American people were far more reluctant to follow their leaders into an unnecessary conflict, than were the German people who were pressing their Kaiser to lead the country into war.

The loyalty felt towards the Kaiser sprang not only from Germany's economic prosperity, but also from the fact that he embodied the unity of the country. 'The German nation has found itself again,' wrote one German émigré, 'and its oneness of mind is symbolised by the Kaiser.'[335]

The sudden emphasis on the distinction between the Kaiser and his people, and laying the blame on him for the war was clearly an attempt to stir up revolution and to ensure that, once the conflict was over, Germany would no longer be a monarchy. Ironically, if there were a distinction between Wilhelm and his subjects, it was summed up by the Italian author and historian, Guglielmo Ferrero, in the American *Atlantic Magazine* in November 1914. Ferrero had met a German intellectual who told him:

"There is only one pacifist in Germany. It is Wilhelm II. But he can do nothing because he is the Emperor."[336]

Chapter 22 – 'They Are Afraid of the Kaiser's Kind Heart'

The charges of cruelty which were levelled against the Kaiser in 1917 were all the more unjust and devastating as they came at a time when his own Generals and Chiefs of Staff had become so exasperated by his opposition to some of their more drastic measures that they had virtually stripped him of all authority. Angered by his refusal to sanction the dropping of gas bombs on London, they mocked him remorselessly for his concern for the welfare of civilians, prisoners-of-war and the families of enemy soldiers who were reported as missing; and when his eyes filled with tears on witnessing the extent of the suffering around Verdun, they accused him of weakness.

The propagandists' portrayal of a merciless warlord was greatly at odds with Wilhelm's actual behaviour in the midst of the conflict, for those who knew him well observed how sickened he was by the carnage and the numerous attempts that he made to 'avoid any unnecessary cruelty'. Since the outbreak of hostilities he had aged visibly and, after visiting Verdun, he was so distressed by the extent of the suffering that he was physically ill for several weeks afterwards. Moreover, on a personal level, he repeatedly demonstrated humanity and kindness, as when, for example, a British prisoner-of-war wrote to him requesting leave to return home to visit his dying mother. Wilhelm granted him two weeks' absence on the understanding that as a gentleman he would give his word to return. Surprisingly, perhaps, the officer duly kept his word but when similar requests were made to the Allied leaders by German prisoners-of-war they were either rejected or ignored.

Wilhelm also withstood the jibes of his Generals and Chiefs of Staff in his efforts to assist an Englishwoman

248

who had written to ask his help in finding her nephews who were reported missing in action.

"...A peal of scornful laughter rose from the other guests at table," wrote Princess Evelyn Blucher. "A German Kaiser they said had work to do other than search for missing English officers. The Kaiser remained silent but, on rising from the table, asked Prince Munster to try and get some news for Lady O."[337]

He continued, too, to try to maintain his relationship with his family in Britain and Russia, sending greetings to an English aunt on her Golden Wedding Anniversary, and forwarding his condolences when, soon afterwards, her husband died. When the four-year-old son of his cousin, Queen Marie of Romania, died, the Chief of Staff suggested using the funeral to Germany's advantage by sending in bombers to strike while the entire Royal Family and members of the government were gathered together. Furious at such heartless suggestion, the Kaiser issued an immediate order that there were to be no attacks in the area until the family had been allowed a decent period of mourning. He was equally concerned for the welfare of his Russian cousins, and was horrified to discover that Cousin George had rescinded his offer of a safe-haven in England for the Imperial Family, on the grounds that the Tsarina, was half-German and 'a Bosch by birth and in sentiment'. Wilhelm, therefore, sent a message via neutral Sweden assuring Nicholas that he and his family would be given a home in Germany, but in view of the political situation, Nicholas declined the offer, leaving Wilhelm to sigh sincerely:

"I have done everything humanly possible for the unhappy Tsar and his family."

Concerned, too, for the welfare of his own people, he sought to raise their morale when news from the Front was distressing, by making a point of walking in the street and lighting a cigarette to show that his hand was not shaking. As he travelled the country, reviewing troops and handing out medals, the British press repeatedly reported that he had fled Berlin in terror and was drifting through his Empire 'like a doomed and restless spirit.' An independent American observer, however, having recently arrived in Germany from London, discovered a very different Kaiser from the one he had expected to see. The news of German reverses, he realised, was disheartening the people, and therefore Wilhelm had embarked on a series of tours to raise morale.

"He was, in actual fact, displaying complete calm, not a little personal courage and producing a vast amount of enthusiasm wherever he went."[338]

A Swedish observer, Sven Hedin, who met him during the war, was filled with admiration for his commitment to his people.

"The German cause," he wrote, "can have no representative than the Kaiser and he seems to have been born for this crisis; for now he feels he has done all in his power to preserve peace, he feels responsible for the development of the destiny of Germany, and with this aim in sight, he consecrates to this cause every sentiment, every thought, every act."[339]

Wilhelm well understood the anguish of parents whose sons had been wounded or killed in battle, for, just two months after the outbreak of war, his nephew, nineteen-year-old Prince Maximilian of Hesse-Kassel, received a fatal shot to the stomach during the attack on Mont de Cats in Flanders. The distress of Maximilian's family was made all the greater when the Belgian priest who buried him refused to reveal the whereabouts of his grave.[ii] Two years later, Maximilian's brother, Friedrich,

---

[ii] Even after the war, despite the intervention of the Pope, the priest and

was also killed in action, having his throat slit by a bayonet in Romania.

Even closer to home Wilhelm worried constantly for the safety of his own sons, all of whom were serving in various capacities, and two of whom were injured in battle in 1914. His favourite son, Eitel-Friedrich, was wounded at Baupaume; and his fifth son, Oskar, who had earned the Iron Cross for bravery, collapsed following an assault in the area of Verdun, suffering from shell-shock.

Rather than hardening him, Wilhelm's anxieties made him more empathetic to the concerns of other parents, but the greater his compassion, the more his Generals sought to side-line him from operations and to keep from him information about plans to which he might object. In April 1916, Princess Blucher recorded that he was:

> "...kept practically under supervision by men like Falkenhayn, who never allows anyone to speak to him alone...They are afraid of the Kaiser's kind heart."[340]

In the late summer of 1916, the Germans' failure to capture Verdun created such a sense of disappointment and anger that it was deemed necessary to completely overhaul the High Command. The obvious choice of replacement for Falkenhayn was a sixty-eight-year-old veteran of the Franco-Prussian War, Paul von Hindenburg, who had returned to service in 1914, taking over command of the Eighth Army and gaining considerable success on the Eastern Front in the Battle of Tannenberg. His victories made him so popular that statues of him appeared across the country and wherever he travelled he was hailed as a conquering hero. Those closest to him realised, however, that the real power behind his success was his deputy, Erich

---

local people refused to return Maximilian's body to his family and it was not until their received a direct appeal from Britain's King George V that they finally allowed him to be reinterred in Hesse-Kassel in 1926.

Ludendorff – a calculating, humourless and highly-strung man who, for all his brilliance as a tactician, had little grasp of the conditions endured by the ordinary soldiers. Wilhelm had been reluctant to appoint the two to a position of power but there appeared to be no one better suited to inspire the army and develop and effective strategies. Within a short time of their appointment, Ludendorff had turned the country into a virtual military dictatorship in which the Kaiser's role was reduced still further to that of a mere figurehead. Such was their authority that 'they made a point of contradicting every order or command that [Wilhelm] gave; [and] he was turned out of the room at Headquarters whenever the telephone rang, so as not to hear the commands and real facts.'[341] When Prince Blucher met him in 1917, he observed that Wilhelm appeared so 'helpless and alone' and, two months later, Blucher's wife commented that he was 'growing more into the shadow of a king and people talk openly of his abdication as though it is very much desired.'[342]

Ludendorff was not prepared to accept the Kaiser's original war aims, for he believed that so much blood had been spilt that Germany deserved territorial compensation for her losses. He developed plans to annex Belgium, parts of Northern France and Poland, while keeping Wilhelm largely in the dark about his schemes to which he was certainly opposed. Unable to restrain his Chiefs of Staff, the Kaiser was forced to retire into the shadows while they took over the government of the country as well as deciding the course of the war. Had he been included in their decisions, he might well have succeeded not only in improving Germany's military operations but also in bringing a swifter end to the conflict. His eldest son, with whom he rarely saw eye-to-eye, recorded that:

> "In the war his personal modesty led to an almost complete exclusion of his own person from the military and organization methods and commands

252

of his Chiefs of Staff. Those of us who had an inside insight into the business of leading military posts could not but regret this fact as we had unreservedly admired the sound judgement and military perception of the Kaiser even in operations on a grand scale."[343]

More impressively, Wilhelm repeatedly sought a means of bringing an end to the slaughter and returning Europe to the *status quo ante bellum*. This idea had already been mooted by the Pope, and in November 1916 – while the Kaiser was drawing up a peace offer – the British Lord Landsdowne circulated a letter to the same end but his suggestion was met with intense criticism from the British cabinet.

That autumn, following successes in Romania, Germany was in a superior position to that of the Allies, who, according to Lloyd George, were 'at their lowest ebb'. There could be no better opportunity, Wilhelm believed, to negotiate a fair peace, even though at that time, there was every prospect of a complete German victory.

"What is wanted," he told Bethmann, "is a moral deed to free the world…from the pressure which weighs on all. For such a deed it is necessary to find a ruler who has a conscience, who feels that he is responsible to God, who has a heart for his own people and those of his enemies, who…possesses the will to free the world from its sufferings. I have the courage. Trusting God, I will dare to take this step."[344]

The following month, Bethmann duly summoned the Reichstag and, in a widely-reported speech, announced that the Kaiser's overriding desire was to restore Germany to peace due to his 'deep moral and religious sense of duty towards humanity and towards the nation.'

Among the offers contained in the note, was the assurance that Belgian independence would be restored and

253

Germany would give financial assistance for the country's economic rehabilitation. Although Hindenburg insisted on inflating the demands and filling the note with arrogant assertions, Wilhelm expressed a willingness to negotiate terms. The message was issued to the Allies and to the Pope, informing them that, although Germany had the resources and ability to continue fighting to victory, 'to avoid further bloodshed and make an end to the atrocities of war [the Central Powers] propose to enter forthwith into peace negotiations.'[345]

Without having seen the proposals, the French Prime Minister, Aristide Briand, dismissed the offer as nothing but 'a ruse, an attempt to weaken the bonds of our alliances'; while a member of the British Cabinet suggested that it was merely a pretence to give Germany 'breathing space that will furnish her with the opportunity to lay fresh plans of aggression.'[346] Another member of the British War Cabinet, Lord Curzon, went to great pains to explain to the House of Lords that the Kaiser only wanted peace to safeguard German interests – which, ironically, was an accurate description of why Wilhelm did not want war in the first place. A few insightful politicians suggested that the proposals should at least be considered, for, as Lord Courtney told the House of Lords, 'you want peace. The German Chancellor wants peace...I hope the answer to the German Government will not shut the door against further explanations.' In December, however, the British Prime Minster, Asquith, was forced to resign, and his successor, David Lloyd George stated that Britain would continue fighting until Germany was defeated. The Russians were equally unimpressed, insisting that the Allies were determined to 'continue the war to a successful end to prevent Germany from establishing her hegemony'.

Ultimately, the Entente powers stated that peace was impossible until Germany agreed to make reparations to France and Belgium, and to disarm by bringing about:

254

"...a settlement calculated to end, once and for all, forces which have contributed a perpetual menace to the nations and to afford the only effective guarantees for the future security of the world."[347]

Rather than agreeing to negotiation, therefore, the Allies refused to cease hostilities until Germany behaved like a conquered nation.

While these proposals were being discussed, President Wilson asked each of the belligerents to state their war objectives. This was not, as has often been suggested, a peace note, nor was it an offer of mediation. Wilson himself explained that he was 'merely proposing that soundings be taken in order that we...may learn how near the haven of peace may be.'[348]

Although Wilson's offer made no mention of the Kaiser's proposals, Wilhelm responded graciously, stating that the President 'has the greatest opportunity every presented to man to make his name immortal – by bringing about peace.'[349]

The Austrians were cautious in their response, as Tisza wrote to Czernin, 'a one-sided announcement of the war aims would simply afford the leader of the belligerent enemy group the opportunity of undoing everything', but he drew attention, too, to the fact that the neutral countries might well speak up for the Central Powers, since:

"All the European neutrals feel that they are more seriously threatened by England than by us. The events in Greece, Romania, etc., as well as England's commercial tyranny, act in our favour, and the difference of our attitude to the peace plans as compared with that of the Entente...will secure neutral sympathy for our group of Powers."[350]

Nothing came of Wilson's proposals; instead, he led his people to war.

Although the Vatican had sent no response to Wilhelm's peace note, the following summer, Pope

Benedict XV sent an envoy, Cardinal Pacelli[kk], to meet him and the Chancellor. The Pope had made numerous appeals for peace and, like Wilhelm, suggested a return to the *status quo ante bellum*. Following the United States' entry into the war, he had become increasingly concerned by Wilson's suggestion that Austria-Hungary – 'the Apostolic Kingdom', which had strong ties to the Vatican – should be dismantled in favour of independence for the different cultures and ethnic groups within the Empire. While Pacelli stressed that the Vatican must remain neutral, Wilhelm warned that, unless the war were brought to a speedy conclusion, 'there was the danger of peace being forced onto the world by Socialists, which would mean the end of the power of the Pope and the Roman Church, even among Catholics!'[351]

At the conclusion of their meeting, Pacelli assured him that he would convey his feelings to the Pope, and within a few weeks Benedict had issued a peace note to all the belligerent nations. Calling for disarmament, freedom of the seas, and the restitution of occupied territories, he also suggested that each side should pay for its own reconstruction – a view which differed from the demands of the Allies, who believed that Germany should pay reparations to both France and Belgium. As early as 1915, however, the Allies had secretly agreed to reject any suggestions put forward by the Vatican, and refused to even consider the Pope's proposals. Colonel House replied to the Vatican on behalf of a somewhat indignant Wilson, who had originally intended to ignore the note altogether. No agreement, he said, could be reached until the German government – and, by implication, the Kaiser – were overthrown, since the object of the war was to 'deliver the free peoples of the world from the menace and the actual power of a vast military establishment controlled by an

---

[kk] The future Pope Pius XII

irresponsible government' which had secretly 'planned to dominate the world.' He concluded that 'we cannot take the word of the present rulers of Germany as a guaranty of anything that is to endure'.

In little more than a year, the planned destruction of the Hohenzollern dynasty would reach fulfilment.

Chapter 23 – 'That I Should Most Faithfully Serve Germany'

In April 1917, the exiled Bolshevik, Vladimir Lenin, returned from Switzerland to St Petersburg, intent on fomenting a second revolution. Unbeknown to the Kaiser, Hindenburg and Ludendorff had secretly assisted his passage through Germany by providing him with funds and a guarded train, in the hope that he would take Russia out of the war, thereby freeing the Germans to concentrate all their attention on the Western Front. When Wilhelm eventually discovered what had happened, he was incensed at the prospect of the spread of Bolshevism and the dangers Lenin would pose for the exiled Russian Imperial Family.

Meanwhile, a fellow-Bolshevik, Leon Trotsky, who had been living in relatively luxury in New York, had also returned to Russia with a substantial sum of money which was alleged to have been given to him by a notable Wall Street banker. Trotsky's voyage had been particularly eventful, for his ship was intercepted by British officials in Halifax, Canada, where, in view of his revolutionary activities, he was detained in Amherst Internment Camp. After four weeks, he was suddenly released allegedly thanks to President Wilson who had put pressure on the British Government to allow him to continue his journey unimpeded.

A couple of months later, in August 1917, an American Red Cross Mission arrived in St Petersburg ostensibly to assist those who had suffered during the February Revolution. Unlike other Red Cross Missions, however, this one was comprised primarily of engineers, photographers, journalists and bankers, led by a director of the Federal Reserve, whose opulent lifestyle – staying in the most luxurious hotel in St Petersburg, sitting in the Imperial Box at the theatre, and adding to his collection of expensive antiques – earned him the epithet the 'American

Tsar'[ll]. Within a month, the few doctors who had accompanied the mission were recalled home, and as a translator and former Tsarist official observed, those members who remained in Russia:

"...shoved aside the problem of relief work and...struck into Russian politics...As time went on and reports of their political activities were published abroad, and the American Government or the Red Cross did nothing to have them removed, the Russians could only conclude that their actions were approved at home."[352]

As Washington published reports of the extent of malnutrition in Russia, the American people generously made donations for the purchase of condensed milk for starving babies, but, unbeknown to the donors, these were delivered instead to the troops of Lenin's Red Army. When, in October 1917, Lenin seized power, he appeared to repay this assistance by granting many railway and reconstruction projects, as well as access to Russian oil, to the families and connections of the Wall Street bankers.

Lenin, as predicted, immediately sued for peace, and, as a Russo-German treaty was prepared, Wilhelm insisted that a clause be included guaranteeing the safety of the former Tsar and his family. His ministers, however, conveniently forgot this stipulation, and when the Treaty of Brest-Litovsk was signed on March 3rd 1918, it made no provision for the protection of the captive Romanovs.

In the spring of 1918, with Russia removed from the conflict, the German Chiefs of Staff concentrated all their efforts on a major offensive along a forty-mile stretch of

---

[ll] The American Consul in Munich drew attention to the sterling work of the American Red Cross in all the combatant countries until Henry Davidson – a partner of J.P. Morgan – was appointed its chairman. 'To the everlasting disgrace of the American Red Cross," wrote the Consul, "Davidson ordered that no attention be paid to the German wounded, and no medicine of any kind be sent them."

the Western Front. 'Operation Michael' – the first stage of *Kaiserslacht* ('the Emperor's Battle') – proved so successful that Wilhelm sincerely believed that victory was in sight. His joy was short-lived, however, as Ludendorff's lack of effective planning and inability to understand the conditions under which the troops were operating, resulted in the storm-troopers moving so quickly that the supply lines could not reach them and they lost all sight of any overall objective. By May, the plan was proving so disastrous that it was necessary to call off the offensive, leaving the disheartened soldiers to question their purpose in fighting at all. To make matters worse, where once the Kaiser's armies had been cheered as they made their way to the Front, now they were met with silence or even jeers. In some places, farmers hurled stones at the windows of passing military trains, while saboteurs uncoupled the carriages from their engines. Already demoralised, the soldiers soon began to lose faith in their officers, for, at the beginning of the war they had been led by highly-experienced and efficient commanders, but the death toll among these skilled officers was so great that there were insufficient competent men to replace them. Consequently, very young officers, straight from the military training schools, were placed in positions of authority which they were incapable of fulfilling.

The troops returning home on leave became even more disheartened when they saw the conditions in which their families were living. Even before the United States' entry into the war, the blockade had caused severe hardship for the civilian population, but from April 1917, the situation became even more dire when Wilson ordered the seizure of neutral Dutch merchant ships in American harbours and a blockade of Dutch ports to prevent any exports from reaching the enemy – a rather strange move in light of the fact that he had led his country to war ostensibly to protect the 'freedom of the seas' and the rights of neutral shipping.

Fish had been a primary import from the Netherlands, and, in the absence of many other foodstuffs, large numbers of Germans had relied on this as a chief source of protein but, with the tightening of the blockade, its consumption fell by seventy-five per cent. At the same time, a lack of fertilizer, a series of poor potato harvests, and the dearth of able-bodied men and horses to work the land, led to the failure of the agricultural programmes which Wilhelm had encouraged. In the winter of 1916-1917, as rice and grain were unavailable, vast numbers of people were reduced to living solely on turnip bread, while boiled basswood blossom was used as a substitute for tea, and ground acorns were used in place of coffee. It was estimated that the result was an average twenty percent drop in weight, and the annual mortality rate increased so dramatically that some observers claimed that between 1915 and 1918, eight-hundred-thousand civilians died of malnutrition and malnutrition-related disease. According to an official report, the effects of emaciation were manifold, including mental impairment, an inability to recover from even mild illnesses, reduced physical capacity, and 'a marked increase in mortality especially among the aged and the youth of school age.'[353] In wintertime, the already malnourished people suffered all the more due to a shortage of fuel for firewood and materials to make warm clothing, and their situation was not helped by the necessity of standing outdoors for hours, queueing for meagre rations. Even the troops suffered, many soldiers being reduced to eating the potatoes and barley that was provided for their horses.

Conditions were equally grave in Austria, where troops on the Italian Front were so hungry that they dug up and ate the corpses of buried horses; and, in May 1918, a group of mutinous Austrian sailors attacked a German grain ship in a desperate effort to abate their intense hunger. In view of the plight of the civilian population and his own inclination to conclude hostilities, in September 1917, the Austro-Hungarian Emperor Karl[mm], visited Wilhelm at his Headquarters in Spa to inform him that he intended to approach President Wilson with a view to negotiating a fair peace. As his own efforts had been repeatedly thwarted, and as President Wilson had already spoken of the dismantlement of Austro-Hungarian Empire, Wilhelm held out little hope that the Allies would be willing to negotiate fairly, but Karl explained that he had no other option since his people were starving, and his armies were mutinying. Thousands of troops had simply abandoned their posts and were marauding through the countryside like bandits, while soldiers of different ethnicities had laid down their arms, refusing to continue to fight for an Empire of which they no longer felt a part.

The *New York Times* greeted Karl's proposal with optimism, stating that here was a real opportunity for peace. Wilson, however, was not inclined to negotiate, replying that:

> "The Government of the United States feels that there is only one reply which it can make to the suggestion of the Imperial Austro-Hungarian Government. It has repeatedly and with entire candour stated the terms upon which the United States would consider peace, and can and will entertain no proposal for conference upon a matter concerning which it has made its position and purpose so plain."

The news from the front was equally depressing for the Kaiser, as, throughout the summer, the joint British, Australian and American forces launched a counter-attack

---

[mm] Emperor Franz Josef died in November 1916, to be succeeded by his great-nephew, Karl, who, since his accession had desperately sought to bring the conflict to a conclusion.

on the Western Front, retaking many positions gained by the Germans during the Kaiserslacht. In just five months, almost one million German soldiers were killed, and many of those who survived were so demoralised that they abandoned their posts.

> "The new 1918 troops in particular," wrote the Kaiser, "were badly tainted with revolutionary propaganda and often took advantage of the darkness of night to sneak away from the firing and vanish into the rear."[354]

Nonetheless, he insisted that the majority of his men continued to carry out their duties faithfully and refused to be beaten; and when, in a desperate attempt to relieve their conditions, he ordered a retreat from Antwerp, his son, the Crown Prince reported that, despite fatigue and months of struggle, they withdrew in a disciplined and orderly manner, taking heart from the prospect of taking up a more advantageous position on the Meuse.

By the end of September it was clear that Germany's ally, Bulgaria, was on the point of total surrender, and there was every reason to believe that Austria-Hungary would quickly follow. Ludendorff, whose own beloved stepson had been killed in the *Kaiserslacht*, was on the verge of a nervous breakdown and, abandoning all hope of victory, called for an immediate armistice. Both Hindenburg and Ludendorff warned Wilhelm that the only means of negotiating a fair peace was to implement various internal reforms to make the country more democratic. The government was therefore rapidly replaced and Wilhelm appointed his liberal-minded cousin, Prince Max of Baden, as Chancellor. Reluctant as he had been to take up the role, Prince Max was horrified to hear Ludendorff's pessimistic descriptions of the state of the army, and initially urged the Kaiser to hold out a little longer in the hope that a brief withdrawal might revitalise the troops and enable them to continue on to victory. Wilhelm, war-weary and described by one observer as looking like 'a white-haired, broken old man', replied that a negotiated armistice was the only available option and the only means of saving the monarchy. On October 6th, therefore, Max informed the Reichstag that a request for an armistice had been sent to President Wilson, in the hope of gaining a fairer peace from America than could be gained through negotiations with France and Britain. In requesting the Armistice, Max stated that the German Government agreed to comply with all of the plans laid out in the President's address to Congress in January 1918 – the 'Fourteen Points' on which Wilson had stated that durable peace could be secured:

1. Open diplomacy – whereby no secret treaties would be arranged between nations and all agreements would be visible to the public.
2. Freedom of the seas in peace and in wartime.
3. An end to all economic barriers in order to enable free trade.
4. A reduction of armaments to the point where each nation held only those weapons which were necessary for its protection.
5. Impartial adjustment of all colonial claims, taking into account the wishes of the native populations.
6. The withdrawal of foreign troops from Russia so that Russia would be free to decide upon her own political development.
7. The evacuation of German troops from Belgium.
8. The restoration of all French territory captured by the Germans, 'and the wrong done to France by Prussia in 1871 in the matter of Alsace-Lorraine, which has unsettled the peace of the world for nearly fifty years, should be righted, in order that peace may once more be made secure in the interest of all.'
9. A readjustment of the Italian borders.

10. The granting of autonomy to the different ethnic groups of Austria-Hungary.

11. The evacuation of foreign troops from the Balkans.

12. The granting of autonomy to the different ethnic groups within the Ottoman Empire.

13. The establishment of an independent Poland.

14. The formation of the League of Nations.

In response to Prince Max's request for an armistice, Wilson's Secretary of State, Robert Lansing, asked for greater clarification of the Germans' intentions. The Foreign Minister, Wilhelm Solf, replied more specifically that Germany would adhere to the Fourteen Points and begin an immediate evacuation of the occupied territories. It is of vital importance to note, therefore, that the Germans agreed to an Armistice *solely on the basis of the Fourteen Points.*

Lansing, however, responded less favourably than Max had anticipated. Referring to a speech by Wilson in which he had stated that it was vital for the Allies to destroy or reduce to impotence, 'any power...that can disturb the peace of the world,' Lansing told the Chancellor that:

"The power which has hitherto controlled the German nation is the sort here described. It is within the choice of the German nation to alter it."

This was clearly not only an attack on the Kaiser, but also an incitement to the German people to revolution.

"Don't you see," Wilhelm gasped when presented with the note, "The object of this is to bring down my House and to set the monarchy aside."[355]

When the note was published in the German press, there was an immediate outpouring of loyalty to the Kaiser, and, as one prominent editor wrote:

"Must they not think a people capable of the depths of treason when they expect it to abandon a dynasty which has been the architect of its greatness throughout the course of a glorious history?"[356]

Nonetheless, rumours began to circulate throughout Germany that the Kaiser's abdication was imminent and that it was likely that his heir, the Crown Prince, would also step down. As the monarchists struggled to correct the error, a third and far more direct response arrived from Wilson. This time he stated plainly that as long the Kaiser remained on the throne, the United States was unable to negotiate and would therefore accept nothing less than an unconditional surrender.

"The hypocritical Wilson has at last thrown off the mask!" Wilhelm said, convinced that, from the moment he had led his country into the war, the President had been intent upon the downfall of the German monarchy.

As newspaper headlines presented Wilson's offer: 'Capitulation or Negotiation', the German people, starving and war-weary, were clearly being coerced into demanding Wilhelm's abdication. The Social Democrats and Independent Socialists were quick to seize their moment, one of them telling the Reichstag, 'The question can no longer be evaded. Shall it be war with the Hohenzollerns or peace without the Hohenzollerns?' – thus planting in the minds of his hearers the myth that the Emperor, renowned until 1914 as 'the Peace-Kaiser', was solely responsible for the war.

In the meantime, the Austrian Emperor wrote to the Kaiser, telling him that he was about to sue for peace and asking whether Germany wished to join with him. Before Wilhelm had replied, the Austrian ministers presented their request to Washington, declaring that with or without the agreement of their allies, they were ready to enter into negotiations and asking for an immediate armistice.

Within days of this request having been sent, revolution erupted in Austria, and, as many regiments turned against the German soldiers who were stationed in their country, Emperor Karl was forced to flee Vienna. Wilhelm was faced with a terrible dilemma, for not only did he believe that he could not renege on his coronation oath as King of Prussia, but, in view of events in Austria and in the light of his knowledge of historical precedents when revolutions followed abdications, he genuinely feared for what would become of Germany without a monarchy.

In view of the desperate situation, Wilhelm, despite protests from his Chancellor, resolved to join his army in Flanders, where, to his relief he was warmly welcomed and greeted with 'wild cheering.' In Berlin, however, Max and the Government were caving into pressure from the Social Democrats who believed that only the Kaiser's abdication would secure a just peace for the country.

"Prince Max's government is trying to throw me out," Wilhelm wrote to Admiral Hintze of the Foreign Office. "At Berlin I should be less able to oppose them than in the midst of my troops."[357]

His absence from the capital, though, was seen by many as a means of avoiding the question of his abdication, and newspapers openly stated that his clinging to the crown was the sole impediment to peace. Prince Max then approached Wilhelm's son, Prince August Wilhelm, and sought to impress upon him the necessity of his father's abdication, and suggested that, in order to save the monarchy, the crown would pass to the Crown Prince's eldest son, for whom – since he was still a child – August Wilhelm could act as Regent. August Wilhelm indignantly replied that he had no intention of advising his father to abdicate.

In the Reichstag, meanwhile, several members of different parties warned of the dangers that would follow abdication, while Wilhem's brother-in-law, Prince Frederick Charles of Hesse – who had also been approached in the hope that he would advise the Kaiser to resign – spoke of the devastating effect that Wilhelm's departure would have upon the army.

As the country was rapidly descending into chaos and it was clear that all hope of victory was lost, the Imperial Admiralty hoped at least to go down in a blaze of glory, and concocted a reckless plan to launch the fleet and simultaneously attack the French coast and face the Royal Navy head-on in an epic sea-battle in the English Channel. Few officers and seamen had any faith in the offensive, and, viewing it as a suicide mission, many failed to return from shore-leave. Others mutinied and abandoned their ships to march through Kiel, urging dockworkers to join them in their protests. As the number of protestors increased, Wilhelm's brother, Henry, was forced to flee the city with a red flag tied to his motor car.

As word of events in Kiel travelled quickly, rioting erupted in several other cities as workers abandoned their factories to form Workers Co-operatives similar to Russian Soviets, which demanded immediate withdrawal from the war.

A horrified Wilhelm received numerous reports from Berlin, informing him that the entire country was turning against him, and so, on November 8th, he summoned the Crown Prince and the Chiefs of Staff to Spa to assess the situation. Ludendorff's successor[nn], General Gröner, presented a devastating picture of a country in a state of revolution, where soldiers were deserting in droves, and the only alternative to his abdication was to lead the loyal regiments against the insurgents, which meant, in effect, provoking a civil war. Several other Generals disagreed, however; and the Crown Prince, who had arrived directly from the battlefield, asserted that the greater part of the army remained committed to his father.

[nn] Ludendorff, on the brink of a nervous breakdown and believing that the Kaiser was about to dismiss him, had resigned on 26th October.

In view of these conflicting reports, Wilhelm asked for immediate assessments from the commanders of all the military divisions before making any decision, but he insisted that, even if he were compelled to abdicate as German Emperor, he could not renege on his oath and would therefore never abdicate as King of Prussia. Nor, he said, would he abandon his troops but rather he would personally lead them back into Berlin in an orderly fashion.

"The army will march back home in good order," Gröner replied brusquely, "but not under the command of Your Majesty."[358]

As these discussions were taking place, frequent messages arrived from the Chancellor, describing the precariousness of the situation as city after city fell into the hands of revolutionaries; and, as the responses came in from the military commanders, the overriding message was clear – the Kaiser could no longer rely on the loyalty of his troops. Finally, Prince Max of Baden telephoned to tell Wilhelm plainly that unless he abdicated at once there was no hope for the monarchy.

"The Kaiser received the news with grave silence," wrote his eldest son. "His firmly compressed lips were colourless; his face was livid and had aged by years. Only those who knew him as I did could penetrate that mask of calmness and self-control, maintained with such an effort."

Realising there was no alternative, Wilhelm prepared a written response for the Chancellor, declaring that he would abdicate as German Emperor 'if further bloodshed can be hindered thereby'; he earnestly wished to avoid civil war; and he would remain King of Prussia and would lead his orderly troops back to the fatherland.

Before the declaration had been finalised, however, there came the devastating news that Prince Max, of his own volition, had already publicly declared that Wilhelm had abdicated both as Emperor and King; and the Crown

269

Prince had also waived his right to the throne. According to Wilhelm, the army was 'shaken to the core' to think that he had abandoned his troops, while Max excused his own actions by stating that the Allies had refused to conclude any durable peace until the Kaiser stepped down.

On hearing this, the Crown Prince offered to return to his regiment and to rally the troops in support of his father, but Wilhelm, refusing to create a civil war, declined the offer and, after much soul-searching and pressure from his Generals, he realised that he had no option but to leave the country.

So it was, on the evening of 9th November, he set out for the Dutch border, a broken man who nonetheless believed that to the end, he was serving his country.

> "I consciously sacrificed myself and my throne in the belief that, by so doing, I was best serving the fatherland...I decided to leave the country since, in view of the reports brought to me, I must needs believe that, by so doing, I should most faithfully serve Germany, make possible better armistice and peace terms for her, and spare her further loss of human lives, distress and misery."[359]

As Wilhelm soon realised, however, this 'sacrifice' was in vain, for the peace terms imposed upon German were designed to utterly destroy the country, which, soon after the Kaiser's departure, erupted into civil war, leading only to 'the disintegration of the army and the nation.'

Chapter 24 – 'Conceived in Lust and Born in Lies'

When the German representatives signed the armistice agreement on November 11th 1918, they accepted all of Wilson's Fourteen Points and, at the Allies' insistence, agreed to comply with a further twenty-one demands, including the surrender of the greater part of their armaments, the High Seas fleet and the submarine fleet; an Allied occupation of the Rhineland; and the immediate release of prisoners-of-war. Since this was merely the ceasefire agreement rather than a capitulation, the Allies insisted that German prisoners-of-war would remain in captivity and the starvation blockade would not be lifted until a formal treaty had been signed.

The terms of the armistice came as terrible blow to the German people who had believed that, in complying with the Fourteen Points, the starvation blockade would be lifted. In actuality, once the agreement was signed, conditions only deteriorated, as the occupation of the Rhineland cut off access to some of the most fertile plains in the country on which the surrounding cities had depended for food. What was more, German fisherman were forbidden from fishing in the North Sea or the Baltic, and, as malnutrition increased, its associated diseases spread even more rapidly.

Six months of negotiations followed the armistice, as representatives from around the world gathered for a Peace Conference in Paris, dominated by Britain's Lloyd George, France's Clemenceau, and the United States' Woodrow Wilson. The German delegates were denied any part in the negotiations and, from the start, it was clear that their country was to be treated as a defeated nation. The streets of Paris were lined with hundreds of captured or surrendered German cannon, and Wilson, driven in an open-roofed car, waved to the adoring crowds like a conquering hero.

> "Cameras and motion picture machines vied with one another to get the best view of Woodrow Wilson, when he smilingly walked up the steps," wrote one Canadian visitor. "The poilus[oo] stood at attention and the crowds displayed the greatest enthusiasm when President Wilson appeared."[360]

Beneath the euphoria, the Paris Peace Conference was characterised by squabbles, secret deals and sinister groups, working behind the scenes to further their own agendas. 'Time and again,' wrote one participant, 'I was visited by delegates claiming that this or that decision was or would be taken in response to the promptings not of land-grabbing governments but by wealthy capitalists or enterprising captains of industry.'[361] Some believed that borders were being redrawn and independent states were being created solely for the establishment of new banks which specific financier families and syndicates had already purchased. One prominent French economist repeatedly demanded answers to the question as to whether or not American and British financiers had made secret deals with the Bolsheviks during the war, in order to secure contracts for the construction of railways and the rights to exploit a vast forest which 'can bring in a revenue of three hundred million roubles a year.'

He never received a satisfactory reply.

After months of wrangling, a treaty was finally signed on 28th June 1919 – five years to the day since the assassination of Franz Ferdinand. Its title – the Treaty of Versailles – was another symbol of Germany's humiliation since an earlier treaty of the same name had concluded their victory in the Franco-Prussian War.

[oo] An informal term for a French Infantryman

'It is a sentence of death!' gasped one German statesman on reading its terms, while a former Ambassador to England concluded that, 'This peace is a peace of violence. It is not based on justice.'

Twelve of Wilson's Fourteen Points – *on which the Germans had agreed to the armistice* – were abandoned to the great advantage of the Allies. The openness that Wilson had called for gave way to numerous private agreements, and, through secret negotiations, Austria-Hungary was dismantled. Despite the promise of free trade, economic barriers were raised against Germany; and while the Central Powers were stripped of their armaments, their former enemies were under no obligation to reduce their military capabilities. Wilson's initial insistence on the 'impartial adjustments of colonial claims', and Asquith's statement that Britain had no intention of expanding her Empire, sounded hollow as Germany's colonies and African rights were picked over and shared out among the Allies, which, together with the acquisition of other possessions, added one-and-a-half-million miles of territory to Britain. Considering that Wilson had claimed that the people of every nation had a right to self-determination, it was somewhat ironic that Egypt, without the consent of the Egyptians, was subsumed into the British Empire; and, without consulting the inhabitants, Alsace-Lorraine was returned to France, despite the fact that, as one American observed, 'the young people are enthusiastically German – are among the most devoted to the German cause in the [recent] war.'[362]

Wilhelm's long-held belief that envy of Germany's economic success had been the chief cause of the war, appeared to be vindicated by the manner in which German trade and markets were destroyed by the terms of the treaty. Not content with the scuppering of the High Seas Fleet, the Allies requisitioned all Germany's large merchant vessels, and half of all smaller vessels, trawlers and crafts. The most

273

prosperous German coal mine was placed under Allied supervision, and the Germans were required to send forty million tonnes of coal – as well as a similar quantity of iron – to their former enemy every year. Taxes were placed on all German imports, but the Germans were forbidden from taxing their exports.

As the Allied forces occupied the Rhineland and parts of East Prussia, they gained access to Germany's richest agricultural and industrial areas; and, with the enforced dismantling of the German air force, numerous designs and patents were seized and handed to Germany's former enemies. Fledgling American pharmaceutical companies purchased German patents for next to nothing, basically stealing the intellectual copyright of dedicated German scientists.

Most devastatingly of all, however, the Germans were compelled to accept full responsibility for the war, and were therefore required to make reparation payments totalling one-hundred-and-thirty-two-billion gold marks – which, with the interest accrued over decades, eventually reached two-hundred-and-sixty-nine billion gold marks, or one-hundred-thousand tonnes of gold.

Even among the former Allies, there were protests about the severity of the treaty. James Ramsay Macdonald, referred to it as unjust, defective and a violation of 'the understanding upon which the Armistice was signed'; and one American commentator explained that:

> "Had all the German people been guilty, and all the Allies as innocent as angels, still this treaty would have been an abomination…It was conceived in lust and born in lies."[363]

In 1920, a group of ex-servicemen from all the combatant countries met in Geneva to discuss the best means of avoiding future wars. Even the British delegates called for a cancellation of the Treaty of Versailles; and, in

March the same year, the United States Senate also refused to endorse it.

From exile in the Netherlands, Wilhelm followed the progress of the Peace Conference with increasing gloom and exasperation. Everything that he had striven to build was being swept away in a few short months, and echoes of 'hang the Kaiser' resounded through of Europe. For a man who had longed to be appreciated and admired, it was excruciating to realise that he was probably the most hated man in the world, and even more painful to know that the majority of the accusations levelled against him were entirely unjust. 'Why do the English hate me so?' he plaintively asked his hosts in Holland, and he was aghast to be told that they held him personally responsible for every atrocity committed during the war.

The Germans had hoped that, by approaching Wilson rather than the Entente with their armistice request, they would receive a fairer deal. Now, realising that his country was being utterly destroyed in his absence, and his abdication had been in vain, Wilhelm had nothing but contempt for the 'Champion Liar of the Age', the American President:

> "Oh Wilson! He is a greater autocrat than I or the Tsar of Russia ever was. He has more power than either of us had. I call him Kaiser Wilson."[364]

In January 1919, a commission, chaired by the United States' Secretary of State, Robert Lansing, was established to inquire into the 'the responsibilities of the authors of the war', and after a relatively brief investigation, it reached the conclusion that Austria-Hungary, abetted by Germany, had premeditated the conflict and deliberately committed acts to make war unavoidable; and that the Central Powers had 'deliberately worked to defeat all the many conciliatory proposals made by the Entente Powers and their repeated efforts to avoid war.'

This must have been galling for Wilhelm to read, in view of the fact that he was the last to mobilise his army, and the efforts to which he had gone to find a peaceful solution. To make matters worse, the 'evidence' for these charges was a number of carefully selected telegrams passed between Berlin and Vienna during the July Crisis, while no mention was made of the numerous letters that Wilhelm had written to his cousins in Russia and England in the weeks following Franz Ferdinand's assassination. The commission stated bluntly that Wilhelm held a war council on July 5th 1914 – an allegation which, as was shown, was clearly untrue[pp] – and that his Norwegian cruise was merely a ruse to distract from his secret preparations for war. Of course, much was made of the Germans' violation of the neutrality of Belgium, including a list of no fewer than thirty-two alleged atrocities from rape and abduction to the poisoning of wells and torture. With supreme irony, in view of the thousands who were dying of malnutrition due to the blockade, the list also included the 'deliberate starvation of civilians'; 'the breach of rules relating to the Red Cross', regardless of the fact that, under the auspices of Davidson, the American Red Cross had refused to treat or deliver medicines to the German wounded; and 'the misuse of flags of truce', when Churchill had actively encouraged British sailors to fly false flags and to disguise Royal Naval ships as neutral vessels.

The damning 'evidence' of the report, demanded a calling to account of those who were deemed responsible for the war, the chief of whom was named as the ex-Kaiser.

"There is little doubt that the ex-Kaiser and others in high authority were cognisant of and could at

---

[pp] See Chapter 15

least have mitigated the barbarities committed during the course of the war. A word from them would have brought about a different method in the action of their subordinates on land, at sea and in the air.'[365]

As a result of these accusations, Article 227 was inserted into the Treaty of Versailles, stating that William Hohenzollern would face an International Tribunal, presided over by judges from the Allied countries, for the 'supreme offence against international morality, the sanctity of treaties, and the essential rules of justice.'[366] On the day that the treaty was signed, a formal note was sent to Queen Wilhelmina and the Dutch Government requesting his extradition. The Dutch, however, refused to cooperate on the grounds that so-doing would be in breach of their neutrality; and, while Wilhelm himself stated that he would willingly have faced the court had he believed that his attendance would in any way profit Germany, as things stood it would only lead to further dishonour for the fatherland.

The Spectator suggested that, despite his promise to 'hang the Kaiser', Lloyd George had never really wanted the trial to take place 'because he thought the risks would be greater than the advantages.'[367] Did those risks include the likelihood that a fair hearing would find him innocent? Or that he might be given an opportunity to express a valid opinion about who had really brought about the war?

Chapter 25 – 'Innocent Before God & Men'

Had the tribunal ever taken place, two specific charges were to be levelled against the Kaiser: that he premeditated and caused the war; and that he conducted it in an illegal manner. Undoubtedly, the greater part of the evidence against him would have been taken from his own words, as writers in the Allied countries set to work, dissecting virtually every speech he had ever made, editing and emphasising those parts which supported the view that he had created such a militaristic climate that war had become inevitable.

As early as 1914, Lloyd George had urged the British people to read the heavily doctored copies of his speeches, which would, he claimed, demonstrate the Kaiser's dangerous lunacy. Propagandists had also frequently drawn attention to the address that he gave to his troops as they set out to crush the Boxer Rebellion:

> "No quarter is to be given…No prisoners are to be made…As the Huns under King Attila made a name for themselves a thousand years ago…so now let the name of Germany go down in China for a thousand years so that a Chinaman will never again look askance at a German."[368]

As presented, these words do indeed appear violently aggressive but there is much dispute as to whether or not what he said was accurately reported or interpreted. The speech, as it appeared in the press, was taken down by a shorthand writer and then translated into English and other languages. The original text, however, reveals quite a different meaning, particularly when it is taken in context. At the time he was speaking, the Boxers were indiscriminately killing Europeans, and the German Envoy had been murdered. Wilhelm, therefore, warned his troops:

> "You know very well that you are to fight against a cunning, brave, well-armed and terrible enemy.

278

When you come face to face with him, no quarter will be given. No prisoners will be taken…"[369]

Clearly then, what was shown as an exhortation to barbarism could, in fact, have been a warning of the dangers that his soldiers were about to face.

Similarly, lines were taken out of context from the numerous addresses in which he spoke of the Germans having their bayonets fixed and their swords sharpened for battle, omitting the previous sentences in which he stressed that Germany wanted peace but *should she come under attack* his soldiers were well-prepared to defend her.

Wilhelm was known for his posturing and his love of the theatrical, and even his greatest detractors had to confess that he was an extremely skilled orator. With his love of Shakespearean language and his passion for German mythology, he carefully crafted his words to create the greatest impact on his hearers.

"The Kaiser is a born orator," wrote the Hungarian, Emil Reich, "He speaks naturally very well and even the style of an address delivered on the spur of the moment, is quite remarkable. Whether he delivers a sermon aboard a ship;…or whether he addresses students at Bonn university, a regiment, labourers, scientific congresses or diplomats; he invariably succeeds in giving point and life and fine shape to his ideas."[370]

Throughout his reign, his people had become accustomed to the drama of his performances and saw them more as an inspiration for devotion to their country than as a call to arms. The Belgian Ambassador, Baron Grendl, was well aware of this fact, and in 1907 he reported to Brussels that, while the foreign press made much of the Kaiser's seemingly bellicose statements:

"Nobody here [in Germany] has thought of interpreting the words of His Majesty in the sense of a threat directed against foreign powers. The habitual style of the Emperor is too well known for people to be under any misapprehension as to the import of his speeches. Nor is it right to doubt the sincerity of His Majesty's pacific intentions. He has furnished sufficient proof of them during a reign of 18 years."[371]

The Irish writer, Stanley Shaw, understood this, too. Writing in 1913, he explained that 'there is much, and to account for, if not quite justify, the Emperor's rhetoric. The peculiarity of Germany's monarchic system placed, and places, the monarch in a patriarchal position not very different from that of Moses towards the Israelites—a leader, preacher, and prophet.'[372]

Even Lloyd George admitted, 'I do not believe he meant all these speeches,' but he argued that by uttering such words Wilhelm was culpable of fostering the Prussians' natural desire for conflict.

A second argument in favour of the Kaiser's determination to lead Germany to war, was the fact that he paid so much attention to strengthening his army and navy. As has been shown, however, he viewed this as a defensive move, since historically Germany had been surrounded by enemies, and, what was more, his neighbours were arming more rapidly than he was. 'The development of military forces of other European powers,' he had said, 'makes it our...imperative duty to look to the increase of our own *defensive* powers.'[373]

"Now, who was really ready for this war?" asked an American diplomat in 1915. "England with the combined navies of Russia, France and Japan, and a peace-footing army of 2,260,000 men, or Germany with her standing army of 672,000 men, her untried navy and her obligations to hard pressed Austria-Hungary on her hands?"[374]

The argument that Wilhelm precipitated war through his encouragement of militarism, therefore fails to stand. As the British playwright, George Bernard Shaw, wrote in 1914,

> "We must not pretend that...militarism and the inevitable war between England & Germany is a Prussian infamy for which the Kaiser must be severely punished. We began it; and if they met us halfway, as they certainly did, it is not for us to reproach them."[375]

As Wilhelm was also accused of dismissing the Entente's efforts to avoid the conflict, particular reference was made to his rejection of Grey's suggestion of July 26th 1914 of a four-power conference. As was shown, Wilhelm rejected the idea on the grounds that it resembled a tribunal against Austria, and the proposed conference would be dominated by members of the Entente. No mention was made, however, of Wilhelm's alternative suggestion of a temporary occupation of Belgrade; nor was there any explanation as to why no answer was given to his request that Britain should exert pressure on France and Russia to avoid war, while he performed the same service to Austria.

Had Wilhelm truly premeditated war with Britain, why would he have waited until 1914? Fourteen years earlier, at the height of the Boer War, most of Europe was fiercely anti-British and, as Wilhelm informed his grandmother, he received several clandestine offers of alliances all of which he ignored. Again, had he wanted war with Russia, there could have been no better time to strike than in 1905 when, suffering an ignominious defeat in the Russo-Japanese War, the country was erupting into revolution. Moreover, the Russian Foreign Minister, Sazanov, is alleged to have stated that 'the German Emperor's love of peace is a guarantee to us that we ourselves can decide on the moment of war.'[376]

The most obvious argument in Wilhelm's defence against the charge of launching a premeditated war, is the fact that he no motive for so doing. As he constantly reiterated, Germany had prospered throughout his twenty-five-year reign and a conflict would bring irreparable damage to the trade on which that prosperity depended. For this reason, as well as for his 'feelings of humanity', he had worked to the very last moment to maintain peace. When war broke out, he had, according to Sven Hedig, a clear conscience because, '...he feels himself in his hear innocent before God and men of having caused this war, and that he has done everything in his power to avoid it.'[377]

Germany's enemies had far more plausible motives for wanting war. As Wilhelm pointed out, Britain resented and feared Germany's economic success; France was anxious to retake Alsace-Lorraine; and Russia, which was economically tied to France, was desperate to acquire new ports and to gain greater influence in the Balkans.

"The aims of the Entente could be gained only through a war; those of Germany only without a war."[378]

Interestingly, in 1930, even President Wilson's adviser, Colonel House, finally admitted, "I do not think the Kaiser either wanted war or planned it."

Regarding the conduct of the war, while it cannot be denied that atrocities were committed by the German army, it has been shown that these were no worse than those committed by the soldiers of the Entente. Moreover, Wilhelm's compassion for the enemy had made him a laughing-stock among his own Generals, and his opposition to the use of gas bombs and frequent calls for a just peace had led to his being side-lined by the Chiefs of Staff. He had not been in favour of the invasion of Belgium; he was horrified by the sinking of the *Lusitania*; and, for months he had withstood the Imperial Admiralty's calls for unrestricted submarine warfare. He had issued a pardon for Edith Cavell; he had pressed for fair treatment of prisoners-of-war; he had attempted to assist the Russian Imperial Family; and on numerous occasions he had put forward peace initiatives, in the hope that Europe could return to the status quo before the war.

Even the members of the commission must have realised that Wilhelm was innocent of the charges levelled against him, for, included in their arraignment is the comment that the tribunal must be 'broad enough to include him *even if he had not directly ordered the violations.'* Some members of the commission argued that legally a sovereign or head of state was responsible solely to his people and therefore they had no authority to bring charges against the Kaiser.

> "The majority of the commission, though, was not influenced by the legal argument. They appeared to be fixed in their determination to try and punish the ex-Kaiser of Germany."[379]

Wilhelm was to be made a scapegoat for the horrors of 1914-1918, but, if, as has been shown, he had neither wanted war, nor, once it had started, sought to prolong it, why was it necessary to vilify him and to suggest that he should shoulder the guilt for such a shameful and horrific catastrophe? More importantly, if neither he nor the Tsar nor the Austro-Hungarian Emperor wanted war, who did, and who had the most to gain from such unimaginable slaughter?

These were questions with which Wilhelm tortured himself during his years in exile and, while it is easy to dismiss his conclusions as 'conspiracy theories' invented to exonerate himself and point the finger of blame elsewhere, he carefully studied documents and theses before reaching the conclusion that some 'secret society' had deliberately engineered the entire conflict. According to his hostess in the Netherlands, Norah Bentinck, he 'plunged himself' into books about Freemasonry, and was amply supplied with the most current literature on the subject by his brother, Henry. From these studies he deduced that masonry was 'a sinister power in world politics and he attributes as much evil-doing to its secret machinations as did our eighteenth-century ancestors to the doings of the 'Illuminati'."[380] He was not referring to the masonic groups which meet in virtually every European city, but rather to the higher echelons whose activities and purpose are kept from even the lowlier members of their society. Queen Victoria, he claimed both in his memoirs and in conversation, had warned him against becoming involved with a specific branch of masonry which was, he said, quite different from that of the majority of Lodges in Britain or in Germany. Franz Ferdinand had openly stated that there was a masonic plot to kill him, and Wilhelm claimed to have been told that 'The Grand Orient Lodge' had not only been instrumental in instigating the war but also, during a meeting in Switzerland in 1917, adopted a resolution to bring about the 'dismemberment of Austria-Hungary, democratization of Germany, elimination of the House of Hapsburg, abdication of the German Emperor...elimination of the Pope and the Catholic Church, elimination of every state Church in Europe.'[381]

It could be argued that the Freemasons provided an easy target quite simply because of the secrecy of their organisation, but Wilhelm was not alone in believing that some form of conspiracy – not necessarily connected with Freemasonry – was behind the instigation and prolonging of the war. Winston Churchill was also convinced that there was an international conspiracy behind the upheavals of the nineteenth and twentieth centuries, writing that, 'from the days of Spartacus-Weishaupt to those of Karl Marx, and down to Trotsky...this world-wide conspiracy for the overthrow of civilization and for the reconstitution of society on the basis of arrested development, of envious malevolence, and impossible equality, has been steadily growing.' As far back as 1876, the British Prime Minister, Benjamin Disraeli, had stated that:

"The government of this country has not only to deal with governments, kings and ministers, but also with secret societies, elements which must be taken into account, which at the last moment can bring our plans to naught, which have everywhere their unscrupulous agents, who incite assassinations and can if necessary lead a massacre."[382]

Even Woodrow Wilson acknowledged this, too, stating in 1913 that:

"Since I entered politics, I have chiefly had men's views confided to me privately. Some of the biggest men in the United States, in the field of commerce and manufacture, are afraid of something. They know that there is a power somewhere so organized, so subtle, so watchful, so interlocked, so complete, so pervasive, that they better not speak above their breath when they speak in condemnation of it."[383]

Wilhelm likewise stated that secret societies had always operated through governments, and, while some were beneficial, the majority were destructive.

"The most dangerous of these organizations hide under the cloak of some ideal object or other – such as active love of their neighbours, readiness to help the weak and poor, and so forth – in order that, with such pretexts as a blind, they may work on their real secret ends."[384]

The Red Cross Mission to Russia was a prime example of this method, as the American people believed in good faith that their donations were to help starving babies and the victims of war and revolution. In reality, they were assisting international industrialists to gain lucrative contracts and access to oil and other natural resources.

Behind these profiteers were cartels of bankers who operated throughout Europe and the United States, making fortunes out of the carnage. Apart from the immediate profits of war – which allegedly allowed, for example, one family of oil magnates to gain $200,000,000, and J.P. Morgan to 'make more in two years than the senior Morgan had made in his life' – even more was to be gained by creating debt. By 1918, virtually all the combatants had borrowed such vast sums from international financiers that they would continuing repaying their loans for almost a hundred years. Not until 9th March 2015 did Britain finally complete her payments for loans granted through bonds in 1917; while the excessive reparation payments demanded of Germany by Treaty of Versailles were designed to ensure that the country would remain beholden to financiers for decades to come.

"Give me control of a nation's money supply, and I care not who makes its laws," said Amschel Rothschild in the late eighteenth century – a maxim which undoubtedly lay behind many of the events in the instigation, prolonging and resolution of the First World War. Wilhelm firmly believed that Wilson acted solely in the interests of the Wall Street bankers, several of whom had family connections in every European court, and, by loaning money to different nations were not only able to continue the war far longer than would otherwise have been the case, but also ensured that, when the conflict was over, the combatant nations would be in their debt. In order to achieve their aims, it was necessary for the United States to participate in the Peace Conference, and this was why – in Wilhelm's opinion – Wilson had brought his country into the war, 'under the influence of powerful financial groups.'[385] Interestingly, in August 1919, the President was asked by Senator McCumber whether he believed that, if Germany had not violated American rights, the United States would have entered the war anyway. Wilson replied, "I do."

'It is no accident,' wrote one American commentator, 'that our peace settlement realizes for the bankers in London and Paris the ambitions with which they approached the war'[386]; while Wilhelm observed that:

286

"The great profit derived by America from the World War consists in the fact that the United States was able to attract to itself nearly fifty per cent of all the gold in the world, so that now the dollar, instead of the English pound, determined the exchange rate."[387]

In 1916, he had predicted that this would be the case, telling his American dentist that while Britain was introducing conscription to build up her army, 'she will see…the dollar replacing the pound as the unit of the world's finance.'[388] This was no indictment of the American people, for Wilhelm was at pains to point out that, had they understood what Wilson was doing, they would not have accepted it. He believed, too, that the Entente countries would not have demanded his abdication, which was a deliberate plan to foment unrest and civil war.

"In view of all this, heavy guilt lies on the shoulders of the American ex-president as a result of his having demanded my abdication under the pretence that it would bring Germany better terms. *In Germany, however, Mr Wilson should never be confused with the American people.*"[389]

Among many accusations levelled against him during the war and after his exile, was the suggestion that Wilhelm was insane. To foster this idea, psychologists were encouraged to produce books and theses which would demonstrate that he was decidedly unbalanced and, as was previously stated, suffering from megalomania, religious mania and an over-inflated ego. By portraying him as mad, his opinions could easily be dismissed without further investigation, but one charge which was never levelled against him by the psychologists was that of 'projection'– 'the attribution of one's own attitudes, feelings, or suppositions to others'. He was, however, obviously the victim of the projections of his detractors. Frequently, for example, he was described as having a desire for world domination, despite the fact that he tirelessly stressed that he simply wished Germany – which was territorially smaller than the state of Texas, and her overseas territories were insignificant compared to those of France and Britain – to live in peace with her neighbours, being free to participate in trade and commerce on an equal footing with the other Great Powers.

Did, one might ask, Wilhelm ever attempt to interfere in the government or domestic affairs of any other nation? Did his peace notes make any mention of a necessary regime change in any of the allied countries? Did he seek to alter the borders of any European country? Or did he attempt to take colonies from any of his neighbours?

As the answers to these questions are all negative, one might ask how then did he plan this world domination? And, more importantly, who *did* insist on interfering in Germany's and Austria-Hungary's internal affairs? Who insisted on the removal of the Kaiser and the Austrian Emperor? And who redrew the map of Europe to deprive many Germans and Austrians of their nationality?

It has been argued that his desire for colonies was a major cause of the First World War, and his imperialism was widely condemned by the leaders of the same countries who thrived on overseas conquests. Britain, it must be remembered, ruled a quarter of the earth's surface, and Wilson's imperialism, though couched in the terms 'moral imperialism', was no different from that of Germany. While Wilhelm openly admitted that Germany needed coaling stations and colonies for trade, Wilson stated in his first message to Congress:

> "Our domestic markets no longer suffice. We need foreign markets. We must build up trade, especially foreign trade."[390]

Over the next few years, he embarked on a naval programme to benefit trade, exactly as Wilhelm had done but, at the same time, saw fit to send troops into various countries whose governments did not reflect his own ideas. In 1915, following the overthrow and murder of the President, he sent American soldiers into Haiti to compel the National Assembly to ratify a convention prepared by the American State Department. The following year, in the midst of a scandal 'in which American politicians in league with American financiers were preying upon San Domingo finances by virtue of political control exerted under the terms of the custom convention', five hundred U.S. marines were sent into the Dominican Republic to force President Jimenez to resign. The same year, American forces were also sent into Nicaragua to enforce the 'Canal Convention' from which the United States gained leases of territory and 'exclusive proprietary rights to construct, maintain and operate, free from all taxation and public charges an inter-oceanic canal across Nicaragua'[391].

The final defamation of the Kaiser, which continues to this day, is the belief that he was not only the forerunner but also a supporter of Adolf Hitler. In the post-war years, reeling under the humiliation of the Treaty of Versailles and the belief that Germany had been betrayed rather than losing the war, it is unsurprising that many German people were originally drawn to the idea of a man who would restore their national honour. Many princes and even the Kaiser himself initially saw in National Socialism (Nazism) a means of regaining pride in their culture and their heritage. It did not take long, however, for Wilhelm to see through the façade, and in 1938 – within a couple of months of Neville Chamberlain's signing of the Munich Agreement with Hitler – Wilhelm gave an interview in which he stated very clearly his opinion of the dictator:

> "There is a man alone, without family, without children, without God....He builds legions but he doesn't build a nation. A nation is created by families, a religion, tradition: it is made up out of

the hearts of mothers, the wisdom of fathers, the joy
and the exuberance of children."

Under Hitler, he stated, Germany had become:

"...an all-swallowing State, disdainful of human
dignities and the ancient structure of our race, sets
itself up in place of everything else. And the man
who, alone, incorporates in himself this whole State,
has neither a God to honour nor a dynasty to
conserve, nor could a past to consult...This man
could bring home victories to our people each year
without bringing them...glory."

His complete disillusionment is obvious as he
compares his vision of the country he had intended to
create, with that which was now ruled by the Nazis:

"But of our Germany, which was a nation of poets
and musicians and artists and soldiers, he has made
a nation of hysterics and hermits, engulfed in a mob
and led by a thousand liars or fanatics."

Are these the words of a belligerent man who had
dreamed of world domination, or rather those of an
Emperor whose devotion to his country and its people had
always been at the forefront of all his endeavours and who
had been made a scapegoat for the crimes of others?

In 1920, Wilhelm, resigned to spending the rest of
his life in exile, purchased a country estate in Doorn in the
Netherlands. In July that year, his youngest son, Joachim,
committed suicide, and nine months later, his wife, Dona,
also died. Wilhelm was not permitted to enter Germany to
attend her interment in the Temple of Antiquities near the
New Palace in Potsdam.

In November 1922, at the age of sixty-three, he
married the widowed, Princess Hermine von Schoenaich-
Carolath, and spent the rest of his life living quietly in
Doorn, writing his memoirs, studying, and watching
Hitler's destruction of Germany with increasing despair. He

died of a pulmonary embolism on 3rd June 1941, and was buried in the mausoleum at Doorn where German monarchists still gather to pay tribute to their former Emperor.

By the same author:

Biography

Queen Victoria's Granddaughters 1960-1918
Queen Victoria's Grandsons 1859-1918
Alice, the Enigma – A Biography of Queen Victoria's Daughter
Dear Papa, Beloved Mama – An intimate portrait of Queen Victoria & Prince Albert as parents

Historical Fiction

Most Beautiful Princess – A Novel Based on the Life of Grand Duchess Elizabeth of Russia
Shattered Crowns: The Scapegoats
Shattered Crowns: The Sacrifice
Shattered Crowns: The Betrayal
The Fields Laid Waste

Novels

The Counting House
By Any Other Name

Children's Books

Wonderful Walter

Poetry

Child of the Moon
The Ragamuffin Sun

References

[1] Bentinck, Lady Norah *The Ex-Kaiser in Exile* (Hodder & Stoughton 1921)

[2] Czernin, Count Ottokar *In the World War* (Cassell & Company 1920)

[3] Shaw, Stanley *William of Germany* (Dublin University 1913)

[4] Shaw, George Bernard *Common Sense about the War* (New Statesman 14th November 1914)

[5] Dickson A.S.A Don *The Kaiser – A Book About The Most Interesting Man in Europe* (Doubleday, Page & Co. 1914)

[6] Gauss, Charles *The German Emperor as shown in his Public Utterances* (Charles Scribner & sons 1915)

[7] Dickson A.S.A Don *The Kaiser – A Book About The Most Interesting Man in Europe* (Doubleday, Page & Co. 1914)

[8] Gauss, Charles *The German Emperor as shown in his Public Utterances* (Charles Scribner & sons 1915)

[9] Legge. Edward *King Edward, the Kaiser and the War* (Grant Richards 1917)

[10] Gauss, Charles *The German Emperor as shown in his Public Utterances* (Charles Scribner & sons 1915)

[11] Bigelow, Poultney *The German Emperor* (New Review, August 1889)

[12] Shaw, George Bernard *Common Sense about the War* (New Statesman 14th November 1914)

[13] Whitman, Sidney *The Life of Emperor Frederick* (Harper & Bros. 1901)

[14] Martin, Theodore *The Life of His Royal Highness the Prince Consort Vol. IV* (Smith, Elder & Co. 1879)

[15] Anonymous *The Empress Frederick – A Memoir* (Dodd, Mead & Co. 1914)

[16] Fulford, Roger (editor) *Your Dear Letter; Private Correspondence of Queen Victoria and the Crown Princess of Prussia 1865-1871* (Evans 1971)

[17] Whitman, Sidney *The Life of Emperor Frederick* (Harper & Bros. 1901)

[18] Fontenoy, La Marquise de *Secret Memories of the Court of Berlin under William II* (DeFau 1909)

[19] Ponsonby, Frederick *Recollections of Three Reigns* (Eyre & Spottiswoode 1957)

[20] Bigelow, Poultney *The German Emperor* (New Review, August 1889)

[21] Wemys, Rosslyn, *The Memoirs and Letters of Sir Robert Morier Vol 2* (Edward Arnold 1911)

[22] Legge. Edward *King Edward, the Kaiser and the War* (Grant Richards 1917)

[23] Fulford, Roger (editor) *Your Dear Letter; Private Correspondence of Queen Victoria and the Crown Princess of Prussia 1865-1871* (Evans 1971)

[24] Ponsonby, Frederick (editor) *Letters of the Empress Frederick* (Macmillan & Co. 1928)

[25] Fontenoy, La Marquise de *Secret Memories of the Court of Berlin under William II* (DeFau 1909)

[26] Wilhelm II, *The Kaiser's Memoirs* translated by Thomas Ybarra (Harper Brothers 1922)

[27] Schwering, Count Axel von *The Berlin Court Under William II* (Cassell & Company Limited 1915)

[28] Schwering, Count Axel von *The Berlin Court Under William II* (Cassell & Company Limited 1915)

[29] Topham, Anne *Memories of the Kaiser's Court* (Methuen and Co. 1914)

[30] Munsterberg, Hugo *The Peace & America* (D. Appleton & Company 1915)

[31] Ramm, Agatha (editor) *Beloved & Darling Child*

[32] Catling, Thomas *My Life's Pilgrimage* (John Murray 1911)

[33] Mackenzie, Sir Morell *The Fatal Illness of Frederick the Noble* (Sampson, Lowe,

Marston, Searle and Rimmington 1888)

[34] Barkeley, Richard *The Empress Frederick* (MacMillan 1956)

[35] Wilhelm II (translated by Thomas Ybarra) *The Kaiser's Memoirs* (Harper & Brothers 1922)

[36] Barkeley, Richard *The Empress Frederick* (MacMillan 1956)

[37] Schwering, Count Axel von *The Berlin Court Under William II* (Cassell & Company Limited 1915)

[38] Schwering, Count Axel von *The Berlin Court Under William II* (Cassell & Company Limited 1915)

[39] Schwering, Count Axel von *The Berlin Court Under William II* (Cassell & Company Limited 1915)

[40] Schwering, Count Axel von *The Berlin Court Under William II* (Cassell & Company Limited 1915)

[41] Wilhelm II (translated by Thomas Ybarra) *The Kaiser's Memoirs* (Harper & Brothers 1922)

[42] Mackenzie, Sir Morell *The Fatal Illness of Frederick the Noble* (Sampson, Lowe, Marston, Searle and Rimmington 1888)

[43] Mackenzie, Sir Morell *The Fatal Illness of Frederick the Noble* (Sampson, Lowe, Marston, Searle and Rimmington 1888)

[44] Ponsonby, Frederick (editor) *Letters of the Empress Frederick* (MacMillan & Co. 1928)

[45] Dickinson, A.S.A *The Kaiser* (Doubleday 1914)

[46] Gould Lee, Arthur *The Empress Frederick Writes to her Daughter, Sophie, the Crown Princess of the Hellenes* (Faber & Faber 1958)

[47] Wilhelm II, *My Early Life* (G.H. Doran 1926)

[48] Adam, Juliette (translated by J.O.P. Bland) *Letters from Foreign Politics* (La Nouvelle Review April 1890)

[49] Dickinson, A.S.A *The Kaiser* (Doubleday 1914)

[50] Wilhelm II (translated by Thomas Ybarra) *The Kaiser's Memoirs* (Harper & Brothers 1922)

[51] Schierbrand, Wolf von (translator and editor) *The Kaiser's Speeches* (Harper & Brothers 1903)

[52] Schoen, Freiherr von (translated by Constance Vesey) *The Memoirs of an Ambassador* (George Allen & Unwin 1922)

[53] Hervier, Paul-Louis *The Two Williams – Studies of the Kaiser & The Crown Prince* (Eveleigh Nash Company 1916)

[54] Davis, Arthur N. *The Kaiser I knew* (Hodder & Stoughton 1918)

[55] Vacaresco, Hélène, *Kings & Queens I Have Known* (Harper & Brothers 1904)

[56] Munsterberg, Hugo *The Peace & America* (D. Appleton & Company 1915)

[57] Ponsonby, Frederick *Recollections of Three Reigns* (Eyre & Spottiswoode 1957)

[58] Fontenoy, La Marquise de *Secret Memories of the Court of Berlin under William II* (DeFau 1909)

[59] Vacaresco, Hélène, *Kings & Queens I Have Known* (Harper & Brothers 1904)

[60] Munsterberg, Hugo *The Peace & America* (D. Appleton & Company 1915)

[61] Anon. *The Real Kaiser* (Melrose Ltd. 1914)

[62] Wilhelm, Crown Prince *Memoirs of the Crown Prince of Germany* (Thornton Butterworth 1922)

[63] Schoen, Freiherr von (translated by Constance Vesey) *The Memoirs of an Ambassador* (George Allen & Unwin 1922)

[64] Munsterberg, Hugo *The Peace & America* (D. Appleton & Company 1915)

[65] Gauss, Charles *The German Emperor as shown in his Public Utterances* (Charles Scribner & sons 1915)

[66] Gauss, Charles *The German Emperor as shown in his Public Utterances* (Charles

Scribner & sons 1915)
[67] Schierbrand, Wolf von (translator and editor) *The Kaiser's Speeches* (Harper & Brothers 1903)
[68] Wilhelm, Crown Prince *Memoirs of the Crown Prince of Germany* (Thornton Butterworth 1922)
[69] Thompson, Robert J. *England & Germany in the War. Letters to the State Department* (Chapple Publishing 1915)
[70] Topham, Anne *Memories of the Kaiser's Court* (Methuen and Co. 1914)
[71] Leutrum, Countess Olga *Court & Diplomacy in Austria & Germany. What I Know* (T. Fisher Unwin 1918)
[72] Wilhelm II, *My Early Life* (G.H. Doran 1926)
[73] Dickinson, A.S.A *The Kaiser* (Doubleday 1914)
[74] Hansard *HC Deb 21 November 1902 vol 115 cc150-98*
[75] Bigelow, Poultney *The German Emperor* (New Review, August 1889)
[76] Bigelow, Poultney *The German Emperor & His Eastern Neighbours* (Charles L. Webster & Co. 1892)
[77] Kennedy, J.M. *The War Lord – A Character Study of the German Emperor from his Letters & Speeches* (Duffield 1914)
[78] Adam, Juliette (translated by J.O.P. Bland) *The Schemes of the Kaiser* (E. Dutton 1918)
[79] Fried, Alfred H. *The German Emperor & The Peace of the World* (Hodder & Stoughton 1912)
[80] Grieb, Conrad K. *Uncovering the Forces of War* (Examiner Books 1947)
[81] Cerf, Barry *Alsace-Lorraine Since 1870* (The Macmillan Company 1919)
[82] Brooks, Sydney *The Real Problem of Alsace-Lorraine* (The North American Review Vol. 206 1918)
[83] Schrader, Frederick Franklyn *1683-1920 – The Fourteen Points & What Became of Them* (Concord Publishing Company 1920)
[84] Adam, Juliette *Letters on Foreign Politics* (La Nouvelle Revue April 1899_
[85] Don Levine, Isaac (editor) *Letters from the Kaiser to the Tsar* (Frederick A. Stokes 1920)
[86] Harrison, Austin *England & Germany* (Macmillian & Co. 1907)
[87] Wilhelm II, *The Kaiser's Memoirs* translated by Thomas Ybarra (Harper Brothers 1922)
[88] Ponsonby, Frederick (editor) *Letters of the Empress Frederick* (Macmillan & Co. 1928)
[89] Bigelow, Poultney *The Berlin Court under William II* (Cassell & Company 1915)
[90] Wilhelm II (translated by Thomas Ybarra) *The Kaiser's Memoirs* (Harper & Brothers 1922)
[91] Bigelow, Poultney *The German Emperor & His Eastern Neighbours* (Charles L. Webster & Co. 1892)
[92] Legge. Edward *King Edward, the Kaiser and the War* (Grant Richards 1917)
[93] Topham, Anne *Memories of the Kaiser's Court* (Methuen and Co. 1914)
[94] Kennedy, J.M. *The War Lord – A character study of the Kaiser from his letters & Speeches* (Duffield & Co. 1914)
[95] Leutrum, Countess Olga *Court & Diplomacy in Austria & Germany. What I Know* (T. Fisher Unwin 1918)
[96] Wilhelm II (translated by Thomas Ybarra) *The Kaiser's Memoirs* (Harper & Brothers 1922)
[97] Schierbrand, Wolf von (translator and editor) *The Kaiser's Speeches* (Harper & Brothers 1903)
[98] Don Levine, Isaac (editor) *Letters from the Kaiser to the Tsar* (Frederick A. Stokes 1920)
[99] Ponsonby, Frederick (editor) *Letters of the Empress Frederick* (Macmillan & Co.

1928)

[100] Alice, Princess, Countess of Athlone *For My Grandchildren* (Evans Bros 1966)

[101] Eckardstein, Baron von *Ten Years at the Court of St James* (Thornton Butterworth 1921)

[102] Eckardstein, Baron von *Ten Years at the Court of St James* (Thornton Butterworth 1921)

[103] Reid, Michaela *Ask Sir James* Eland 1987

[104] Suffield, Lord *My Memoirs 1830-1913* (Herbert Jenkins Ltd. 1914)

[105] Hansard *HC Deb 14 February 1901 vol. 89 cc72-162*

[106] Marie Louise, Princess *My Memories of Six Reigns* (Evans 1956)

[107] Lewis, Evans *The Germans in Africa* (Oxford University Press 1914)

[108] Lewis, Evans *The Germans in Africa* (Oxford University Press 1914)

[109] Hobhouse, Emily *The Brunt of the War* (Methuen & Co. 1902)

[110] Wilhelm II (translated by Thomas Ybarra) *The Kaiser's Memoirs* (Harper & Brothers 1922)

[111] Don Levine, Isaac (editor) *Letters from the Kaiser to the Tsar* (Frederick A. Stokes 1920)

[112] Fried, Alfred H. *The German Emperor & The Peace of the World* (Hodder & Stoughton 1912)

[113] Lusk, Hugh H. *The Real Yellow Peril* (North American Review Vol. 186)

[114] Gauss, Charles *The German Emperor as shown in his Public Utterances* (Charles Scribner & sons 1915)

[115] Wile, Frederic William *Men Around the Kaiser* (Maclean 1913)

[116] Schierbrand, Wolf von (translator and editor) *The Kaiser's Speeches* (Harper & Brothers 1903)

[117] Schierbrand, Wolf von (translator and editor) *The Kaiser's Speeches* (Harper & Brothers 1903)

[118] Dickinson, A.S.A *The Kaiser* (Doubleday 1914)

[119] Gooch, G.P. *The Life of Lord Courtney* (Macmillan & Co. 1920)

[120] Hansard *HL Deb 30 July 1906 vol 162 cc288-324*

[121] Fried, Alfred H. *The German Emperor & The Peace of the World* (Hodder & Stoughton 1912)

[122] Palmer Chambers, Miriam *The Origins of the Entente-Cordiale* (University Thesis for the George Washington University 1927)

[123] Bruce, Stewart E. *The War Guilt and the Peace Crime of the Entente Allies* (F.L. Searle & Co 1920)

[124] Thompson, Robert J. *England & Germany in the War. Letters to the State Department* (Chapple Publishing 1915)

[125] Nevins, Allan *Henry White; Thirsty Years of American Diplomacy* (Harper & Brothers 1930)

[126] Wells, H.G. *Social Forces in England & America* (Harper & Brothers 1914)

[127] Hansard *HL Deb 09 March 1908 vol 185 cc1072-7*

[128] Hurd, Archibald *The Command of the Sea* (Chapman & Hall 1912)

[129] Schwering, Count Axel von *The Berlin Court Under William II* (Cassell & Company Limited 1915)

[130] Legge. Edward *King Edward, the Kaiser and the War* (Grant Richards 1917)

[131] Legge. Edward *King Edward, the Kaiser and the War* (Grant Richards 1917)

[132] Legge. Edward *King Edward, the Kaiser and the War* (Grant Richards 1917)

[133] Czernin, Count Ottokar *In the World War* (Cassell & Company 1920)

[134] Eckardstein, Baron von *Ten Years at the Court of St James* (Thornton Butterworth 1921)

[135] Schwering, Count Axel von *The Berlin Court Under William II* Legge. Edward *King Edward, the Kaiser and the War* (Grant Richards 1917)

[136] Jeyes S.H. *Mr Chamberlain His Life & Public Career* (Sands & Co. 1903)
[137] Eckardstein, Baron von *Ten Years at the Court of St James* (Thornton Butterworth 1921)
[138] Czernin, Count Ottokar *In the World War* (Cassell & Company 1920)
[139] Wilhelm, Crown Prince *Memoirs of the Crown Prince of Germany* (Thornton Butterworth 1922)
[140] Eckardstein, Baron von *Ten Years at the Court of St James* (Thornton Butterworth 1921)
[141] Hammer S.C. *William the Second* (Houghton Mifflin Company 1917)
[142] Wilhelm II (translated by Thomas Ybarra) *The Kaiser's Memoirs* (Harper & Brothers 1922)
[143] *European Politics During the Decade Before the War as Described by Belgian Diplomats* (The German Foreign Office 1915)
[144] Wilhelm II (translated by Thomas Ybarra) *The Kaiser's Memoirs* (Harper & Brothers 1922)
[145] Grelling, Dr. Richard *Belgian Documents* (Hodder & Stoughton 1919)
[146] Grelling, Dr. Richard *Belgian Documents* (Hodder & Stoughton 1919)
[147] Alexander, Grand Duke *Twilight of Royalty* (Ray Long & Richard R. Smith Inc. 1932)
[148] Wilhelm, Crown Prince *Memoirs of the Crown Prince of Germany* (Thornton Butterworth 1922)
[149] Schoen, Freiherr von (translated by Constance Vesey) *The Memoirs of an Ambassador* (George Allen & Unwin 1922)
[150] Don Levine, Isaac (editor) *Letters from the Kaiser to the Tsar* (Frederick A. Stokes 1920)
[151] Don Levine, Isaac (editor) *Letters from the Kaiser to the Tsar* (Frederick A. Stokes 1920)
[152] Schrader, Frederick Franklyn *1683-1920 – The Fourteen Points & What Became of Them* (Concord Publishing Company 1920)
[153] Don Levine, Isaac (editor) *Letters from the Kaiser to the Tsar* (Frederick A. Stokes 1920)
[154] Don Levine, Isaac (editor) *Letters from the Kaiser to the Tsar* (Frederick A. Stokes 1920)
[155] Don Levine, Isaac (editor) *Letters from the Kaiser to the Tsar* (Frederick A. Stokes 1920)
[156] Gooch G.P. & Temperley, Harold (editors) *British Documents on the Origins of the War 1898-1914 Vol. VII* (1932)
[157] Grelling, Dr. Richard *Belgian Documents* (Hodder & Stoughton 1919)
[158] Grelling, Dr. Richard *Belgian Documents* (Hodder & Stoughton 1919)
[159] Harrison, Austin *England & Germany* (MacMillan & Co, 1907)
[160] The Adelaide Advertiser 5th November 1910
[161] Grelling, Dr. Richard *Belgian Documents* (Hodder & Stoughton 1919)
[162] Hammer S.C. *William the Second* (Houghton Mifflin Company 1917)
[163] Hammer S.C. *William the Second* (Houghton Mifflin Company 1917)
[164] Wilhelm, Crown Prince *Memoirs of the Crown Prince of Germany* (Thornton Butterworth 1922)
[165] Don Levine, Isaac (editor) *Letters from the Kaiser to the Tsar* (Frederick A. Stokes 1920)
[166] Ponsonby, Frederick *Recollections of Three Reigns* (Eyre & Spottiswoode 1951)
[167] Hansard *HL Deb 16 February 1909 vol 1 cc1-5*
[168] Legge, Edward *King Edward, the Kaiser and the War* (Grant Richards 1917)
[169] Legge, Edward *The Public & Private Life of Kaiser William II* (Eveleigh Nash 1915)
[170] Legge. Edward *King Edward, the Kaiser and the War* (Grant Richards 1917)
[171] Wilhelm II (translated by Thomas Ybarra) *The Kaiser's Memoirs* (Harper & Brothers

1922)

[172] Suffield, Lord *My Memoirs 1830-1913* (Herbert Jenkins Ltd. 1914)

[173] Wilhelm II (translated by Thomas Ybarra) *The Kaiser's Memoirs* (Harper & Brothers 1922)

[174] Graves, Dr Karl Armgaard, *The Secrets of the German War Office* (McBride, Nast & Company 1914)

[175] Graves, Dr Karl Armgaard, *The Secrets of the German War Office* (McBride, Nast & Company 1914)

[176] *The Times* July 22nd 1911

[177] Gooch G.P. & Temperley, Harold (editors) *British Documents on the Origins of the War 1898-1914 Vol. VII* (1932)

[178] Wilhelm II (translated by Thomas Ybarra) *The Kaiser's Memoirs* (Harper & Brothers 1922)

[179] Don Levine, Isaac (editor) *Letters from the Kaiser to the Tsar* (Frederick A. Stokes 1920)

[180] Carnegie, Andrew *An Autobiography of Andrew Carnegie* (Constable & Co Ltd 1920)

[181] Carnegie, Andrew *An Autobiography of Andrew Carnegie* (Constable & Co Ltd 1920)

[182] Gooch G.P. & Temperley, Harold (editors) *British Documents on the Origins of the War 1898-1914 Vol. IX* (1932)

[183] Fried, Alfred H. *The German Emperor & The Peace of the World* (Hodder & Stoughton 1912)

[184] Fried, Alfred H. *The German Emperor & The Peace of the World* (Hodder & Stoughton 1912)

[185] Fried, Alfred H. *The German Emperor & The Peace of the World* (Hodder & Stoughton 1912)

[186] Seton-Watson R.W. *German, Slav & Magyar* (Williams & Northgate 1916)

[187] Czernin, Count Ottokar *In the World War* (Cassell & Company 1920)

[188] Czernin, Count Ottokar *In the World War* (Cassell & Company 1920)

[189] Gooch G.P. & Temperley, Harold (editors) *British Documents on the Origins of the War 1898-1914 Vol. IX* (1932)

[190] Don Levine, Isaac (editor) *Letters from the Kaiser to the Tsar* (Frederick A. Stokes 1920)

[191] Don Levine, Isaac (editor) *Letters from the Kaiser to the Tsar* (Frederick A. Stokes 1920)

[192] Don Levine, Isaac (editor) *Letters from the Kaiser to the Tsar* (Frederick A. Stokes 1920)

[193] Leutrum, Countess Olga *Court & Diplomacy in Austria & Germany. What I Know* (T. Fisher Unwin 1918)

[194] Grelling, Dr. Richard *Belgian Documents* (Hodder & Stoughton 1919)

[195] Ludwig, Ernest *Austria-Hungary and the War* (J.S. Ogilvie Publishing 1915)

[196] Czernin, Count Ottokar *In the World War* (Cassell & Company 1920)

[197] Czernin, Count Ottokar *In the World War* (Cassell & Company 1920)

[198] Czernin, Count Ottokar *In the World War* (Cassell & Company 1920)

[199] Gooch G.P. & Temperley, Harold (editors) *British Documents on the Origins of the War 1898-1914 Vol. XI* (1932)

[200] Morgenthau, Henry *Ambassador Morgenthau's Story* (Doubleday, Page & Company 1919)

[201] Ludwig, Ernest *Austria-Hungary and the War* (J.S. Ogilvie Publishing 1915)

[202] Leutrum, Countess Olga *Court & Diplomacy in Austria & Germany. What I Know* (T. Fisher Unwin 1918)

[203] Wilhelm II (translated by Thomas Ybarra) *The Kaiser's Memoirs* (Harper & Brothers 1922)

[204] Bradshaw Fay, Sydney *The Origins of the World War Vol II* (The Macmillan

Company 1928)

[205] Bradshaw Fay, Sydney *The Origins of the World War Vol II* (The Macmillan Company 1928)

[206] Schoen, Freiherr von (translated by Constance Vesey) *The Memoirs of an Ambassador* (George Allen & Unwin 1922)

[207] Ludwig, Ernst *Austria-Hungary & the War* (J.S. Ogilvie Publishing 1915)

[208] Beck, James M. *The Evidence of the Case* (G.P. Putnam's & Son 1915)

[209] William, Crown Prince of Germany *Memoirs of the Crown Prince of Germany* (Charles Scribner's Sons 1922)

[210] Bunsen, Maurice de *Despatch From His Majesty's Ambassador at Vienna Respecting the Rupture of Relations with the Austro-Hungarian Government* (January 1 1915)

[211] Onkenn, Herman (translated by William Wallace Whitelock) *Modern Germany in Relation to the Great War* (Mitchell Kennerley 1916)

[212] Paléologue, Maurice *An Ambassador's Memoirs* (G.H. Doran 1925)

[213] Gibbs, Philip *The Soul of the War* (William Heinemann 1915)

[214] Bentinck, Lady Norah *The Ex-Kaiser in Exile* (Hodder & Stoughton 1921)

[215] Onkenn, Herman (translated by William Wallace Whitelock) *Modern Germany in Relation to the Great War* (Mitchell Kennerley 1916)

[216] 'A Russian' *Russian Court Memoirs 1914-1916* (Herbert Jenkins Limited 1917)

[217] Beck, James M. *The Evidence of the Case* (G.P. Putnam's & Son 1915)

[218] Buchanan, Sir George *My Mission to Russia Vol. 1* (Cassell & Company Ltd. 1923)

[219] Wilhelm II (translated by Thomas Ybarra) *The Kaiser's Memoirs* (Harper & Brothers 1922)

[220] Buchanan, Sir George *My Mission to Russia Vol. 1* (Cassell & Company Ltd. 1923)

[221] *Daily Graphic* July 31st 1914

[222] Alice, Princess, Countess of Athlone *For My Grandchildren* (Evans Bros 1966)

[223] Bruce, Stewart E. *The War Guilt and the Peace Crime of the Entente Allies* (F.L. Searle & Co 1920)

[224] Dickinson, A.S.A *The Kaiser* (Doubleday 1914)

[225] Paléologue, Maurice *An Ambassador's Memoirs* (G.H. Doran 1925)

[226] A Russian' *Russian Court Memoirs 1914-1916* (Herbert Jenkins Limited 1917)

[227] Bentinck, Lady Norah *The Ex-Kaiser in Exile* (Hodder & Stoughton 1921)

[228] McGuire, James T. *The King, The Kaiser & Irish Freedom* (The Devin-Adair Company 1915)

[229] Buchanan, Sir George *My Mission to Russia Vol. 1* (Cassell & Company Ltd. 1923)

[230] Paléologue, Maurice *An Ambassador's Memoirs* (G.H. Doran 1925)

[231] Paléologue, Maurice *An Ambassador's Memoirs* (G.H. Doran 1925)

[232] McGuire, James K. *What Germany Could do for Ireland* (Wolfe Tone Company 1916)

[233] Gooch G.P. & Temperley, Harold (editors) *British Documents on the Origins of the War 1898-1914 Vol. XI* (1932)

[234] Wilhelm II (translated by Thomas Ybarra) *The Kaiser's Memoirs* (Harper & Brothers 1922)

[235] Gooch G.P. & Temperley, Harold (editors) *British Documents on the Origins of the War 1898-1914 Vol. XI* (1932)

[236] Gooch G.P. & Temperley, Harold (editors) *British Documents on the Origins of the War 1898-1914 Vol. XI* (1926)

[237] Marie Louise, Princess *My Memories of Six Reigns* (Evans 1956)

[238] Gooch G.P. & Temperley, Harold (editors) *British Documents on the Origins of the War 1898-1914 Vol. XI* (1926)

[239] Gooch G.P. & Temperley, Harold (editors) *British Documents on the Origins of the War 1898-1914 Vol. XI* (1926)

[240] Bruce, Stewart E. *The War Guilt and the Peace Crime of the Entente Allies* (F.L. Searle & Co 1920)

[241] Blucher, Princess Evelyn *An English Wife in Berlin* (E. Dutton & Co. 1921)

[242] Legge. Edward *King Edward, the Kaiser and the War* (Grant Richards 1917)

[243] Gaffney, Thomas St. John *Breaking the Silence* (Horace Liveright 1930)

[244] Thompson, Robert J. *England & Germany in the War. Letters to the State Department* (Chapple Publishing 1915)

[245] Davis, Arthur N. *The Kaiser I knew* (Hodder & Stoughton 1918)

[246] Davis, Arthur N. *The Kaiser I knew* (Hodder & Stoughton 1918)

[247] Gooch G.P. & Temperley, Harold (editors) *British Documents on the Origins of the War 1898-1914 Vol. XI* (1926)

[248] Wilhelm II (translated by Thomas Ybarra) *The Kaiser's Memoirs* (Harper & Brothers 1922)

[249] Drinker Bullitt, Ernesta *An Uncensored Diary from the Central Empires* (Doubleday, Page and Company 1917)

[250] Perry Chitwood, Oliver *The Immediate Causes of the Great War* (Thomas Y. Crowell Company 1918)

[251] Fuehr, Alexander *The Neutrality of Belgium* (Funk & Wagnalls 1915)

[252] Gooch G.P. & Temperley, Harold (editors) *British Documents on the Origins of the War 1898-1914 Vol. VIII* (1932)

[253] Eltzbacher, Paul (translated by S. Russell Wells) *Germany's Food – Can it Last?* (Hodder & Stoughton 1915)

[254] Drinker Bullitt, Ernesta *An Uncensored Diary from the Central Empires* (Doubleday, Page and Company 1917)

[255] Freytag-Loringhoven, Baron von *Deductions from the World War* (G.P. Putnam's Sons 1918)

[256] Blatchford, Robert *The War that was Foretold* (Reprinted from the Daily Mail 1914)

[257] Legge, Edward *The Public & Private Life of Kaiser Wilhelm* (Everleigh Nash 1915)

[258] Goschen, Sir Edward *The True Story of A Scrap of Paper* (George Barrie's Sons 1915)

[259] Munsterberg, Hugo *The Peace & America* (D. Appleton & Company 1915)

[260] Legge, Edward *The Public & Private Life of Kaiser Wilhelm* (Everleigh Nash 1915)

[261] Anonymous *The Real Kaiser* (Dodd, Mead & Company 1914)

[262] Schwering, Count Axel von *The Berlin Court Under William II* (Cassell & Company Limited 1915)

[263] Hintze, Professor Otto (translated by William Wallace Whitelock) *Modern Germany in Relation to the Great War* (Mitchell Kennerley 1916)

[264] Blucher, Princess Evelyn *An English Wife in Berlin* (E. Dutton & Co. 1921)

[265] Thompson, Robert J. *England & Germany in the War. Letters to the State Department* (Chapple Publishing 1915)

[266] Cobb, Irvin *Speaking of Prussians* (G.H. Doran Company 1917)

[267] Cobb, Irvin *Speaking of Prussians* (G.H. Doran Company 1917)

[268] Protheroe, Ernest *A Noble Woman – The Life Story of Edith Cavell* (The Epworth Press 1916)

[269] Protheroe, Ernest *A Noble Woman – The Life Story of Edith Cavell* (The Epworth Press 1916)

[270] Gaffney, Thomas St. John *Breaking the Silence* (Horace Liveright 1930)

[271] Meyer, Eduard (translated by Helen S. White) *England – Its Political Organization and Development and the War Against Germany* (Ritter and Co. 1916)

[272] Mattern, Johannes *Germany's Alleged Atrocities – England's Most Effective Weapon* (The Open Court Publishing Company 1915)

[273] Thompson, Robert J. *England & Germany in the War. Letters to the State Department* (Chapple Publishing 1915)

[274] *Egyptian Delegation to the Peace Conference Collection of Official Correspondence* (Published by the Delegation 1919)

[275] Crozier, F.P. *Brass Hat in No Man's Land* (Jonathan Cape & Harrison Smith 1930)

[276] Drinker Bullitt, Ernesta *An Uncensored Diary from the Central Empires* (Doubleday, Page and Company 1917)
[277] McGuire, James T. *The King, The Kaiser & Irish Freedom* (The Devin-Adair Company 1915)
[278] Bentinck, Lady Norah *The Ex-Kaiser in Exile* (Hodder & Stoughton 1921)
[279] Anon. *The Real Kaiser* (A. Melrose Ltd. 1914)
[280] Blatchford, Robert *The War that was Foretold* (Reprinted from the Daily Mail 1914)
[281] Gaffney, Thomas St. John *Breaking the Silence* (Horace Liveright 1930)
[282] Grelling, Dr. Richard *Belgian Documents* (Hodder & Stoughton 1919)
[283] Shaw, George Bernard *Common Sense about the War* (New Statesman 14th November 1914)
[284] Fullerton, William Morton *Hesitations, The American Crisis and the War* (Doubleday, Page & Company 1916)
[285] *National Souvenir of Prince Henry's Visit to the United States* (Voelcker Brothers 1902)
[286] Don Levine, Isaac (editor) *Letters from the Kaiser to the Tsar* (Frederick A. Stokes 1920)
[287] Schierbrand, Wolf von (translator and editor) *The Kaiser's Speeches* (Harper & Brothers 1903)
[288] Munsterberg, Hugo *The Peace & America* (D. Appleton & Company 1915)
[289] Schrader, Frederick Franklyn *1683-1920 – The Fourteen Points & What Became of Them* (Concord Publishing Company 1920)
[290] McGuire, James T. *The King, The Kaiser & Irish Freedom* (The Devin-Adair Company 1915)
[291] *Los Angeles Times* July 31st 1914
[292] Cobb, Irvin S. *Speaking of Prussians* (George H. Doran & Company 1917)
[293] Horne, Charles F. (Editor) *Source Records of the Great War Vol. IV* (National Alumni 1923)
[294] Rintelen, Captain Franz von *Dark Invader – War Time Reminiscences of a German Naval Intelligence Officer* (Penguin 1933)
[295] Rintelen, Captain Franz von *Dark Invader – War Time Reminiscences of a German Naval Intelligence Officer* (Penguin 1933)
[296] Davis, Arthur N. *The Kaiser I knew* (Hodder & Stoughton 1918)
[297] 'Historicus Junior' *The 'Lusitania Case'* (Hugh H. Masterson, June 1915)
[298] Harris, Frank *England or Germany?* (The Wilmarth Press 1915)
[299] Collman, Charles *War Plotters of Wall Street* (The Fatherland Co. 1915)
[300] *Wall Street Journal* (19th June 1915)
[301] 'Historicus Junior' *The 'Lusitania Case'* (Hugh H. Masterson, June 1915)
[302] Blucher, Princess Evelyn *An English Wife in Berlin* (E. Dutton & Co. 1921)
[303] Gerard, James W. *My Four Years in Germany* (George H. Doran & Company 1917)
[304] Davis, Arthur N. *The Kaiser I knew* (Hodder & Stoughton 1918)
[305] Wise, Jennings C. *Woodrow Wilson Disciple of Revolution* (1937)
[306] Gerard, James W. *My Four Years in Germany* (George H. Doran & Company 1917)
[307] Munsterberg, Hugo *Tomorrow - Letters to a Friend in Germany* (D. Appleton & Company 1916)
[308] Turner, John Kenneth *Shall it Be Again?* (B.W. Huebsch Inc. 1922)
[309] Memorandum of the German Government in Regard to Incidents Alleged to Have Attended the Destruction of a German Submarine and its Crew by the British Auxiliary Cruiser "Baralong" on August 19, 1915
[310] Grey, Sir Edward *Memorandum to the American Ambassador in London December 1915*
[311] Curtin, Dr Thomas *The Land of Deepening Shadow* (Grosset & Dunlop 1917)
[312] Rintelen, Captain Franz von *Dark Invader – War Time Reminiscences of a German*

Naval Intelligence Officer (Penguin 1933)

[313] Pitcher Okie, Howard *America & the German Peril* (William Heineman 1915)

[314] Mach, Edmund von *German's Point of View* (A.C. McClurg & Co. 1915)

[315] Picton, Harold *The Better German in times of War* (The National Labour Press 1918)

[316] Munsterberg, Hugo *Tomorrow - Letters to a Friend in Germany* (D. Appleton & Company 1916)

[317] Wilhelm II (translated by Thomas Ybarra) *The Kaiser's Memoirs* (Harper & Brothers 1922)

[318] Schrader, Frederick Franklyn *1683-1920 – The Fourteen Points & What Became of Them* (Concord Publishing Company 1920)

[319] Wise, Jennings C. *Woodrow Wilson Disciple of Revolution* (1937)

[320] Wise, Jennings C. *Woodrow Wilson Disciple of Revolution* (1937)

[321] Linchowsky, Prince Karl *My Mission to London 1912-1914* (Cassell & Co. 1917)

[322] Marble Gale, Oliver (Editor) *Americanism – Woodrow Wilson's Speeches on the War* (The Baldwin Syndicate 1918)

[323] Marble Gale, Oliver (Editor) *Americanism – Woodrow Wilson's Speeches on the War* (The Baldwin Syndicate 1918)

[324] Turner, John Kenneth *Shall it Be Again?* (B.W. Huebsch Inc. 1922)

[325] Turner, John Kenneth *Shall it Be Again?* (B.W. Huebsch Inc. 1922)

[326] Turner, John Kenneth *Shall it Be Again?* (B.W. Huebsch Inc. 1922)

[327] Horne, Charles F. (Editor) *Source Records of the Great War Vol. V* (National Alumni 1923)

[328] Prince, Morgan *The Psychology of the Kaiser* (Richard G. Badger 1915)

[329] Ackerman, Carl W. *Germany the next Republic?* (George H. Doran 1917)

[330] Roscoe Thayer *Volleys from a Non-Combatant* (Doubleday, Page & Company 1917)

[331] Hansard HC Deb 04 April 1917 vol 92 cc1419-80

[332] Churchill, Winston *A Traveller in War Time* (Macmillian & Company 1918)

[333] Munsterberg, Hugo *The Peace & America* (D. Appleton & Company 1915)

[334] Blucher, Princess Evelyn *An English Wife in Berlin* (E. Dutton & Co. 1921)

[335] Munsterberg, Hugo *The Peace & America* (D. Appleton & Company 1915)

[336] Bartlett Bridgeman, Helena *An American Woman's Plea for Germany* (*The Fatherland 1915)*

[337] Blucher, Princess Evelyn *An English Wife in Berlin* (E. Dutton & Co. 1921)

[338] 'An American' *Can Germany Win?* (C. Arthur Pearson 1914)

[339] Hervier, Paul-Louis *The Two Williams – Studies of the Kaiser & The Crown Prince* (Eveleigh Nash Company 1916)

[340] Blucher, Princess Evelyn *An English Wife in Berlin* (E. Dutton & Co. 1921)

[341] Blucher, Princess Evelyn *An English Wife in Berlin* (E. Dutton & Co. 1921)

[342] Blucher, Princess Evelyn *An English Wife in Berlin* (E. Dutton & Co. 1921)

[343] Wilhelm, Crown Prince *Memoirs of the Crown Prince of Germany* (Thornton Butterworth 1922)

[344] Bentinck, Lady Norah *The Ex-Kaiser in Exile* (Hodder & Stoughton 1921)

[345] Carnegie Endowment for International Peace *Official Communications Relating to Peace Proposals 1916-1917 Pamphlet No. 23* (Carnegie Endowment 1917)

[346] Henderson, Arthur *Speech to the British Parliament* (The Times, London December 16th 1916)

[347] Carnegie Endowment for International Peace *Official Communications Relating to Peace Proposals 1916-1917 Pamphlet No. 23* (Carnegie Endowment 1917)

[348] Carnegie Endowment for International Peace *Official Communications Relating to Peace Proposals 1916-1917 Pamphlet No. 23* (Carnegie Endowment 1917)

[349] Davis, Arthur N. *The Kaiser I knew* (Hodder & Stoughton 1918)

[350] Czernin, Count Ottokar *In the World War* (Cassell & Company 1920)

[351] Wilhelm II (translated by Thomas Ybarra) *The Kaiser's Memoirs* (Harper & Brothers

1922)

[352] Kalpaschnikov, Andrei *A Prisoner of Trotsky's* (Doubleday, Page & Co. 1920)

[353] Kellogg, Vernon *Germany in the War and After* (The Macmillian Company 1919)

[354] Wilhelm II (translated by Thomas Ybarra) *The Kaiser's Memoirs* (Harper & Brothers 1922)

[355] Ludwig, Emil (Translated by Ethel Colburn Mayne) *Kaiser Wilhelm II* (London 1926)

[356] Beaumont, Maurice (Translated by E. Ibbetson James) *The Fall of the Kaiser* (George Allen & Unwin 1931)

[357] Beaumont, Maurice (Translated by E. Ibbetson James) *The Fall of the Kaiser* (George Allen & Unwin 1931)

[358] Wilhelm, Crown Prince *Memoirs of the Crown Prince of Germany* (Thornton Butterworth 1922)

[359] Wilhelm II (translated by Thomas Ybarra) *The Kaiser's Memoirs* (Harper & Brothers 1922)

[360] Callahan, Edith *Glimpses of the Paris Peace Conference* (Catholic Messenger Press 1920)

[361] Dillon, Dr E.J. *The Inside Story of the Peace Conference* (Harper & Brothers 1920)

[362] Bartlett Bridgeman, Helen *An American Woman's Plea for Germany* (*The Fatherland 1915*)

[363] Bruce, Stewart E. *The War Guilt and the Peace Crime of the Entente Allies* (F.L. Searle & Co 1920)

[364] Bentinck, Lady Norah *The Ex-Kaiser in Exile* (Hodder & Stoughton 1921)

[365] *Report of the Violations of the Laws and Customs of the War* (The Clarendon Press 1919)

[366] Hansen, Henry *The Adventures of the Fourteen Points* (The Century Co. 1919)

[367] *The Spectator* 31st January 1920

[368] Kautsky, Karl *The Guilt of Wilhelm Hohenzollern* (Skeffington & Son 1920)

[369] Gauss, Charles *The German Emperor as shown in his Public Utterances* (Charles Scribner & sons 1915)

[370] Reich, Emil *Germany's Madness* (Dodd, Mead and Company 1910)

[371] Grelling, Dr. Richard *Belgian Documents* (Hodder & Stoughton 1919)

[372] Shaw, Stanley, *William of Germany* (Trinity College 1913)

[373] Schierbrand, Wolf von (translator and editor) *The Kaiser's Speeches* (Harper & Brothers 1903)

[374] Thompson, Robert J. *England & Germany in the War. Letters to the State Department* (Chapple Publishing 1915)

[375] Shaw, George Bernard *Common Sense about the War* (New Statesman 14th November 1914)

[376] Wilhelm II (translated by Thomas Ybarra) *The Kaiser's Memoirs* (Harper & Brothers 1922)

[377] Hervier, Paul-Louis *The Two Williams – Studies of the Kaiser & The Crown Prince* (Eveleigh Nash Company 1916)

[378] Wilhelm II (translated by Thomas Ybarra) *The Kaiser's Memoirs* (Harper & Brothers 1922)

[379] *Report of the Violations of the Laws and Customs of the War* (The Clarendon Press 1919)

[380] Bentinck, Lady Norah *The Ex-Kaiser in Exile* (Hodder & Stoughton 1921)

[381] Wilhelm II (translated by Thomas Ybarra) *The Kaiser's Memoirs* (Harper & Brothers 1922)

[382] Disraeli, Benjamin *Speech at Aylesbury* (1876)

[383] Woodrow Wilson, Thomas *The New Freedom* (1913)

[384] Wilhelm II (translated by Thomas Ybarra) *The Kaiser's Memoirs* (Harper & Brothers 1922)

[385] Wilhelm II (translated by Thomas Ybarra) *The Kaiser's Memoirs* (Harper & Brothers 1922)

[386] Turner, John Kenneth *Shall it Be Again?* (B.W. Huebsch Inc. 1922)

[387] Wilhelm II (translated by Thomas Ybarra) *The Kaiser's Memoirs* (Harper & Brothers 1922)

[388] Davis, Arthur N. *The Kaiser I knew* (Hodder & Stoughton 1918)

[389] Wilhelm II (translated by Thomas Ybarra) *The Kaiser's Memoirs* (Harper & Brothers 1922)

[390] Turner, John Kenneth *Shall it Be Again?* (B.W. Huebsch Inc. 1922)

[391] Turner, John Kenneth *Shall it Be Again?* (B.W. Huebsch Inc. 1922)

CPSIA information can be obtained
at www.ICGtesting.com
Printed in the USA
LVHW011601190220
647496LV00012B/861